A Crash Course in
TEENAGE
Survival

John Bytheway

BOOKCRAFT
SALT LAKE CITY, UTAH

Library of Congress Cataloging-in-Publication Data

Bytheway, John, 1962–
A crash course in teenage survival : what I wish I'd known in high school, the first and second semesters / John Bytheway.
  p. cm.
Includes index.
Summary: Offers advice for teenagers about such topics as self-esteem, prayer, friendship, morality, dealing with tragedy, learning to love the scriptures, and more.
  ISBN 1-57345-930-5 (pbk.)
  1. Teenagers—Religious life. 2. Teenagers—Conduct of life. 3. High school students—Religious life. 4. High school students—Conduct of life. 5. Mormon Church—Membership. 6. Church of Jesus Christ of Latter-day Saints— Membership. [1. Christian life. 2. Conduct of life. 3. Mormons.] I. Title.

BX8643.Y6 B96 2001
248.8'3—dc21   2001002393

Printed in the United States of America   72082-6805

10   9   8   7   6   5   4   3   2   1

Contents

CONTENTS

Summer School

Second Semester

Acknowledgments

Let me explain—No, there is too much. Let me sum up . . .

I'm grateful that the folks at Deseret Book have decided to take my first two books, *What I Wish I'd Known in High School* and *What I Wish I'd Known in High School: The Second Semester* and combine them into one, *A Crash Course in Teenage Survival*. A lot has happened since the first two books were published, so we decided to update a few things, include some more recent quotes, and add a chapter or two.

When I wrote the first two books, I was a young single adult who was still going to church dances and trying to get dates. My perspective then was much closer to what most teens are going through, so we decided to leave those chapters alone, even though I'm now married and have a few new perspectives. (Some things haven't changed, though, and high school is still wonderful, awful, great, terrible, fulfilling, and frustrating.) We called the new chapters "Summer School." Those chapters cover things like making friends, making decisions, and making it through tough times.

Thanks for letting me explain, I mean, sum up. Now, let's get over to the auditorium for orientation!

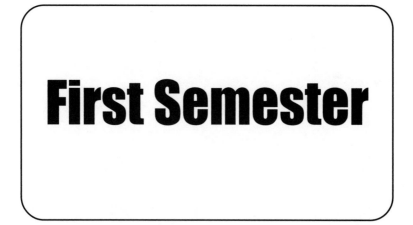

First Semester

Orientation

or, About the Guy Who Wrote This

Hi. Welcome to the orientation for this course, "A Crash Course in Teenage Survival." My name is John, and I wrote what you're reading. If you were sitting next to me, hearing me say these words instead of reading them yourself, you'd hear a slight lisp because of my retainer. So feel free to imagine the lisp whenever you read a word with the letter "s." The people at the orthodontist's office tell me the lisp will go away as I get used to the retainer, so stop imagining the lisp in about, um, Fourth Period.

First off, I suppose I should introduce myself. As I mentioned, my first name is John, and my last name is a prepositional phrase that you've probably said a million times: Bytheway. Take a wild guess about how to pronounce that. Yup, just like it sounds. By the way. That's really it. (My cousin Miriam is mentioned in the Bible—see Deuteronomy 24:9.)

Once I took a date to a restaurant. (I did, I got a date—my parents held a special fast, and I got a date.) The waitress said, "There's going to be a wait until a table opens up; can I take your name?" I thought to myself, *Here we go again,* then I said, "Yeah, it's Bytheway."

She looked at me blankly, as if she were waiting for me to finish my sentence. Then she said, "By the way . . . what?"

"No, Bytheway is my name," I replied.

She put her hands on her hips and said, "Uh-uh."

"Yeah, that's it," I said.

"I'll bet you get teased about that."

I should've paused for a few seconds, given her a confused look, and said, "Why?" but I didn't. I just said, "Yeah, I get teased about it a lot."

"Where does that name come from?" she asked.

I tried to keep a straight face and answered, "It's Japanese." (I wonder if she believed me.)

One time I was playing Pictionary® with some friends, and after the game was over, someone suggested we each "draw" our own name. I thought about it a minute and drew this:

See that? Yeah, it looks like a forest-service restroom, but it's also a *John by the way!* Get it? A sanitary self-portrait! (You're probably thinking, "Oh great. I buy this book to learn something, I'm four paragraphs into it, and the author's drawing Pictionary® bathrooms.") Yes, friends, we're gonna break the fun meter today. So next time you go camping, and "nature calls," you'll think of me. There's a nice thought. Now, let's see if there's any *useful* information in here.

Perhaps you're wondering why I wrote this book. Good question. To be honest, I've been writing this book since I was a sophomore in high school. I didn't actually sit down and start typing until much later, but I've been trying to find the right words to explain certain things for a long time. I remember one high-school day when I felt a little frustrated. (Ever happen to you?) I ended up at the school library looking for a book that hadn't been written. The book I wanted wasn't about math or history or social studies, or any subject I had in school. I wanted answers about things teachers don't normally talk about, for example: What does it mean to be popular? Why do some people treat me differently when we're alone than they do when their other friends are around? Why do I feel good some days and rotten other days? Am I moody? Is there life after high school? And so on and so on.

What I've tried to do here is write the book I was looking for all those years ago, the book explaining all the things I wish I had known when I was in high school. But before we go any further, there's just one thing I'd like to say:

Congratulations! You're reading a book!

Your parents are probably in the kitchen doing high fives. I know you read textbooks, but this one is different. Books from school you *have* to read; this one's just for fun. So I'll try to write it that way.

Seriously, though, what have you ever learned from doing Play Station? Or watching *sit*-coms on TV? Admit it! *Not much!* A mental diet of TV and video games will give you indigestion of the brain. Well, all of that is about to change. Yes, fellow travelers, the Starship o' Knowledge is about to leave Spacedock.

So here's the deal. You read this instead of watching TV, and I'll try to make it every bit as exciting as the shows you're missing (if not *more* exciting). There will be some class periods that may not be totally fun or funny, but they will be something better: *Interesting or Fascinating or Intriguing* or even **TESTIMONY BUILDING.** When was the last time prime time did that?

Now I'd like to introduce something you'll be seeing a lot of in this book. You see, I don't know very much, but I love to read the words of people who do. So I'll be repeating what others with fine minds (like yours) have said throughout history. Yes indeed, I think it's time to dip into the well of "Great Quotage" for a "GQ" (Great Quote). We'll use GQs throughout the book, and I think you'll like them. In fact, I highly recommend that you start a GQ collection of your own. Okay, here's the first one I saw on the wall of a high school in Southern Utah:

> The more you read, the more you know.
> The more you know, the smarter you grow.
> The smarter you grow, the stronger your voice,
> In expressing your view, or making your choice.

Knowledge is power! And that's what reading is all about. There is an unbelievably large universe of information out there, and you can explore it because you can read. I hope you will read many books after you finish this one—I'll even recommend a few from time to time as we go along together.

As you may have noticed, this course is called "A Crash Course in Teenage Survival." I thought about calling it other things, like "There Is Life after High School," or "This Too Shall Pass." But the main point is that you are going to make it—and make it big. Your high-school experience is not a forecast for your life. If things are not so hot now, don't worry! Things get better. People grow up! (Well, some of them do.) They feel less of a need to put other people down, make judgments, and gossip about friends. I survived—in fact, my life really began after I was out of high school. Right now, though, you're in the middle of it, so let's talk about how to make it through.

This book was written with three goals in mind. First of all, as with any book, you should expect to learn things you didn't know before. Second, as you travel through the pages, you ought to enjoy the ride! Third, and most important, a book should make you want to be better than you were when you picked it up. So those are the goals—in short: learn things, have fun, and make changes.

One more thing. *This is your book.* I hope you will use a highlighter when you read, and mark it up! (Have your scriptures handy too, so you can mark the ones we talk about.) Highlight what you like or what you have questions about. Underline, write notes in the margin, or whatever. That way, when you thumb through this book at another time, you'll remember what stood out to you before. If you'll do that much, I'll try to make the book as interesting, informative, and relevant as possible. Deal? Deal.

Oh, and by the way, enjoy the course!

First Period: Social Scene 101

Popular. Yes, Popular.
This Chapter Is, Like, So Totally Popular, Okay?

Popularity ends on yearbook day,
but respect lasts forever.

What does it mean to be popular? I'll tell you. I'm not sure. Fact is, it's different wherever you go. Some people are popular in one school, but they might not be in another. Certain extracurricular activities are popular in some schools and not in others. No doubt, you know exactly what the cool things are in your school: the "right" clothes to wear, words to say, music to listen to, activities to try out for, and everything else.

Who figures all this out? Is there a Coolness Club that meets after school and decides what is cool and what isn't? Do they publish a list, or does everyone just know? Does the media figure it out for us? Do those most admired or most visible in our school have an influence? Maybe we're all just following someone and we don't know who!

Oooh, that's a frightening thought, because we could follow them right into nowhere.

Well, what does it mean to be popular, then? I think you already know. Being popular means a lot of people know who you are, and maybe admire you for your self-assurance.

Here's a different question: Who are the people you most respect in your school? (I'm choosing my words carefully— not the *most popular*, but *most respected*.) Chances are, they're the ones who are friendly to everyone. They're nice to those who are in "their group," but also to those who are not. They're not "two-faced."

Perhaps you've watched one of these people and noticed

how he or she seems to be everyone's friend. And maybe something inside you said, "That's the right way to be; it's the way people ought to be, and I would like to be that way too." When you look up to someone like that, it's called respect. That's what we really ought to be aiming for, isn't it? *Respect.* Stay with me, and I'll tell you how to get it.

Have you ever had a TV dinner? You know, one of those microwaveable things with food in different compartments? Sometimes we treat people like TV dinners. I don't mean we heat them in the microwave, but we do put them into compartments.

I don't know the names for the compartments in your school, but here are some that I've heard: "These are the jocks, these are the loners, these are the skaters, these are the popular people, like, okay?" And it's almost as if someone is standing over the compartments saying, "All right, nobody move! Hey—you can't talk to him, you're not popular (whack, whack)! Get back in your place!"

Sound familiar? Putting people into compartments is unkind, and it can hurt. And believe me, you were not sent to earth to hurt people. You have more important things to do.

Here's another GQ:

> Jesus was the only teacher tall enough to see over the walls that divide the human race into compartments. (Frank Crane)

Did you know that the scriptures talk about these kinds of things? They do. Read carefully. Jesus said,

> For if ye love them which love you, what reward have ye? do not even the publicans the same?
> And if ye salute your brethren only, what do ye more than others? do not even the publicans so? (Matthew 5:46–47)

See my point? Nephi taught us to liken the scriptures unto ourselves (see 1 Nephi 19:23). If we were to "liken" that scripture unto high school, how would it sound? How about this:

> If you're only nice to the people that are nice to you, big deal; what do you want, a gift certificate? Everyone does that. And if you only say "hi" in the hall to the people that say "hi" to you, what are you doing more than anyone else?

Maybe you know people who are different when they're alone than when they're with their friends. They might say "hi" to you if they're alone, but with their group they act like they've never seen you before. (I see you're nodding your head.) The apostle Paul said, "Be of the *same mind* one toward another" (Romans 12:16; emphasis added).

Do you want to be popular? Better yet, do you want to be respected? Then no matter how others treat you, be "of the same mind" toward others, not "double minded" or "two-faced." This makes life a whole lot easier because you don't have to put on a new personality to match who you're with. That's too much work! When you're of the same mind you're always yourself, no matter who you're talking to—it's much better. (Besides, being two-faced gets expensive. You have to buy two hair dryers, two curling irons, two toothbrushes, and you're always running out of electrical outlets.)

Being "of the same mind" means you can reach out to others too. There are people in your school who don't have many friends. What can you do about it? Well, when you see someone walking down the hall, eyes on the ground, no friends in sight, you be the one to say "hi." It's just a little word, but actions speak louder than words. Saying "hi" also says, "You're an important person—it doesn't matter whether you're in my 'compartment' or not. I'm not ashamed to recognize you, in front of all these people, as a worthwhile human being and a child of God."

You can really make a person's day, just by saying "hi." And if *that's* true, just imagine what a difference you could make if you were to call that person by name. Try it sometime. Find out the name of someone who needs a boost. (I'll bet you can think of someone right now.) Next time you see this person in the hall, say, "Hi, _____" (insert name here).

Let's imagine it happening. One day, you're walking down the hall and you say, "Hi, Jared," and you just keep walking down the hall. Just a casual "Hi, Jared," and you keep right on going. Now what's Jared doing? He's thinking (imagine his thoughts echoing, like in the movies): "How did he know my name?" And you, my friend, have just made a miracle. Someone was just made to feel important . . . by you. You're still walking down the hall, and he's standing with his mouth open, watching you walk away. You never know what burdens your classmates may be carrying, and a simple, friendly "hi" can make a lonely person's world turn from darkness to day.

Of course, we need to be careful about that. It has to be real, or, better said, *you* have to be real. This isn't something to *do,* this is something to *be.* If you walk up to someone and say, "Hi, I'd like to make you my personal service project for the month," it will probably backfire. The caring has to come from the inside out. If we change only how we act on the outside, or in other words our *behavior,* we might seem condescending and rude. If we really desire from the inside out to help people, we have to change our *nature.* Then our actions will naturally follow—we will not have to fake it. President Ezra Taft Benson said:

The Lord works from the inside out. The world

works from the outside in. . . . The world would shape human *behavior,* but Christ can change human *nature.* (*Ensign,* November 1985, 6; emphasis added)

Now, perhaps you're a student leader in your school: a student-body officer, a cheerleader, a class officer, or something else. Good for you! That's great. No doubt that takes a lot of time and energy, and, hopefully, it's a lot of fun too. Amidst all the good times, just remember who helped you get there!

> And in nothing doth man offend God, or against none is his wrath kindled, save those who confess not his hand in all things, and obey not his commandments. (D&C 59:21)

The Lord had a hand in your getting that leadership role. You are in a great position to make miracles happen in your school. People look up to you and they will follow you, so lead! Make it the cool thing to do to be kind and accepting to everyone. As the saying goes, "It's nice to be important, but it's more important to be nice."

There's one more thing that makes this whole idea a little complicated. It's called boys and girls together in the same place and everyone trying to figure out who likes whom. For example, if they're not careful, boys can "train" the girls *not* to be nice. Sometimes a girl tries to be nice to a boy and he assumes, "Oh . . . she must like me," when the girl was only trying to be friendly. This can cause so many problems for the girl that she may decide, "Forget this—every time I try to be nice to a guy he misunderstands, and then I have to tell him I just want to be friends, and then he might say I'm stuck up, and YUCK! this just isn't worth it, so I just won't talk to boys." Can you see how easily that can happen? Sometimes we train people not to be nice.

So what's the point? The point is, chill! Let people be nice just to be nice. If a girl likes you in an "I-wish-you'd-ask-me-out" way, you'll know. Girls know how to send that message too. This problem can occur the other way around, when girls misunderstand guys who are just trying to be nice, so perhaps we all need to chill. (Editor's note: The word *chill* in this case means "calm down." It will probably go out of style someday, so we thought we'd let you know what it means in case it already has. If so, please replace the word *chill* with something more modern like "disengage warp engines," or "stare off into space and sing a Gregorian chant," which also means "calm down." Thank you.)

Just one more rather serious thought to go with all this. If Jesus were to visit your high school, where would he go? What group would he spend his time with? We'll answer that question by asking another: Where did he go when he was on the earth? He spent his time with the lonely, the outcast, the lepers, those who didn't fit in—and he healed them. Using Jesus' example as our guide, what should we do?

George Albert Smith was one of the presidents of the Church. When I was in seminary, our teacher showed us George Albert Smith's "creed" or code of conduct. This is good stuff—I'll never forget it. It's divided into ten statements, which I'll share with you here. (The ones that stuck out most in my mind are italicized.)

1. I would be a friend to the friendless and find joy in ministering to the needs of the poor.

2. I would visit the sick and the afflicted and inspire in them a desire to be healed.

3. I would teach the truth to the understanding and blessing of all mankind.

4. I would seek out the erring one, and try to win him back to a righteous and happy life.

5. I would not seek to force people to live up to my ideals, but rather love them into doing the thing that is right.

6. I would live with the masses and help to solve their problems that their earth life may be happy.

7. I would avoid the publicity of high positions and discourage the flattery of thoughtless friends.

8. *I would not knowingly wound the feelings of any, not even one who may have wronged me, but would seek to do him good and make him my friend.*

9. I would overcome the tendency to selfishness and jealousy and rejoice in the success of all of the children of our Heavenly Father.

10. *I would not be an enemy to any living soul.* Knowing that the Redeemer of mankind has offered unto the world the only plan that would fully develop us, and make us really happy here and hereafter; I feel it not only a duty, but a privilege to disseminate this truth (*Sharing the Gospel with Others*, comp. Preston Nibley [Salt Lake City: Deseret News Press, 1948], 1).

Aren't those great goals? To be "a friend to the friendless," and "not be an enemy to any living soul." Can you imagine what a different world we would have if everyone lived by President Smith's creed!

How do you become popular? I'll tell you. Stop trying, and forget it. Be you. Focus on being who God wants you to be, and the rest will happen. You will be respected. It is much better to be respected than to be popular. Hmmm, that sounded profound, can I say that again? *It is better to be respected than to be popular.* And who knows, maybe you'll be both. You'll be popular *because* you're respected. You won't have to go off to college remembering regrets from high school.

Besides, popularity can be a fleeting thing. I remember

some of my classmates from back in junior high school. I remember observing some who were so confident, so popular. They wore all the right clothes; they said all the right things. I watched them a lot, because I guess I kind of admired their confidence. I wanted to be like that.

Years passed. One day when I was a senior in high school, I thought about some of those people I had looked up to in junior high. Where did they go? Many of them weren't in the limelight anymore. Something happened. They were the ones who had started dating early, who had started partying before everyone else. They got ahead of themselves, and many of them blew it. They made mistakes and damaged their reputations. And it seemed like another group of students—the ones who were a little quieter in junior high—kind of stepped up into their spots and took over. Interesting.

Anyway, if you're not "popular," please, don't spend one calorie of energy worrying about it. It's not that big a deal. There is life after high school: Your experience there is not a forecast for your life. You're in much better company if you spend your energy getting acquainted with your Father in Heaven, and being "popular" with or known by him.

All you have to do is do the best you can at being you—and that shouldn't be too hard. You've been doing it since you were born. Popular people don't get that way by imitating others—they're popular because they're comfortable being themselves. Make sense? I hope so. As Og Mandino once said:

> Be yourself. Try to be anything else but your genuine self, even if you deceive the entire world, and you will be ten thousand times worse than nothing. . . . You have been blessed with special skills that are yours alone. Use them, whatever they may be, and forget about wearing another's hat. A talented chariot driver can win gold

and renown with his skills. Let him pick figs and he would starve. No one can take your place! Realize this and be yourself. You have no obligation to succeed. You have only the obligation to be true to yourself. Do the very best that you can, in the things you do best, and you will know, in thy soul, that you are the greatest success in the world. (*The Greatest Success in the World* [New York: Bantam Books, 1981], 94)

I love that! I want to change one word, though. "You have no obligation to *be popular!* You have only the obligation to be true to yourself." Live your life by your values, and you'll earn respect. I'll say it one more time: It is better to be respected than to be popular. Popularity ends on yearbook day, but respect lasts forever. Why do I say forever? Well, the last time I saw most of my high school classmates was on graduation day. Unfortunately, the last thing I remember about a few of them is how mean they were. (I'm hopeful that they've changed. I'm hopeful that we all have.) Other students I remember well because I had such great respect for them—I still do. That's why I say respect lasts forever. So here's the question: *What lasting memory do you want to leave in the minds of your classmates?*

On your graduation day, many of you will grab your yearbooks and try to summarize your high-school years in one or two sentences. Which tribute would you rather see: "I didn't know you very well, but I always respected you for the way you lived, and the way you treated others. Thank you for being a friend when I felt like I didn't have one," or, "No way! You were like, so totally popular, okay?"?

As for high school, you have three or four years to do it, and the rest of eternity to think about it. Thanks for listening, and I'll see you in Second Period. Don't be late!

Second Period: Self-Esteem 101

Real Estate and Real Esteem: Finding a Foundation for Your Self-Worth

The least, the most inferior spirit now upon the earth . . . is worth worlds.
—*Brigham Young*

Your local bookstore has thousands of books on self-esteem. Listen to the words they use: *self-esteem, self-confidence, self-image, self-worth* . . . all these "self" words. What do they all mean? Sounds kind of self-*ish,* doesn't it? (At the North Pole, among Santa's crew, they use the words "elf-worth," "elf-confidence," and "elf-esteem." Ho, ho, ho.)

Writers through the years have used such words to mean different things. So before we go on, we need to decide what *we* mean by "self-esteem." Should we say that having good self-esteem means that we'll always feel good about ourselves? Yes. I mean, no. Well, maybe. Wait a sec . . . I mean, we'd better not. Because, if we *always* feel good about ourselves, there's probably something wrong. Sometimes we feel bad for good reasons. Listen to Nephi: "O wretched man that I am! Yea, my heart sorroweth because of my flesh; my soul grieveth because of mine iniquities" (2 Nephi 4:17).

Would we say that Nephi had "low self-esteem"? Of course not. Each of us *ought* to feel like Nephi did when confronted with our weaknesses—and we ought to respond the way he did, too: "I know in whom I have trusted. . . . My God hath been my support. . . . He hath filled me with his love" (2 Nephi 4:19–21).

Real, appropriate self-esteem, the kind everyone ought to have, has so little to do with self, and so much to do with God, that perhaps *self-esteem* isn't the best word to describe

25

it. Self-esteem, the way many in the world define it, places too much reliance on self, and not enough on God.

Have you ever been confused about this? I have. First we're told to be meek, humble, and submissive. Then we're told to have self-confidence—a positive attitude—and to believe in ourselves. Which one is it? Or is it a little of each? Fortunately, we can use our knowledge of the gospel as we struggle to figure this out. Elder James E. Faust gave a marvelous definition of appropriate self-esteem specially tailored for Latter-day Saints:

> The self-esteem to which I refer is something different. It is not blind, arrogant, vain love of self, but is self-respecting, unconceited, honest esteem of ourselves. It is born of inner peace and strength. (*Reach Up for the Light* [Salt Lake City: Deseret Book, 1990], 31)

There's the definition we want! And for the rest of this book, we're going to use the term *self-esteem* the way Elder Faust defined it: an honest, self-respecting, unconceited opinion of ourselves. So, should we *always* feel good about ourselves? Perhaps not. But we can enjoy the inner peace that comes from knowing that we are important to the Lord! He loved us enough to send his Son (see John 3:16), and he rejoices when we repent (see D&C 18:13). We may not always feel like it, but we are worthwhile. You, and I, and everyone else on earth is of great worth. Maybe we could make a bumper sticker that says, "Got worth?" Yes we do. That's a fact we know from the scriptures!

> Remember the worth of souls is great in the sight of God. (D&C 18:10)

You may be asking, "Well, if I'm of such great worth, why do I feel like I'm riding an emotional roller coaster? Why do I have so many ups and downs?" Good questions. Some of those things are just a part of growing up. However, one problem may be that you're building your foundation in the wrong place. Young or old, we *must* build on solid ground or we'll never feel stable.

Let's say you're going to build a house, and you're looking for a nice piece of land. Your real-estate agent fumbles through his listings and says,

"Say, I know a great area, and it's really cheap!"

"What's it called?" you ask.

"Landslide Hills."

"Why is it called that?"

"Well, because, uh, one day you'll be living on the north side of the street, and you'll hear a loud rumbling noise, a few pictures will fall off the walls, and then you'll be on the south side of the street."

"Uh, no, I don't think so."

"Well, let's see, I have some property next to a big river. The Petersons used to live there. Yup, 1016 Backstroke Drive."

"Are they still there?"

"No, they floated downstream last spring. Now they're at 1216 Backstroke Drive."

"Wow. What else have you got?"

"I believe two homes are up for sale on the fault line—let's see, yes! One home at 907 Achy Quaky Heart Circle, and one at 486 D. Fault Drive."

"Hmmm. Do you have anything with a better foundation?"

"How firm a foundation?" (Ha, ha.)

"I want something that will remain standing through rainstorms and floods and winds . . . you know, something rock solid."

"Oh—you want to build on a rock."

"Yes, of course; I thought you would take that for granite."
(Geology joke.)

When you're looking to build something important, something that you hope will remain standing, you want to build on solid ground. But it's especially tempting to build self-esteem on not-so-solid ground. The world tells us that worth comes from fame, wealth, awards, appearance, status, and so on. That is risky real estate! If you build there, you're taking your chances. Hop in the SUV, buckle up, let's check out a few of those spots, and you'll see what I mean.

LANDSLIDE HILLS—THE WAY OTHERS TREAT US

Hmmm, this looks nice. We could build our self-worth around our friends, or around the way others treat us. Friends are great! Choose your friends wisely, they say, because friends can make such a difference in your life. It's the best feeling in the world to have good friends who make you feel like you belong.

Some of my favorite high-school memories didn't happen anywhere near school, but just driving around with my friends. I can't even remember what we did half the time, but we always kept our standards high. We would laugh, go places, eat, visit girls . . . it was so much fun. I believe we could outparty any sorority or fraternity on this earth; we could have more fun, more laughs, stay up later—then wake up the next morning, remember everything we did, and not feel the least bit guilty (because we kept our standards).

So maybe that's it: Happiness and self-worth come from friends. That's where we'll build. Should we stop reading this chapter now because we've figured it out? Well, no. Friendship is a good support, but it's not a foundation for permanent self-esteem. Friends are great, but they can slip and slide and avalanche away too. Some friendships can be more like rivalries. One friend of mine had a landslide in her friendship neighborhood. She expressed it like this:

> One day they're your friend, and the next day they're your enemy. It's like they're saying, "Okay, today I'll be your friend, but tomorrow, I'm going to tell everyone what you told me about so and so, and you'll wonder why I'm trying to ruin your life. Then on another day, I'll be your friend again, and act like nothing happened. Your job, of course, is to forgive me every time, because no matter what, it's your fault.

Yuck. Thus the familiar saying, "With friends like that, who needs enemies?" I suppose those problems are ordinary in young friendships, but you, my friend, are not ordinary. And someone as extraordinary as you must be an extraordinary friend. We'll keep our good friendships, but we'd better not build on Landslide Hills, or we'll be comin' down the mountain. Let's pack up and move out—fasten your seat belt and pass the Twinkies. Okay, where else should we look? Let's check out the river!

BACKSTROKE DRIVE—OUR APPEARANCE

Hey, this is nice! Backstroke Drive looks really attractive. Why don't we try building our self-esteem on our appearance? You know, our clothes, our looks, our "image." Kind of tempting, huh?

I have a seminary-teacher friend named Kim Peterson. He gave a wonderful talk once where he passed out score cards and had all the youth "rate" certain people on a scale of 1 to 10. He held up a picture of a supermodel and all the boys gave her a 10. (Of course all the girls scored her in the 1 to 2 range.) Then he held up a picture of a male movie star, like Tom Cruise. This time the girls gave the 10s and the guys the 1s and 2s. He showed many more pictures, and everyone was having a good time. Then came the teaching moment; the next picture Brother Peterson pulled out was a portrait of Jesus. Confusion fell over the room. No one knew what to do! Some held up a 10; others tried to combine cards to make bigger numbers. The room became quiet because the game didn't seem to make sense anymore. Then Brother Peterson made a profound statement: "There is something wrong with a system where Jesus Christ and Tom Cruise get the same score."

What a great insight! There *is* something wrong with that system! And yet we use it every day to judge ourselves and to judge others. We are daily taught by the media to appreciate very few body types, and we often seem to value people only if they are good looking. I think Leo Tolstoy said it very well:

> It is amazing how complete is the delusion that beauty is goodness. (From *The Kreutzer Sonata,* as cited in *The Oxford Dictionary of Quotations,* 3d ed. [Oxford: Oxford University Press, 1979], 551)

People are valued for what's inside, not for the package they come in (see 1 Samuel 16:7 . . . of course, you already know this because it's a scripture mastery verse). Besides, with time the package will change. We don't love our grandmas because they are supermodels; we love them because of the quality of their hearts. Someday, everyone's "package" will be resurrected, and their status will be based on the beauty in their hearts and the purity of their lives.

Yup, better not build on Backstroke Drive. If we do, our self-esteem will float away like the other homes built on the riverbank. Back in the truck, Chuck. Now, what was the other place the agent mentioned?

ACHY QUAKY HEART CIRCLE OR D. FAULT DRIVE—OUR ACCOMPLISHMENTS

Why don't we base our self-esteem on our accomplishments? Because it's earthquake city, that's why. Please don't misunderstand. We believe in setting and achieving goals and everything else, and we know these things can make us feel happy. But we're looking for the *best* place to build, not just a good place. Keep setting your goals and working to achieve them, and never give up! Be a goal setter, but don't build your self-worth there. If you judge yourself solely by your accomplishments, you will always be able to find someone who can do more or better, and you may be tempted to make comparisons. In the words of Max Ehrmann:

> If you compare yourself with others, you may become vain or bitter. (In *Favorite Quotations from the Collection of Thomas S. Monson* [Salt Lake City: Deseret Book, 1985], 272)

We don't want vainness or bitterness, we want happiness! Besides, the real, worthwhile accomplishments are not flashy trophies, awards or degrees, cars, CDs, stereos, or other possessions. They're more often quiet acts of service and a life of devotion.

Many things make us happy for a while, but only a few things can help us be happy for a long time. We're not talking about the perma-grin-on-your-face happiness that makes you want to hug the bus driver and the grocery checker, but a quieter kind of happiness: a content feeling. Maybe the best word to describe that feeling is *peace,* or *inner peace,* as Elder Faust said. Where can we turn for peace? Not on D. Fault Drive, or Achy Quaky Heart Circle. If you build on Achy Quaky, all you'll have is shake and bakey. (Ah, poetry.)

So far we've checked out three places, and none of them worked out. There are hundreds of other places where we could find a foundation for our self-worth, but we're about to run out of gas! Where is the best place? We want a strong, durable foundation that will last for a lifetime.

GET A PLACE ON THE ROCK

It's been said that wise people learn from experience, and superwise people learn from others' experience. Well, we know of an experienced "ancient realtor" who can tell us where to build! He recommends a place for building not only self-esteem, but a whole life! His name is Helaman, and here's what he said to his sons, and to all of us (another scripture mastery verse):

And now, my sons, remember, remember that it is upon the rock of our Redeemer, who is Christ, the Son of God, that ye must build your foundation; that when the devil shall send forth his mighty winds, yea, his shafts in the whirlwind, yea, when all his hail and his mighty storm shall beat upon you, it shall have no power over you to drag you down to the gulf of misery and endless wo, because of the rock upon which ye are built, which is a sure foundation, a foundation whereon if men build they cannot fall. (Helaman 5:12; see also Luke 6:48)

Here's another great real-estate tip:

Wherefore, if you shall build up my church, upon the foundation of my gospel and my rock, the gates of hell shall not prevail against you. (D&C 18:5)

Now we're getting somewhere! Like we said before: Real, appropriate self-esteem has much more to do with God than it has to do with self. The rock-solid foundation on which to build our self-esteem is the Savior! The gospel! Our true identity as children of God! That's the foundation that won't slip or slide, quake or flood. Let's examine this real estate for real esteem in a little more detail.

YOUR IDENTITY AS A CHILD OF GOD

Sometimes people describe a teenager as having an "identity crisis." When people said that to me, I thought they meant I'd lost my wallet. I'd pull it out and look at my driver's license. "My I.D. looks fine," I'd say. "I don't think it's having a crisis."

Sometimes we say, "You're a child of God," and expect that to clear everything up. Sometimes we forget to explain what being a child of God means. I'm not sure any of us will understand completely what it means until after this life, but we'll do the best we can with what we know now. What does being a child of God mean?

A child of God: It means God is your Father. Our Father in Heaven is the very best father you can possibly imagine. He is perfect. He is the father of your spirit. Have you ever thought about what that means? Let's take a closer look. If you've ever worked on your genealogy, you've seen a pedigree chart. (Once at a youth conference I held up a pedigree chart, and one of the deacons said, "Hey, it's the NCAA tournament!")

Your name is written on a single line, and that line splits into double lines. On those lines, you write the names of your father and your mother. Those lines also each split into two more, where grandparents' names are listed, and so on, and so on, back thousands of years. With enough information, you would eventually get back to our first parents, Adam and Eve. That would be a *huge* chart; that would fill a large room! But, and this is important, that chart is the genealogy of your *body,* not your spirit. It shows only your mortal past, not your

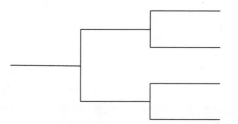

spiritual past. What would a pedigree chart for your *spirit* look like? Elder Boyd K. Packer once said:

> You are a child of God. He is the father of your spirit. Spiritually you are of noble birth, the offspring of the King of Heaven. Fix that truth in your mind and hold to it. However many generations in your mortal ancestry, no matter what race or people you represent, *the pedigree of your spirit can be written on a single line. You are a child of God!* (*Ensign,* May 1989, 54; emphasis added)

Who is the real you, anyway? Is it your body or your spirit? Your spirit, of course! It's been around a lot longer than your body. And what is earth life for? In a nutshell, to get your spirit to take charge of your body! (Why do you think we have fast Sunday? Hmmm?)

If your spirit is the real you, then who is your real father? Right, my friend, your Father in Heaven is *more* your father than your earthly father, because your spirit is more "you" than your body is. You've heard it hundreds of times before, but hopefully it means a little more this time: God is *your Father.* That means he knows you better than you know yourself. And that means you must come to know him too.

In fact, why not take a minute and think of all the things that might startle you when you see heaven for the first time: your new body, the streets, the trees, the animals, seeing all the ancient prophets you've read about! Think of all that might startle you, then read this next quote (it's my number-one favorite of all time). It was spoken by Ezra Taft Benson, a prophet of God:

> Nothing is going to startle us more when we pass through the veil to the other side than to realize *how well we know our Father and how familiar His face is to us.* (*The Teachings of Ezra Taft Benson* [Salt Lake City: Bookcraft, 1988], 24; emphasis added)

Brigham Young was a prophet too, and he said this:

> I want to tell you, each and every one of you, that you are well acquainted with God our Heavenly Father. . . . You are all well acquainted with him, for there is not a soul of you but what has lived in his house and dwelt with him year after year; and yet you are seeking to become acquainted with him, when the fact is, you have merely forgotten what you did know. (*Discourses of Brigham Young,* comp. John A. Widtsoe [Salt Lake City: Deseret Book, 1975], 50)

> If we could see our Father who dwells in the heavens, we should learn that we are as well acquainted with him as we are with our earthly father; and he would be as familiar to us in the expression of his countenance, and we should be ready to embrace him and fall upon his neck and kiss him, if we had the privilege. . . . And there is no other one item that will so much astound you, when your eyes are opened in eternity, as to think that you were so stupid in the body. (Brigham Young, *Journal of Discourses,* 8:30)

Convinced? I hope so. He is real. And he knows you. I'll repeat: Being a child of God means that God is your Father. All the might and power and glory and majesty you can possibly imagine is possessed by *your Father.* What else does "I am a child of God" mean?

A child of God: It means he listens. Maybe you have a best friend. Chances are, one of the things that makes this friend so wonderful is that he or she listens to you and understands you. Think of the person on this earth who listens to you and cares for you the very, very best. I have a friend like this. If I want to talk to him about something, he stops whatever he is doing. He closes the door, comes out from behind his desk, sits down in front of me, and listens; he listens to every word. He listens with his eyes and with his heart as well as with his ears. He listens to me as if I were the most important person in the world. My friend is a wonderful man, but he is imperfect. Think about this—if an imperfect man can listen that well, imagine how your perfect Father in Heaven can listen! Imagine how much he can care! Elder H. Burke Peterson said:

> I want you to know that I know that whenever one of Heavenly Father's children kneels and talks to him, he listens. I know this as well as I know anything in this world—that Heavenly Father listens to every prayer from his children. I know our prayers ascend to heaven. No matter what we may have done wrong, he listens to us. (*Ensign,* June 1981, 73)

Heavenly Father is much more than a friend. And Heavenly Father is interested in his children. He is totally selfless. His work and his glory is to bring to pass our success! (See Moses 1:39.) Throughout the scriptures he is constantly inviting us to pray and talk to him. You have never read a scripture that said, "Behold, only pray between 8:00 and 5:00, because, hey, we're busy up here." The invitations to pray are constant and varied: "Seek me diligently and ye shall find me; ask, and ye shall receive; knock, and it shall be opened unto you" (D&C 88:63). "Pray always, and I will pour out my Spirit upon you, and great shall be your blessing" (D&C 19:38). He wouldn't make the invitation if he didn't intend to listen. Being a child of God means that you have a Father who is intensely interested in you—he listens.

A child of God: It means help in overcoming temptation. In the Pearl of Great Price there is a wonderful story. It's only twenty-two verses long, but it gives us a great example of how to fight temptation. It shows us how Moses overcame the adversary by remembering who he was. Read this slowly—

this is good. It starts in the book of Moses, chapter one, verse three:

> And God spake unto Moses, saying: Behold, I am the Lord God Almighty, and Endless is my name; for I am without beginning of days or end of years; and is not this endless?
>
> And, behold, thou art my son. (Moses 1:3–4)

Okay, I have to stop you: Did you hear that? Moses just learned from a very *good source* who he was. God said, "Thou art my son." When Joseph Smith saw the Father and the Son, he said their "brightness and glory defied all description"! Imagine this beautiful and glorious being looking at *you* and saying, "*Thou* art my son." I imagine Moses thinking, "Me? Really?"

> Wherefore look, and I will show thee the workmanship of mine hands; but not all, for my works are without end, and also my words, for they never cease. . . .
>
> And I have a work for thee, Moses, my son; [there, it happened again—Moses is still learning about his identity] and thou art in the similitude of mine Only Begotten. (Moses 1:4, 6)

Wow. What a wonderful thing to say—in other words, "Moses, you're my son, and you look like Jesus," or, "You are like Jesus," or, "Your mission is to be like Jesus."

> And mine Only Begotten is and shall be the Savior, for he is full of grace and truth. . . .
>
> And now, behold, this one thing I show unto thee, Moses, my son, for thou art in the world, and now I show it unto thee. (Moses 1:6–7)

There's the third time Moses was called a son of God. In fact, every time the Lord says, "Moses," he adds "my son." Why do you suppose the Lord would do that? Do you think it's important? Do you think it made an impression? We'll find out very soon.

Next, Moses saw a wonderful vision. He saw the world and all of its inhabitants. How many is all? (He saw you.) When the vision was over, Moses was exhausted and fell unconscious for "the space of many hours." When Moses awoke, he made a wonderfully humble statement:

> Now, for this cause I know that man is nothing, which thing I never had supposed. (Moses 1:10)

What happens next is fascinating. But first, a question: Who would really like to mess up your understanding of who you are? Right. Satan. Well, take a wild guess who shows up next. Listen:

> And it came to pass that when Moses had said these words, behold, Satan came tempting him, saying: Moses, son of *man,* worship me. (Moses 1:12; emphasis added)

What do you suppose Satan is trying to do? Now remember, three times God called Moses "my son." As soon as God leaves, Satan comes along and tries to undo everything. The first thing he attacks is Moses' understanding of who he is. He calls Moses a "son of man." I imagine Moses thinking to himself, "Wait a minute. God said I was his son, and this being says I am a son of man. Hmmm . . . one of these things is not like the other." Moses responds beautifully.

> And it came to pass that Moses looked upon Satan and said: Who art thou? For behold, I am a son of God, in the similitude of his Only Begotten; and where is thy glory, that I should worship thee? (Moses 1:13)

Did Moses believe all he had heard? Yes! Moses heard and believed everything he was told by God. And when temptation stared him in the face, he said, "Who are you? I am a son of God." As you know, everything in the scriptures is there for a reason. Now, why do you suppose this event is recorded for *you* to read? Could it be that *you* have just been given a tool for how to respond to temptation? Could it be that if we truly understand who we are, sinning will be the farthest thing from our minds?

Perhaps Satan doesn't appear to you directly, but the world sure does: Hey, you wanna watch this video? Hey, have you seen this Web site? Hey, try this, everyone does. Or, in more subtle ways, the world says you have to be popular, you have to dress like this, you have to talk like this, you have to listen to this kind of music, or you won't fit in. How can you respond? By answering to yourself (if not out loud), "Who are you? I am a son of God."

For young women, understanding your identity is so important that every Sunday you're asked to stand up and recite your values. Why? So that when temptation comes along you will already know how to respond: "Who are you? We are daughters of our Heavenly Father who loves us, and we love him. We will stand as witnesses of God at all times in all things, and in all places . . ." Well, you know the rest.

Moses asked, "Who art thou? and where is thy glory that I should worship thee?" You can do the same by identifying temptations for what they really are. What? Watch that video? Where's the glory in doing that? What? Spread gossip about someone else? Where's the glory in that? What? Relax my standards on a date? I don't do that kind of stuff. Where's the glory in that? I am a daughter of God.

Three times Moses heard it, and I'll bet you've heard it more times than that. Modern apostles and prophets communicate with the Lord too. Over and over again they try to help you by reminding you who you are. (Good to review, when you're feeling blue.) Elder Vaughn J. Featherstone said:

It is not difficult to understand why the great God in heaven has reserved these special spirits for the final work of the kingdom prior to his millennial reign. . . . This generation will face trials and troubles that will exceed those of their pioneer forebears. Our generation has had some periods of respite from the foe. The future generation will have little or none. . . . This is a chosen generation. . . . I believe today's [LDS youth] will lead the youth of the world through the most trying time in history. (*Ensign,* November 1987, 27–29)

Wow. Did you hear that? Our trials and troubles will exceed those of the pioneers? No doubt you've heard inspiring stories from Church history about pioneers and handcarts, about unbelievable difficulties and trials. Perhaps our trials won't be the same *kind* as the ones the pioneers had, but in some ways they will be even more difficult. Father in Heaven sent you here because of his faith that you can do it. Okay, here's another favorite, from President Ezra Taft Benson:

For nearly six thousand years, God has held you in reserve to make your appearance in the final days before the Second Coming of the Lord. Every previous gospel dispensation has drifted into apostasy, but ours will not. . . . God has saved for the final inning some of his strongest children, who will help bear off the kingdom triumphantly. And that is where you come in, for you are the generation that must be prepared to meet your God. . . . Make no mistake about it—you are a marked generation. ("In His Steps," *1979 Devotional Speeches of the Year* [Provo, Utah: Brigham Young University Press, 1980], 59)

Identity is important. No matter what others say about you, or what you *think* they say (sometimes we imagine things worse than they are), now you know what *prophets* think. Others may say you're overweight or different or dumb, but God has shared with prophets who you *really* are. Who are you going to believe? I suggest believing God and his prophets. Being a child of God means help in overcoming temptation.

A child of God: It means he wants your success and he will be your ally. An ally is a friend who supports you, who will fight for you and help you when the chips are down. Your Father is a powerful ally. What father would not want his children to succeed? What father would not help his children fight their battles? There will be battles—spiritual battles—and the weapon you need is a testimony. President Ezra Taft Benson said:

> You have been born at this time for a sacred and glorious purpose. It is not by chance that you have been reserved to come to earth in this last dispensation of the fulness of times. Your birth at this particular time was foreordained in the eternities. You are the royal army of the Lord in the last days. You are "youth of the noble birthright." (*Hymns,* 1985, no. 225.) In the spiritual battles you are waging, I see you as today's sons of Helaman. (*Ensign,* May 1986, 43)

Sometimes people ask, "Why are there so many wars in the Book of Mormon?" Well, take a look around. We're at war right now. It's not a war with swords and spears, it's a war of principles; it's a war for your soul and mine. The war in heaven is continuing here on earth, and the Book of Mormon tells us how we can prevail. (We'll talk more about the Book of Mormon in Fourth Period.) Listen to the feelings of Elder Boyd K. Packer about your generation:

> It is my conviction that your generation is better and stronger than was mine. Better in many ways. I have the

faith that you young men and young women can meet the world on its own terms and conquer it. (*Ensign,* May 1989, 54)

"Meet the world on its own terms and conquer it." That's quite a statement, but it's true, because "If God be for us, who can prevail against us?" (JST Romans 8:31). The world cannot win because "they that be with us are more than they that be with them" (2 Kings 6:16). Even when you feel alone, remember that God and one other person makes a majority. Being a child of God means that God wants you to succeed and he is your ally.

All of this may be a little bit hard to understand. I know it was difficult for me to understand when I was young because, well, I was young. I thought other things brought self-esteem. When I got new clothes and put them on I felt an *immediate* lift. When I won a trophy or did well on a test, there was an immediate difference in how I felt about myself that day. Perhaps you don't feel the same kind of instant lift when you say to yourself, "I am a child of God," but be patient. As you come to know your Father in Heaven better, as you learn more about the gospel, and as your testimony grows, you will come to realize that you are built on the only foundation that really lasts—a foundation that can withstand anything the world throws at you.

Have we talked about this enough? I hope so. Yes, you are a child of God, but this isn't the end of self-esteem, it's only the beginning. Now you have to act like a child of God. ("We believe that as we come to accept and *act upon* these values . . .") You have a CTR ring, now you have to choose the right. If you know who you are, but ignore the commandments, of course you won't feel good.

Do you remember the letter you got from the First

Presidency? What's that? you say. What letter? You know, that letter from the Presidency of the Church?

Okay, it wasn't addressed to you personally (you'll get one of those when you go on a mission), but to all the youth of the Church. It's in the pamphlet *For the Strength of Youth*. There's a wonderful statement in your letter that relates to self-esteem. It says, "You can't do wrong and feel right" (4). The same idea has been expressed in many other ways too, but none better than this one: "Wickedness never was happiness" (Alma 41:10; see also Helaman 13:38).

The way to be happy is to be righteous. Isn't it amazing that something so incredibly obvious is ignored, denied, and even ridiculed by most people most of the time? You can't build lasting happiness on wealth, fame, appearance, or selfish pleasure, because the secret to happiness is righteousness. Gee, maybe that's why the Plan of Salvation is also called "The Plan of Happiness"! Listen to President Benson:

> One of Satan's most frequently used deceptions is the notion that the commandments of God are meant to restrict freedom and limit happiness. Young people especially sometimes feel that the standards of the Lord are like fences and chains, blocking them from those activities that seem most enjoyable in life. But exactly the opposite is true. The gospel plan is the plan by which men are brought to a fulness of joy. (*The Teachings of Ezra Taft Benson*, 357)

You mean, living the commandments makes us happy? Yes! You mean, standards help us maintain self-esteem? YES! You mean, wickedness never was happiness? YES, YES, YES! "Joy and happiness come from living the way the Lord wants you to live and from service to God and others" (*For the Strength of Youth*, 19). That's it. Search all you want, but that's it. To feel good, strive to be good. To feel loved, love and serve others.

Something wonderful happens to people who build on the proper foundation: Their language changes! For example, they no longer say, "I *can't* date till I'm sixteen, I *can't* drink, I *can't* see that movie, I *can't* do anything!" Instead, they say, "I *don't want to* date till I'm sixteen, I *don't want to* drink, I *don't want to* see that movie, I *don't want to* do anything against *my* standards." What's the change? Simple. Obedience has become a quest, instead of an irritation. (See C. Terry Warner, *Repenting of Unrighteous Feelings,* Ricks College Devotional Address, March 1, 1983.) Think about *that* one for a while—it's profound.

Well, friends, it's been a long day. We've covered a lot of ground, but we finally found a place to begin building our self-esteem. Good thing Helaman was there to help us. Now that you've found your foundation, does that mean you'll never have another bad day, or never feel down again? Nope. Sorry. No guarantees. Helaman didn't say it would never rain or flood again; he just said you'll be safe when the rains and floods come. And that's because you're built on a rock—a sure foundation—a foundation whereon if teenagers build they cannot fall. Your foundation is Christ, and he knows exactly what it's like to feel lonely, rejected, and misunderstood. He can help you make it through. Yes, there will be rain and floods and hail, but you'll have inner peace. You'll hear the thunder boom and the hail beat upon the house, but you'll be warm and cozy, sitting by the fire of your testimony, wrapped in a robe of righteousness, safely inside your home, built on a rock.

Your homework assignment for this class is to read *For the Strength of Youth.* (If you don't have a copy of the pamphlet, call your Young Men or Young Women leader and they'll give you one.) Read it! Please! Read every word of it! Its high standards are the building code for your life. We've found our foundation, and now we need floors, walls, and a roof. The foundation is the Lord; your life, built to the highest standards, is the rest. Congratulations on your new home, my friend—a home that will last. You did it! You got a place on the Rock.

EXTRA CREDIT

"A Prophet's Counsel and Prayer for Youth," Gordon B. Hinckley, *New Era,* January 2001, 4–15.

"To Young Women and Men," Boyd K. Packer, *Ensign,* May 1989, 53–59.

"To the Young Women of the Church," Ezra Taft Benson, *Ensign,* November 1986, 81–85.

"To the 'Youth of the Noble Birthright,'" Ezra Taft Benson, *Ensign,* May 1986, 43–46.

Third Period: Chastity 101

The Plan of Happiness:
The "Why" behind the Law of Chastity

*Humanity will rise or fall through its
attitude toward the law of chastity.
—Mark E. Petersen*

Good evening, folks, I'm Steve Goodguy, and welcome to 'Quiz Show for Dummies' Are the contestants ready?" *(Look left and smile for the camera.)* "Alrighty, away we go! And here's today's first stumper!

"Question 1: Why can't you shift from 'D' into 'P' while driving down the freeway?"

BZZZZZZT!

"Yes, Jack, your answer, please."

"Two words: Transmission explosion. (Important Driver's Ed safety tip: 'P' means 'Park,' not 'Pass.') Shifting into Park on the freeway causes Dad great physical and emotional discomfort."

"Okay, next question: "How much wood would a woodchuck chuck, if a woodchuck could chuck wood?"

BZZZZZZT!

"Yes, Diane."

"Four."

"Um . . . Sure, um, okay, very good.

Question 3: "If 'pro' is the opposite of 'con,' then what is the opposite of 'progress?'"

BZZZZZZT!

"Go ahead, Michael."

"Con-gress?"

"Wonderful, contestants! and now we'll take a break to hear from our sponsor, Chicken Soup for the Stomach . . .

BZZZZZZT! CLUNK, CLUNK, click.

We interrupt this ridiculous introduction to continue with this chapter. (In case you're wondering what happened in the game show, Jack went on to the idiot round and won the bus trip to Flagstaff.)

Hi, it's me. It's your author again. Welcome back to the book. Let's see, what class are we in? Oh yes. Chastity 101. Okay, here we go. The questions above were relatively easy to answer, and perfect for a game show. Some questions, however, require a little more thought (you'll never see *these* on a TV quiz show):

Question: Why can't I date until I'm sixteen?

Question: Why am I told to date only those with high standards?

Question: Why do we have to obey the law of chastity?

Question: Why can't I see any movie I want?

Question: Why can't I drink?

Question: Why do we have all these rules!?

Good questions, huh? And as we observe the behavior of those on television, in movies, in magazines, and even among our friends at school, questions like those are bound to come up. The idea of getting up in the morning and asking, "Gee, how many restrictions should I place on myself today?" seems strange to most of the world. They may not realize (yet) that real freedom comes from living by the rules. Being "free" means being the master of our passions, not their slave.

Okay, our thirty seconds are up, and it's time for our answer. BZZZZZZZZZZT! Mr. Goodguy, we can answer not only the six questions above, but every question about the standards we choose to live by; and we can answer in only four words: *The Plan of Salvation.*

Simple. The Plan of Salvation is the "big picture" that gives us all the answers. It's the map for our journey through time. Studying the Plan of Salvation is the best way to understand the commandments! In the light of "The Plan," the "whys" behind our standards—especially the law of chastity—are easy to see. Elder Boyd K. Packer explained:

> Without a knowledge of the gospel plan, transgression seems natural, innocent, even justified. *There is no greater protection from the adversary than for us to know the truth—to know the plan!* (*Our Father's Plan* [Salt Lake City: Deseret Book, 1994], 27; emphasis added)

The Plan of Salvation has many names. Among them are the plan of redemption (see Alma 12:32) and the plan of happiness (see Alma 42:8, 16). Let's use the last one, because we all want to be happy. And believe it or not, that's exactly what life is for. The Prophet Joseph Smith said:

> Happiness is the object and design of our existence; and will be the end thereof, if we pursue the path that leads to it; and this path is virtue, uprightness, faithfulness, holiness, and keeping all the commandments of God. (*Teachings of the Prophet Joseph Smith,* sel. Joseph Fielding Smith [Salt Lake City: Deseret Book, 1976], 255–56)

And who can forget these four oft-quoted words (especially since we've already used them in the book—but that's okay; scriptures never wear out): "Wickedness never was happiness" (Alma 41:10)?

By now you may be thinking, "This all sounds really nice, John, but happiness was not what I felt when I had to tell this totally gorgeous guy that I couldn't go out with him because I wasn't old enough," or, "Happiness is not what I experience when everyone at school makes fun of me because they know I'm saving myself for marriage."

You've got a point. But are you talking about short-term happiness or long-term happiness? Are you talking about feeling good now, or feeling great later? The Plan of Salvation is definitely a long-term thing (it's about as long-term as you can get), and there is a far greater happiness ahead if we can endure a few short-term trials on the way. Sometimes standards may seem like a pain—and maybe they are. It may cause a little bit of pain to stick to your standards, but doing so will mean much less pain, and therefore much more happiness, later on. As the old saying goes, "There are two kinds of pain in life: the pain of *discipline,* and the pain of *regret.* Discipline weighs ounces, while regret weighs tons." Which kind of pain do you prefer: a little now, or a lot later? Obviously, what we want in the eternities is much more important than what we want short-term. In fact, as someone once said, "The chief cause of failure and unhappiness in life is in trading what we want most for what we want at the moment."

Well, what do we want most? Happiness. And we're in luck, because The Plan is designed to give us *maximum* happiness! There are blessings beyond imagination waiting for us if we love our Father in Heaven and stick to his Plan. You may have quite an imagination, but the best you can imagine doesn't come close to what God has prepared for his faithful children.

Okay, here's another game show question: Imagine the most wonderful, beautiful, peaceful, happy place you possibly can—we'll call it heaven. Do you think you have a good imagination? BZZZZT. Sorry, you weren't even close. You can't imagine it, I can't imagine it, and Paul could only describe it like this:

> Eye hath not seen, nor ear heard, neither have entered into the heart of man, the things which God hath prepared for them that love him. (1 Corinthians 2:9)

Wow, what a promise! Once again, what's the ultimate

objective for each of us? To dwell with God in a state of "never-ending happiness" (Mosiah 2:41; Alma 28:12). As you know, in order to get there, we must take certain steps:

Come to earth and receive a body. (Done that.)

Be baptized. (Done that. If you're reading this and you *haven't* done that, I have a couple of friends I'd like you to meet.)

Develop faith. (Working on that.)

Obey the commandments. (Working on that.)

Have a celestial marriage. (This means not only being married in the temple, but working with your partner to make your temple marriage a "celestial" marriage. Working on that.)

Endure to the end. (Working on that too.)

Now, if Heavenly Father's objective is to get us to heaven, or, in other words, to "bring to pass the immortality and eternal life of man" (Moses 1:39), what would Satan's objective be? BZZZZZZT! Right! To keep us from getting there! If Moses 1:39 could be called the Lord's "Mission Statement," then this next scripture could be called Satan's mission statement: "For he [Satan] seeketh that all men might be miserable like unto himself" (2 Nephi 2:27).

If this is true, what will Satan try to do? What is his agenda? Simple. *Stop the Plan of Salvation.* Can he do that? No. The Plan will happen—it is happening. But he can try to slow it down, or to cause difficulties along the way (remember the Garden of Eden?). A perceptive teen (like yourself) once asked, "If Satan knows he's going to lose, why does he keep fighting against God?" Good question. Even if Satan does know he will eventually lose, some things are still up for grabs—the individual souls of you and me! He is trying to take captive as many souls as he can (see Moses 4:4). Earth life, then, is a battle for *our souls*. And how do we protect ourselves in this battle? We live our standards. (Hint: *talking* about our standards is nice too, but *living* them is what protects us.)

Let's get specific. Knowing that Satan wants to frustrate The Plan, what do you suppose he will do first? Exactly. *Prevent spirits from coming to earth.* How will he do this? He'll do all in his power to promote abortion. He'll convince people to have no children. He will raise fears about overpopulation and encourage governments to make laws that limit the number of children couples can have. He'll do whatever he can to keep those spirits from coming!

What if the spirits get here anyway? (I mean, you and I and everyone else on the planet did.) Well, one of the steps of The Plan listed above was to have a celestial marriage. In order to enter the temple and receive the ordinance that makes possible a celestial marriage, we must obey what? BZZZZZZT! Right! The law of chastity!

The law of chastity is the number-one commandment Satan will try to get us to break! The most powerful weapon in his arsenal of misery is immorality. Prophets have warned us about it throughout time. President Ezra Taft Benson said:

> The plaguing sin of this generation is sexual immorality. This, the Prophet Joseph said, would be the source of more temptations, more buffetings, and more difficulties for the elders of Israel than any other. (*A Witness and a Warning* [Salt Lake City: Deseret Book, 1988], 74. See also Journal of Discourses, 8:55)

The power to bring children into this world is the most sacred power God has given us, and he has told us that it is to be used only by those who are lawfully married. But Satan tries to make the sacred seem cheap, common, low, and only for selfish pleasure. He wants people to tell dirty stories and jokes, taking sacred things and making them sound vulgar and crude. He promotes sex without responsibility, without the commitment of marriage (or any commitment at all). "Do what you want, live it up! It doesn't matter—just protect yourself." It's like saying, "Don't break the speed limit, but if you do, here's a radar detector—practice safe speeding." Most of the time, when the world uses the term "safe sex" what they really mean is "safe immorality" and that's a contradiction in terms—there's nothing safe about it.

Satan also attacks marriage and families. He does everything he can to make marriage look old-fashioned, outdated, like too much of a commitment, too much responsibility. He persuades people to decide, "Why don't we just live together?"

Is his strategy working? Well, take a look around. Anyone who is awake can see that traditional homes and families are under attack, and the attacks will continue. I read the most chilling quote the other day, and it comes from a leader in a movement that claims to be trying to help women:

> Since marriage constitutes slavery for women, it is clear that the women's movement must concentrate on attacking marriage. Freedom for women cannot be without the abolition of marriage. (Sheila Cronen, as cited in Rush Limbaugh, *The Way Things Ought to Be* [New York: Pocket Books, 1992], 188)

Gee, thank you for that inspiring thought. It reminds me of another quote from President Harold B. Lee:

> Satan's greatest threat today is to destroy the family, and to make a mockery of the law of chastity and the sanctity of the marriage covenant. (*The Teachings of Harold B. Lee* [Salt Lake City: Bookcraft, 1996], 227)

Satan fights this battle on many fronts—he finds many

ways to disrupt The Plan. For example, besides being addictive and destructive, pornography exploits and demeans people (mostly women and children). It sends the message that people are to be valued only as objects—not as spirit individuals, each with a mind and a heart. It also sends the false message that "looks" are more important than anything else, and that we don't have to control our thoughts (see *For the Strength of Youth,* 11).

How does the Word of Wisdom fit into all this? The Word of Wisdom is about the health of our bodies, but it's also about our spirits! What did we, as spirits, fight to keep in the premortal existence? BZZZZZZT! Right: our agency—an essential part of The Plan. What does drinking, or smoking, or drug abuse, or pornography, or *any other addictive behavior* do? Right again—little by little, such behaviors cause us to give away our agency, the very thing we fought to keep! See how it all fits?

Observe the world! Use your brain and your perceptivity, and you'll notice things every day that can be traced back to Satan's basic goal of undermining the Plan of Happiness. Look closely, because Satan is in disguise. Read this description of him, given by the First Presidency:

> He is working under such perfect disguise that many do not recognize either him or his methods. There is no crime he would not commit, no debauchery he would not set up, no plague he would not send, no heart he would not break, no life he would not take, no soul he would not destroy. He comes as a thief in the night; he is a wolf in sheep's clothing. (*Messages of the First Presidency,* comp. James R. Clark, 6 vols. [Salt Lake City: Bookcraft, 1965–75], 6:179)

We must remain alert and recognize what Satan is trying to do. What does Satan want teenagers and young adults to think? Simple. He wants them to think they are a bunch of misfit weirdos if they're not out being immoral every weekend. Get them to think they're pitiful nobodies if they've never been kissed! Get them to feel discouraged and lonely because they're eighteen and they don't date much! And get them to blame that discouragement not on Satan, where it belongs, but *on their standards!* Don't you fall for it! Your tough standards are protections, not punishments! Their purpose is to save your life, not to make it hard. Yes, they make you different from the world, but who wants to be like the world? It's gross!

If I were speaking to you from a lectern or a pulpit instead of a laptop, I would clench my fist and pound the pulpit to give emphasis to these words. My friend, you don't need to compromise! You don't need to descend to the standards of the world! You live a higher standard; you live on a higher plane; you set your sights on the stars, not in the gutter. High standards are made to match the high quality of your spirit. May I repeat? *High standards match the high quality of your spirit!*

It's easy to get really hyper about this topic because too many teenagers think they're in some kind of race: a race to date, a race to have a boyfriend or girlfriend, a race to kiss or be kissed. May I say to you in the spirit of friendship, if you're eighteen and you've never been kissed, *big deal!* If you're eighteen and you've never been on a date, *big whoop!* This is not a race! And even if it were a race, those who cross the finish line first are usually losing—losing virtue and self-respect, and seriously jeopardizing their chances of obtaining the "never-ending happiness" promised in the celestial kingdom (see Mosiah 2:41).

Satan is the enemy of the Plan of Happiness. He is the enemy of romance, and the enemy of love. His plan is the plan of misery. His plan is to ruin our chances for exaltation. So, if we're going to make it back to our Father in Heaven, we'd better come up with a battle plan of our own. Basically, it comes down to your right to choose how you're going to live your life. You can either float along with the popular drift of the world, do what everyone else does, "go with the flow"—or you can set your sights on higher ground, and choose a higher course consistent with the quality of your spirit.

You don't have to apologize to the world about your standards! They'll do what they choose to do, and you'll do what you choose to do. They'll be accountable for their choices, and you'll be accountable for yours. Hmmm, sounds like "Choice and Accountability." Ever heard that phrase?

One of the few things you can really control in life is your standards. You can't change your eye color, your height, the shape of your nose—but you can absolutely choose your standards. You can stand up and say to the world, "This is who I am! This is what I believe! This is what I'll do, and this is what I won't do!"

At this point, you may be thinking, "This is kind of a stretch. Just because I go out with a guy when I'm fifteen, that doesn't mean I'll mess up the whole Plan of Salvation!" That's true, but you have to understand how clever Satan is. He has his own version of "line upon line, precept on precept." I call it "lie upon lie, decept on decept." He'll encourage you to make little compromises at first. Just little things at the beginning. He just wants you to take some small steps along one of his paths: a path of saying, "Oh, it's not that bad"; a path of minor compromises here and there. But little steps lead to medium steps, and then giant steps. Before you know it, you've traveled farther than you realize—and the farther you go, the harder it is to turn around. One of

Satan's more clever lies is this one: "You can do what you want now, and repent later." He neglects to point out how hard that repenting might be.

So what's the solution? Don't start on the path—not even a step. Don't try hand-to-hand combat with Satan; just stay off his turf. Satan is patient, and he's very experienced. If you start dating when you're fourteen, or fifteen, then he's got even more time to work on getting you to think that maybe it's not that bad to violate the law of chastity. And once you think it, he'll begin to move you "lie upon lie" and tempt you to condone it, and move you that much closer to doing it.

As W. Jeffrey Marsh once said, "the path to the tree of life does not go through the great and spacious building"—it avoids it entirely. In order to stay on the path of happiness, you need to choose *right now* how you're going to behave regarding physical affection.

WHAT DO KISSES MEAN?

One of the fun things about working with teenagers is interpreting their body language. If you're giving a talk that bores them, teenagers don't have any problem letting you know. They'll yawn, fall asleep, rest their heads on their hands, sigh loudly, and set their alarm watches to go off. Some will even rest their heads on the bench in front of them and fall asleep. That's why you see a red indentation on the foreheads of many deacons as they walk out of meetings. (Can you imagine anyone falling asleep in meetings? Or English class?)

All of us can communicate loud and clear without using words. In fact, as the old saying goes, "Actions speak *louder* than words." With that idea in mind, let's ask some questions. If you put your arm around someone on a date, what are you saying (without using words)? How about, "I like you." Fair enough? Okay. What if you hold hands with your date? That's a notch or two higher, isn't it? Maybe that's like saying, "I really like you." What if you kiss your date? What are you saying? *What do kisses mean, anyway?*

My seminary teacher tried to explain that to a bunch of us sixteen-year-olds one day. He said, "Class, guys and girls are different." Wow. Several people passed out on the spot, and someone said, "I knew there was something different about them!" Okay, I'm not being fair, because that's not all he said. What he really said was, "Guys and girls are different, and sometimes expressions of affection mean different things to different people. Generally speaking, when a girl is being kissed, she may be thinking, 'Oh . . . this means he likes me; he really cares for me.'" Of course, all of us were intensely interested in this topic but we were trying not to act like it. He continued, "When a boy is kissing a girl, *he* may be thinking, 'Wow, this feels good. I'd like to do this again very soon.'" You may laugh at first, but think about that for a minute. Can you see the potential for problems?

Different people interpret kisses differently. Can you see how easily a *mis*communication or a *mis*understanding can happen? We communicate loud and clear with our actions, and if we're not careful, we could be telling lies! Listen to Elder Marvin J. Ashton:

> A lie is *any* communication given to another with the intent to deceive. . . . A lie can be effectively communicated without words ever being spoken. (*Ensign,* May 1982, 9)

You mean you can be dishonest by kissing someone? *Yes.* If putting your arm around someone means "I like you," and holding hands means "I really like you," than maybe kisses mean "I love you." What do you think? Some will say, "I don't know about that; I don't think kisses mean I love you." Perfect. That makes the point even better. Maybe kisses mean something different to you than they do to me, or to him, or her. And that's exactly why we have to be careful—because we could be telling lies with our actions. This is a major reason why people get hurt, and why there's painful heartaches. Kisses are wonderful, but they are powerful and should be handled with great care.

My friend Randal Wright wrote about a young man who bragged that he had kissed more girls in one day than anyone else in his stake (see "The Dating Years, Charting a Safe Course," by Randal A. Wright, in *Feeling Great, Doing Right, Hanging Tough* [Salt Lake City: Bookcraft, 1991], 105). He felt he had set a "record." To him, kissing was some kind of contest! I wonder how the girls felt about this. At the time they may have thought, "Wow. This boy really cares for me." Did they know he was just going for a record? Did they realize that each girl he kissed was only a notch on the way to his "goal"? Do you think it would have hurt their feelings to know that? President Thomas S. Monson said, "Men, take care not to make women weep, for God counts their tears" (*Ensign,* November 1990, 47).

What has happened to kissing? Doesn't it mean anything anymore? Listen to President Spencer W. Kimball:

> Kissing has been prostituted and has degenerated to develop and express lust instead of affection, honor, and admiration. To kiss in casual dating is asking for trouble. *What do kisses mean* when given out like pretzels, and robbed of sacredness? (*The Teachings of Spencer W. Kimball,* Edward L. Kimball, ed. [Salt Lake City: Bookcraft, 1982], 281)

Finally, the answer from a prophet: Kisses are sacred and are meant to express affection, honor, and admiration. In contrast, if you give out your kisses like free samples at the grocery store, what are they worth? Well, about the same as free samples at the grocery store!

I met a wonderful eighteen-year-old once (he's now a returned missionary) who wrote his feelings about kisses in the following poem:

Kisses

The more the dollar is printed, the less each one is worth.
And so it is with kisses you've given since your birth.
The value of your kisses, a sample cannot measure,
Nor is your kiss more worthy if it's said to give one pleasure.
The more and more you give away, the better your kiss is
*   known.*
And to all the world, your kiss is cheap, and your affection
*   shown.*
But if you save your kisses, no matter what the cost,
You'll find as time moves forward, a chance you've saved, not
*   lost!*
Then when you find the one you love, with whom you'll live
*   life through,*
Think of the worth of a perfect kiss, if saved for only you . . .
(Alvin W. Jones III, used by permission)

What an interesting poem, and what a sharp young man! Imagine a poem like that being written by a teenage boy these days! All that chosen generation stuff must be true. Alvin reminds us that kissing isn't a contest! You can save your kisses, and "you'll find as time moves forward, a chance you've saved, not lost."

One of my friends had an interesting experience at a wedding reception. As she was going through the line, the bride pulled her aside and said, "Do you know what I regret?"

My friend said, "What?"

"I regret that I have kissed so many guys."

"Really?"

"Yes. I asked my husband, 'How many girls have you kissed?' and he said, 'Um . . . I think three.'"

This bride was a little embarrassed, because she had given out kisses like pretzels. When you go to your wedding, you don't want regrets to go with you. You just want bridesmaids and flowers and cake and a clean, worthy young man or young woman who stuck to his or her standards, as you did.

In short: Save your kisses; you may need them one day. Look forward to that wedding day, and plan for it. How do you want to feel as you kneel at the altar? How do you want to feel about your past when you're looking into the eyes of your new husband or wife? Well, you can make it happen just the way you want if you plan it now!

A BATTLE PLAN OF OUR OWN

I attended a standards night where someone asked, "How far can we go before we have to see the bishop?" What an awful question! Imagine a skydiver asking, "How close can I get to the ground before I have to open the parachute?" In order to save us from thinking that we can fall at eighty miles an hour and pull the ripcord "just in time," our prophets and leaders have given us some help. Much of that help is found in—you guessed it—*For the Strength of Youth.* Here's part of what it says: "In cultures where dating is appropriate, do not date until you are sixteen years old." It also says, "Since dating is preparation for marriage, date only those with high standards, who respect your standards, and in whose company you can maintain the standards of the gospel of Jesus Christ" (7).

Okay, down to brass tacks. What about expressions of affection? What will you decide? Of course, this is a very personal subject. Your parents, your bishop, and your Young Men and Young Women leaders can help you. In addition to accepting the counsel from the Church, some teenagers (sharp teenagers like you, who read books and make their own decisions) set several standards for themselves. Here's an example:

Ultimate goal:

To gain eternal life. In order to do this, I must marry "the right person, in the right place, by the right authority" (Bruce R. McConkie, New Era, January 1975, 38).

Dating goal:

To have fun, to meet many different people, to begin to identify qualities I'd like in my future spouse.

Church standards:

I will not begin dating until I'm sixteen.

I will date only those with high standards, who respect my standards, and in whose company I can maintain the standards of the gospel of Jesus Christ.

Personal standards:

I will save my kisses; I will realize that I will be much more respected for what I withhold than for what I allow.

I will realize that late at night I don't think as clearly, and I am more vulnerable. Therefore, I will set a reasonable curfew for myself.

A teenager who lives by these high standards will avoid a lot of problems. Unfortunately, some "spiritual skydivers" feel they can fall much farther than others before pulling the ripcord. They place themselves in danger of not being able to stop before they hit the ground. They are flirting with disaster. President Kimball counseled against French kissing, or the "soul kiss," because it places one in that kind of danger:

> What is miscalled the "soul kiss" is an abomination and stirs passions to the eventual loss of virtue. Even if

timely courtship justifies the kiss it should be a clean, decent, sexless one like the kiss between mother and son, or father and daughter. (*Teachings of Spencer W. Kimball,* 281)

Are those high standards? Yes. Can you live them? Yes. And *it's better to have high standards and postpone a few things than to have low standards and lose everything.*

Around Christmastime we place all the beautiful gifts under the tree, and we "postpone" opening them until Christmas morning. If we wanted to, we could sneak in and open all our presents before Christmas, but it would ruin the fun and the anticipation. Experimenting too early with expressions of affection is like opening all your presents before Christmas. It's not nearly as nice as waiting for the appropriate time. You see, you are working on a wonderful gift. You've been working on it since you were born, and only you can give it! You don't want to share it until the time is just right. On some exciting future day, you'll be able to give this gift to someone else. The gift you've been working on all your life, is you! Elder Jeffrey R. Holland taught:

> On your wedding day the very best gift you can give your eternal companion is your very best self—clean and pure and worthy of such purity in return. (*Ensign,* November 1998, 77)

Many in the world would laugh at our standards. Let them laugh if they want to. Paul said, "I am not ashamed of the gospel of Christ" (Romans 1:16), and neither are we. We just want to be clean. Being clean feels better than guilt and remorse. John Taylor said, "When men say unto us, 'you are not like us' we reply, 'we know it; we do not want to be. We want to be like the Lord'" (*Journal of Discourses,* 11:347).

Who wants to trade a few moments of pleasure for weeks and months of guilt and pain? It's just not worth it. When you return home from your dates, you want to be able to sleep peacefully. When the morning comes, and much of your spiritual and mental alertness returns, you want to be able to look yourself in the mirror and smile with joy. Listen to Elder Russell M. Nelson:

> Above all, courtesy to companions cannot be defiled by disobedience to the law of chastity. That sin is joy's deadly poison. The first morning's glance in the mirror cannot reflect joy if there is any recollection of misdeeds the night before. The surest step toward joy in the morning is virtue in the evening. (*Ensign,* November 1986, 68)

We could go on for pages and pages (some of you are afraid I will). There are so many reasons to keep the law of chastity! But it all goes back to the Plan of Happiness. And even if we don't fully understand all the "whys," we can understand that God loves his children, and gives us commandments because of that love. Sometimes we have to obey even if we don't know why.

> And after many days an angel of the Lord appeared unto Adam, saying: Why dost thou offer sacrifices unto the Lord? And Adam said unto him: I know not, save the Lord commanded me. (Moses 5:6)

If you still don't understand, follow the example of Adam, like my friend Amber did:

> And after many days, the bishop of the ward interviewed Amber, saying, Why dost thou not date until thou art sixteen? And Amber said unto him: I know not, save the Lord commanded me. (Amber's journal, page 5, line 6)

Elder Boyd K. Packer praised young people like Amber and promised them blessings:

Oh, youth . . . the requirements of the Church are the highway to love, with guardrails securely in place . . . with help along the way. How foolish is the youth who feels that the Church is a fence around love to keep him out. . . . How fortunate is the young person who follows the standards of the Church, *even if just from sheer obedience or habit,* for he will find rapture and a joy fulfilled. (*Ensign,* October 1982, 66; emphasis added)

CLASS REVIEW

Now, let's see if we can summarize Third Period in a few words: The Plan of Salvation is the Plan of Happiness. Study it! Learn it! Understand it! Satan will tempt you "lie upon lie" in the areas that will frustrate your goal of exaltation. One of the main areas is the law of chastity. Your personal standards are protections, not punishments. They will help you in the battle for your soul. If, after all you've read, you still don't understand, obey anyway because you love the Lord and want to follow his commandments. Happiness is why you're here, and the Plan of Salvation is the highway to happiness.

Okay, that's it! See you next hour, and don't be tardy!

BZZZZZZT, Clunk, Clunk, BZZZZZZT, click.

Thank you for being with us on "Quiz Show for Dummies!" That's all the time we have tonight, folks, but join us again next time for another brain-stumper extravaganza. I'm Steve Goodguy, reminding you that when skydiving, remember your parachute, and for best results, pull the ripcord! Good night, everybody!

EXTRA CREDIT

"Personal Purity," Jeffrey R. Holland, *Ensign,* November 1998, 75–78.

Of Souls, Symbols, and Sacraments, Jeffrey R. Holland (Salt Lake City: Deseret Book, 2001).

Why Say No When the World Says Yes? Randal A. Wright, comp. (Salt Lake City: Deseret Book, 1993).

"Bridle All Your Passions," Bruce and Marie Hafen, *Ensign,* February 1994, 14–18.

"The Gospel and Romantic Love," Bruce C. Hafen, *Ensign,* October 1982, 64–69.

"Breaking Up without Going to Pieces," M. Gawain Wells, *Ensign,* June 1982, 58–61.

Assembly

"The Way, the Truth, and the Life"

*We must know Christ better than we know him;
we must remember him more often than we
remember him; we must serve him more valiantly
than we serve him.... What manner of men
and women ought we to be? Even as he is.*
—*Howard W. Hunter*

Are you having fun reading this book? I hope so. I've had fun writing it, too. This chapter will be a little different. As you recall, in the Orientation I mentioned that some chapters in this book might not be as fun or as funny as others, but they would be something better, like interesting or testimony building. This is one of those chapters. In the book of Ecclesiastes it says:

To every thing there is a season, and a time to every purpose under the heaven:

A time to be born, and a time to die; a time to plant, and a time to pluck up that which is planted;

A time to kill, and a time to heal; a time to break down, and a time to build up;

A time to weep, and a time to laugh; a time to mourn, and a time to dance. (Ecclesiastes 3:1–4)

One sign of maturity is the ability to understand the proper time and place for things. Some people say that teenagers have a hard time being serious. That's not true. Some people also say that teenagers don't read books. Wrong again. Obviously, they have never met you. I have learned over and over again never to underestimate teenagers. Let 'em know you're serious and give it to 'em straight, and they'll listen. So, what time is it now? It's time to talk about what's most important. This is the most serious chapter in the book. But it's also the best, because of what we get to discuss.

On the Brigham Young University campus, there is a

building called the Testing Center. Hundreds of different exams from hundreds of different classes are administered in this building designed especially for giving people tests. At the front counter the attendant gives you the test you need, along with a computer answer sheet and a #2 pencil. Then you find a chair and sit down and take your test.

If you visited the Testing Center, especially during final exams, you would notice a few things. People look tired and drained. They are usually on edge and they keep to themselves. Nobody likes taking a test. I have never seen anyone in the Testing Center look like they're about to burst with joy. Why should they? It's a place where you go to take tests.

You've decided—and it was the right decision—to take this massive exam called earth life. It is difficult and dangerous. Don't be too surprised if at times it feels like you're taking a test. You are. That's why you're here.

Once, at a youth conference in a faraway state, I noticed a young man who hung around the walls. He was dressed in black and had a kind of scowl on his face. Later, a kind bishop asked me if I wouldn't mind paying some attention to this boy. (I'll call him Brett.) As inconspicuously as I could, I maneuvered my way next to Brett and began to talk. At length he began to respond, still looking down at the floor with the same scowl on his face. I asked him about his family and he told me that his dad had been killed by a drunk driver when he was five. I began to understand why he was angry. Throughout the conference I tried to notice him. When I'd put my arm around his shoulder, he'd make a gun out of his hand and shoot me. Every time I touched him he'd make a gun and shoot—my head, my arm, my stomach. What do you think that meant?

At the service project I was glad to see him involved and working. When I walked by to say "hi," I noticed that he had a terrible broken blister on his hand. He had—purposely, I'm sure—raked and raked while holding the handle in the same spot until the skin next to his thumb was completely gone and the area was bloody and raw. I said to him, "That's gotta hurt." And without lifting his eyes he said, "I'm really used to pain." This world is a big Testing Center. Sometimes the tests are brutal. Brett was taking a difficult test. My guess is that he was full of anger—anger at the world, anger at people, maybe even God.

At another youth conference I met a young lady who had been repeatedly abused by her father. She too was taking a test, a terribly difficult one. Among those who are reading this book there is pain and there is hurt. There are grudges and jealousies and feelings of betrayal. Please read this next part as closely as you know how to. Pay attention not so much to what is written, but to your feelings—see if the Spirit will verify what you are reading. If you are one who has endured that kind of trial, listen. God did not want those things to happen. They are not your fault. God gave people agency and asked them to choose him, their Father. But some are without affection and hate their own family (see Moses 7:33). We knew in the pre-earth life that agency could be a dangerous thing for some who could not handle it. God has made it very clear how he feels about those who offend his little ones (see Luke 17:2). Again, if you have suffered such pain, please listen: It is not your fault. Your wounds can be healed, and your pain can be relieved.

I read once in the *Church News* this explanation from a therapist:

> Some families have many bad sins and habits passed on from one generation to another. The Lord wants to help families like these. He chooses brave and valiant

spirits who will . . . refuse to pass [the abuse] on.
("Mormon Forum," 6 May 1989, 15)

A few weeks later I found myself in Alabama at a youth conference. Toward the end of my talk on a different subject, I thought about sharing this idea on abuse. I resisted until I felt prompted again. This time I shared the idea—God sends strong individuals into families to break the cycle—and I closed my talk.

After picking up my things and speaking to a few of the youth gathered around the podium, I walked up the aisle of the auditorium. I saw a young couple, both in tears. They explained to me that they both came from homes where they had been abused, and that on this night, for the first time, they understood that they may have been sent to break the horrible cycle. I felt humbled, but I also felt joy—not so much that I might have been inspired, but that I had just learned for myself, firsthand, how much God loves and wants to reach out to those who have been abused. Yes, there is pain and unspeakable hardship. You are not alone. Friends, bishops, and professionals lend necessary support and counsel. And there is one who willingly died so that He could take all the pain away. This earth is a difficult place—it is a place to take tests.

I wish there were more time to adequately cover this sad subject, but there is not. Bad things happen to good people. Bad things happened to Nephi, bad things happened to Abraham, bad things happened to Job, bad things happened to Abinadi, bad things happened to Joseph Smith, and bad things happened to Jesus. And perhaps bad things will happen to all of us. But bad things, if we strive to be agents instead of victims, can push us closer to God. He can heal our wounds and help us in our pain.

And he [the Son of God] shall go forth, suffering pains and afflictions and temptations of every kind; and this that the word might be fulfilled which saith he will take upon him the pains and the sicknesses of his people. (Alma 7:11)

The Atonement is not just for sinners (see Bruce C. Hafen, *The Broken Heart* [Salt Lake City: Deseret Book, 1989], 1). Alma didn't even mention sin in that scripture. Jesus died to save us not only from our sins, but also from our pains and our sicknesses—the dark, lonely, helpless feelings from the things that happen *to* us. He experienced those feelings so that we can know that he knows exactly how we feel. The Atonement is infinite and eternal (see 2 Nephi 9:7; Alma 34:10, 12). Jesus can heal our wounds and help us in our pain.

Therefore, fear not, little flock; do good; let earth and hell combine against you, for if ye are built upon my rock, they cannot prevail. (D&C 6:34; see also Helaman 5:12)

If I could be your big brother for a minute, I would tell you that my greatest learning has come from my greatest pain. The hardships you endure will fill you with love and compassion for your fellow beings. They'll give you patience and understanding and a deep respect for those around you who also suffer. Imagine how absurd it would be to ask God to save us from all pain, hardship, and disappointment. "Save me, Father, from all the things that will help me to become kind and loving and wonderful and more like thee."

My friend Kenneth Cope wrote a song a few years ago called "Hear Them Cry." I asked him what it meant, and he explained it to me. The cry of a newborn baby is a signal that a new life has begun. As we grow older, through childhood and into the teenage years, we are told such things as, "Big boys and big girls don't cry." We learn not to "wear our heart on our sleeve." We keep our hard times and problems to ourselves, maybe sharing them with only a few. Things that would have made us cry years ago, we simply endure as we grow older. But we still cry inside. If we are willing to "listen between the lines," we can hear the cries of those around us. In a world full of pains of all kinds, certainly this is not a time to ignore each other. Jesus said, "If ye are not one ye are not mine" (D&C 38:27). As you progress on your journey closer to God, you will notice that the way you see other people will change. The Prophet Joseph Smith said:

> The nearer we get to our heavenly Father, the more we are disposed to look with compassion on perishing souls; we feel that we want to take them upon our shoulders, and cast their sins behind our backs. (*Teachings of the Prophet Joseph Smith,* sel. Joseph Fielding Smith [Salt Lake City: Deseret Book, 1976], 241)

There was a young man in my high school who was close to God. I watched him one day do something that broke all the rules of how "popular" people are supposed to act. We were all socializing in a part of the building we called "jock hall." This was where all the cool, popular people hung out. Rodney, a tough kid and an all-star hockey player, walked down the stairs leading to "jock hall." But instead of joining the social people in the hall, Rodney heard one of those silent cries. He walked to the doorway of the Special Education room. A teacher was wheeling a severely mentally and physically handicapped boy into the hall. I watched out of the corner of my eye as Rodney, who later went on to play hockey at Cornell University, knelt on the hard floor and talked to that handicapped boy. "Hi, how are you doing today?" he began. The boy couldn't even respond—but you could see a brightness in his eyes because he knew someone was being nice to him. Rodney finished his mostly one-way conversation and continued down the hall. I knew that there was something really right about what I had just seen. To be like Jesus, we must listen for the cries of those around us. High school can be a cruel place, and you can lighten the load for many if you're in tune.

If Jesus had been born here and now, how would we treat him? When we think back to such things as the scourging and the crucifixion, it's hard to imagine how people could be so cruel. Nobody crucifies anyone in our time. What if Jesus came here today? A poet tried to imagine it:

When Jesus came to Golgotha, they hanged him on a tree.
They drove great nails through hands and feet, they made a calvary,
They crowned him with a crown of thorns, red were his wounds and deep,
For those were crude and cruel days, and human flesh was cheap.
When Jesus came to our town, they simply passed him by.
They never hurt a hair of him! They merely let him die.
For men had grown more tender; they would not give him pain!
They only passed on down the street, and left him standing in the rain.
(G. A. Studdert-Kennedy. Cited in Gerald N. Lund, *Jesus Christ, Key to the Plan of Salvation* [Salt Lake City: Deseret Book, 1991], 46)

Could it be that even we, as members of the Church, leave Jesus standing in the rain? None of us would think of torturing anyone the way Jesus was tortured—but maybe the temptation we face is to take Jesus and his sacrifice for granted. "Oh, it doesn't matter if I do this; I can repent later, Jesus will suffer for it." Jesus said, "Behold, I stand at the door, and knock" (Revelation 3:20). "Oh well, I can answer it later—this is a good show."

Did you know that if you were to pick up your Bible and read all the words that Jesus spoke, it would take you less than an hour? But we have shows to watch, activities to attend, and music to listen to—and Jesus is left standing in the rain. Perhaps it's time we make the study of Jesus Christ and his gospel a major priority in our lives. Jesus said: "Learn of me, and listen to my words" (D&C 19:23). King Benjamin said, "For how knoweth a man the master whom he has not served, and who is a stranger unto him, and is far from the thoughts and intents of his heart?" (Mosiah 5:13).

How far is Jesus from the thoughts and the intents of our hearts? "Yeah, Jesus is there, but it's just something I'm not into right now. I'll do what I want now, and when the time for a mission or marriage comes around, I'll repent." People with that attitude obviously believe in Jesus, but it's hard to imagine that they really love him.

How do we come to love Jesus? We "learn of [him], and listen to [his] words" (D&C 19:23). Eventually, we may begin to understand how much he loves us. Elder David B. Haight said:

> If we could feel or were sensitive even in the slightest to the matchless love of our Savior and his willingness to suffer for our individual sins, we would cease procrastination and "clean the slate," and repent of all our transgressions. (*Ensign,* May 1988, 23)

One way to get to know people is to see them in many different situations. People's true colors come shining through when times are hard. Perhaps, then, if we want to get to know Jesus, we can learn about what he did and what he said when things were the very hardest, when he was tired, discouraged, and alone.

Did Jesus try to get out of things that were difficult? No. Even when he knew what horrible events were soon to come to pass, he said, "Nevertheless not as I will, but as thou wilt" (Matthew 26:39). Jesus suffered for us in Gethsemane. Elder Boyd K. Packer described it like this:

> He, by choice, accepted the penalty for all mankind for the sum total of all wickedness and depravity; for brutality, immorality, perversion, and corruption; for addiction; for the killings and torture and terror—for all of it that ever had been or all that ever would be enacted upon this earth.
>
> In choosing, He faced the awesome power of the evil one who was not confined to flesh nor subject to mortal pain. That was Gethsemane! (*Ensign,* May 1988, 69)

What would make Jesus willing to do that? It was his love for us. In the Doctrine and Covenants we read: "For behold, I, God, have suffered these things for all, that they might not suffer if they would repent" (D&C 19:16). What made him able to endure it? Maybe he was thinking of how much he loved you.

Did Jesus have courage? A band of men carrying lanterns, torches, and weapons came to take Jesus. Jesus "went forth" and asked, "Whom seek ye?"

> And they said, Jesus of Nazareth. Jesus answered . . . I am he: if therefore ye seek me, let these go their way. (John 18:7–8)

Even in the midst of his peril, he was thinking of his disciples, asking his captors to let them go. Did Jesus have dignity?

> And when he had scourged Jesus, he delivered him to be crucified.
>
> Then the soldiers of the governor took Jesus into the

common hall, and gathered unto him the whole band of soldiers.

And they stripped him, and put on him a scarlet robe.

And when they had platted a crown of thorns, they put it upon his head, and a reed in his right hand: and they bowed the knee before him, and mocked him, saying, Hail, King of the Jews!

And they spit upon him, and took the reed, and smote him on the head.

And after that they had mocked him, they took the robe off from him, and put his own raiment on him, and led him away to crucify him. (Matthew 27:26–31)

Jesus didn't cry out. He didn't say anything. He stood in silent dignity. What made him able to endure it? Maybe he was thinking of how much he loved you. We must not leave him "standing in the rain."

Did Jesus have self-restraint?

And when they had blindfolded him, they struck him on the face, and asked him, saying, Prophesy, who is it that smote thee? (Luke 22:64)

Jesus didn't answer. He didn't say, "Hey, I don't deserve this," as we sometimes do. He just let these things happen. Jesus endured all kinds of indignities from the very people that he came to save. In the words of Bruce R. McConkie:

They took him to Annas, to Caiaphas, to Pilate, to Herod, and back to Pilate. He was accused, cursed, and smitten. Their foul saliva ran down his face as vicious blows further weakened his pain-engulfed body. With reeds of wrath they rained blows upon his back. Blood ran down his face as a crown of thorns pierced his trembling brow. But above it all he was scourged, scourged with forty stripes save one, scourged with a multithonged whip into whose leather strands sharp bones and cutting metals were woven. (*A New Witness for the Articles of Faith* [Salt Lake City: Deseret Book, 1985], xiii–xiv)

What made him able to endure it? Maybe he was thinking of how much he loved you.

Did Jesus know how to forgive?

> Father, forgive them; for they know not what they do. (Luke 23:34)

> And the world, because of their iniquity, shall judge him to be a thing of naught; wherefore they scourge him, and he suffereth it; and they smite him, and he suffereth it. Yea, they spit upon him, and he suffereth it, because of his loving kindness and his long-suffering towards the children of men. (1 Nephi 19:9)

Did Jesus love us? "Greater love hath no man than this, that a man lay down his life for his friends" (John 15:13). We can stand here and say, this is the way, but Jesus is the only one who could say, "I am the way." We can talk about Jesus and say, this is the truth; Jesus can say, "I am the truth." We can point and say, this is the light. Jesus can say, "I am the light." If ever in your life you don't know which way to go, ask yourself, "What would Jesus do?" because he *is* the way.

The kind of peace and love and support that you will need to get through this Testing Center of life are available. They are not found in music groups or celebrities or movies. They are not found in clubs or cars or credit cards. The world has done so little for you. The world is not the place to find peace. Jesus Christ is the Prince of Peace. He is your friend, but he is much more than a friend. He is the Son of God. He is the Lord God Omnipotent. He is so powerful! He is kind and loving and he knows exactly how to help you through life. He has proven his love for you by what he did and how he suffered, and he has left you the scriptures so that you can read about his love. He is the way, the truth, and the life. He stands at the door and knocks. And if you open the door, he will come in! (Revelation 3:20).

Fourth Period: Scriptures 101

The Book of Mormon and High School

*No member of this Church can stand approved in
the presence of God who has not seriously and
carefully read the Book of Mormon.*
—Joseph Fielding Smith

When I began work on this book, I knew I wanted to use a lot of scriptures from the Book of Mormon. I wanted to follow the Church's counsel to read and—

NEWS FLASH! We interrupt this chapter to bring you a UBS Special Report. Here's Dan Lather in New York.

Good evening. An archeological discovery of profound significance was unearthed today in upstate New York. Reporter Connie Chum is on the scene. Connie?

Connie: Thanks, Dan. Mel Johnson had no idea what lay ahead as he began to clear land this morning near his farm. About fifty feet from where I'm standing, Johnson's shovel hit what seemed to be a large stone. The stone was actually the lid of a large stone box buried perhaps a thousand years ago by an ancient American.

With some difficulty, Johnson opened the box and stared in amazement at the greatest archeological find of the twenty-first century: a six-inch-thick book, written on six-by-eight-inch plates of gold alloy, weighing approximately fifty pounds. Ecstatic archaeologists from seventeen major universities are en route to New York to study the characters on the plates, which appear to be an ancient hieroglyphic language.

Translating the plates could take years, but archeologists, scientists, and anthropologists are hoping the strange characters hold the key to unlocking age-old mysteries concerning the origin, history, and culture of the ancient

inhabitants of the Americas. Certainly a productive day for Mel Johnson. This is Connie Chum reporting from Palmyra, New York. Watch for more details tonight on the UBS World News. Dan?
We now return to your regularly scheduled programming.

Wow. What if the Book of Mormon had been discovered like that? Can you imagine the excitement? Scientists would go bananas! Perhaps the world would pay more attention to the Book of Mormon if it had been the lead story on prime-time news, but the Lord doesn't work that way. He requires faith. When Jesus was born in Bethlehem, who knew about it first? Leaders of government? Roman emperors? Scholars and philosophers? Ancient news reporters? No. Humble shepherds watching their flock (and a whole bunch of Nephites on the other side of the planet—see 3 Nephi 1:13).

Similarly, there were no scholars and scientists called by the Lord to bring forth the Book of Mormon. It all started with a fourteen-year-old boy and a prayer. In order for people to believe in the Book of Mormon today, they must begin with faith. Faith will often ask us to believe things when "common sense" tells us not to. *But*—and this is the great part—we have more than faith: we have evidence. We may start with faith, but we have more. We have the book! No one can deny that we have a book! It exists! It is here! It's right there, sitting on your nightstand. (You didn't leave it at seminary again, did you?) And doubters and skeptics and honest seekers of truth alike can read it and find out for themselves if it's true. President Ezra Taft Benson said:

> We do not have to prove the Book of Mormon is true. The book is its own proof. All we need to do is read it and declare it. The Book of Mormon is not on trial—the people of the world, including the members of the Church, are on trial as to what they will do with this

second witness for Christ. (*A Witness and a Warning* [Salt Lake City: Deseret Book, 1988], 13)

You heard it from a prophet. *We're* the ones on trial! Will we use the Book of Mormon? You bet we will. We must! And if we're not using it, we must repent and start using it. Here's President Benson again:

> The Book of Mormon has not been, nor is it yet, the center of our personal study, family teaching, preaching, and missionary work. Of this we must repent. (*A Witness and a Warning,* 75)

As I was trying to say before I was interrupted by the UBS News, I wanted to use a lot of Book of Mormon scriptures in this book. Who was the Book of Mormon written for, anyway? The people in the 1400s? No. What about the people in the 1500s? No. The 1600s? No. 1700s? NO! The Book of Mormon was written for us! Right now! You and me! Ancient prophets saw *our day* and wrote to *us.* They didn't always sugarcoat their message, either!

> I speak unto you as if ye were present, and yet ye are not. But behold, Jesus Christ hath shown you unto me, and I know your doing. And I know that ye do walk in the pride of your hearts; and there are none save a few only who do not lift themselves up in the pride of their hearts. (Mormon 8:35–36)

Wow. Moroni saw us, and he really let us have it. Because these voices from the dust (2 Nephi 33:13) saw our day with all its challenges and problems, the Book of Mormon becomes a book of solutions to help us make it through high school and through life in general.

I've shared with you quotes from many different sources so far, but the book we can't do without is the Book of Mormon. If it were the only reference available, this book could still be written. I'll show you. Let's go through every-thing we've covered so far, and we'll see how it all came from the Book of Mormon.

FIRST PERIOD: POPULARITY

In First Period we talked about putting people in compart-ments, the same way food is divided in TV dinner trays. Hmmm, where did that idea come from? The Book of Mormon!

> There were no robbers, nor murderers, neither were there Lamanites, nor any manner of -ites; but they were in one, the children of Christ, and heirs to the kingdom of God. (4 Nephi 1:17)

Sound like high school? "These are the Jock-ites, these are the Loner-ites, these are the Popular-ites . . ." I guess human nature hasn't changed much in 1500 years. (Fortunately, you have *Divine* Nature.)

President Ezra Taft Benson said that the people in the Book of Mormon who seemed to have the greatest difficulty with pride were the learned and the rich (*A Witness and a Warning,* 79). And whenever that combination came to-gether, the people would be divided:

> And they began to be divided into classes. (4 Nephi 1:26)
>
> And the people began to be distinguished by ranks, according to their riches and their chances for learning; yea, some were ignorant because of their poverty, and others did receive great learning because of their riches. (3 Nephi 6:12)

So what's the solution from the book of solutions? Some strong words from Jacob. Here it comes!

> Because some of you have obtained more abundantly than that of your brethren ye are lifted up in the pride of your hearts . . . let not this pride of your hearts

destroy your souls! Think of your brethren like unto yourselves . . . the one being is as precious in his [God's] sight as the other. (Jacob 2:13, 16–17, 21)

And another great statement from Alma: "Ye shall not esteem one flesh above another, or one man shall not think himself above another" (Mosiah 23:7).

SECOND PERIOD: SELF-ESTEEM

In Second Period we talked about real estate and real esteem. Do you know where those ideas come from? The Book of Mormon!

Nephi showed us that sometimes we feel not-so-good for a reason (see 2 Nephi 4:17). Nephi turned to God for comfort, as we should. We received great counsel from Helaman about building our foundation on the rock, which is Christ (see Helaman 5:12). We learned from Alma that you can't do wrong and feel right: "Wickedness never was happiness" (Alma 41:10). Helaman taught the same principle in different words:

Ye have sought for happiness in doing iniquity, which thing is contrary to the nature of that righteousness which is in our great and Eternal Head. (Helaman 13:38)

Lehi is short, sweet, and to the point in this verse: "And if there be no righteousness there be no happiness" (2 Nephi 2:13).

We also receive a great promise from King Benjamin (this is a favorite of mine):

I would desire that ye should consider on the blessed and happy state of those that keep the commandments of God. For behold, they are blessed in all things, both temporal and spiritual; and if they hold out faithful to the end they are received into heaven, that thereby they may dwell with God in a state of never-ending happiness. O remember, remember that these things are true; for the Lord God hath spoken it. (Mosiah 2:41)

And we will remember, remember. Deal? Deal.

THIRD PERIOD: THE LAW OF CHASTITY

Oh, boy, where do we start? There is so much in the Book of Mormon about the law of chastity that we couldn't fit it all in here, so let's just choose a few. Here's one of my favorites. Alma talked to each of his sons, Helaman, Shiblon, and Corianton. This is one of the things he said to Shiblon:

Use boldness, but not overbearance; and also see that ye bridle all your passions. (Alma 38:12)

Notice Alma's careful choice of words. What is a bridle? What do we use it for? Horses. Why? Because horses are evil, wicked, mean, bad, and nasty, right? Of course not! Horses are powerful and very useful when they are controlled. The scripture does not say "kill your passions." Have you ever tried to ride a dead horse? They won't cooperate.

Some of you who still have your thinking caps on from Third Period are thinking, "Hmmm, there are some religions that *would* say 'kill your passions.' Some believe that the way to be closest to God is never to marry, to be celibate." You're right. Thanks to the Restoration, we have Alma's counsel to "bridle all your passions." But we haven't finished the scripture. He says more. And this is the best part: " . . . bridle all your passions, *that ye may be filled with love*" (Alma 38:12; emphasis added).

What does this say to those who are single? It says (excuse the pun), if we can just hold our horses, life will be so much nicer for us. We can be "filled with love."

After Alma speaks to Shiblon, he speaks to Corianton, and lets us know just how serious the law of chastity is.

Thou didst do that which was grievous unto me; for thou didst forsake the ministry, and did go over into the land of Siron among the borders of the Lamanites, after the harlot Isabel. . . .

Know ye not, my son, that these things are an abomination in the sight of the Lord; yea, most abominable above all sins save it be the shedding of innocent blood or denying the Holy Ghost? . . .

Now my son, I would that ye should repent and forsake your sins, and go no more after the lusts of your eyes, but cross yourself in all these things; for except ye do this ye can in nowise inherit the kingdom of God. (Alma 39:3, 5, 9)

Did you notice how Alma tied the law of chastity to the Plan of Salvation in that last line? Just like we did in Third Period! Isn't this fun?

ASSEMBLY: THE WAY, THE TRUTH, AND THE LIFE

In the Assembly chapter we talked about the Savior, and the Book of Mormon talks about the Savior too! Its whole purpose is to testify of Christ. In fact, some form of the Savior's name is used an average of every 1.7 verses. The Book of Mormon is, in reality, Another Testament of Jesus Christ.

As you remember from Second Period, the Book of Mormon prophet Helaman told us to build our lives "upon the rock of our Redeemer, who is Christ" (Helaman 5:12). Helaman's advice is priceless. Look around you! You'll notice that too many people build their foundations on music groups, sports heroes, celebrities, popularity, wealth, or some other soft foundation. The Book of Mormon tells us that we must build our lives on Christ, and nowhere else! (Not even on youth speakers or authors!)

Prophets in the Book of Mormon teach and testify of

Christ. We learned from Alma that Jesus suffered to save us not only from our sins, but also from our pain caused by the difficult things that happen *to* us. King Benjamin reminded us that we will be like strangers to Jesus if he is "far from the thoughts and intents of [our] heart" (Mosiah 5:13). And we learned from Nephi that Jesus died for us not because he was forced to, or even because he was "supposed to," but because of "his loving kindness and his long-suffering towards the children of men" (1 Nephi 19:9).

So far, we've reviewed everything up to Fourth Period, which is this chapter! And the things in Fifth Period and beyond are a surprise. So let's stop the chapter-by-chapter review, and talk about some other interesting things in the Book of Mormon. There is so much to learn, and so many things yet to be discovered!

SOMETIMES, IT'S JUST HARD

Some time ago I received a nice letter from a young woman who told me that she didn't need a "spiritual overhaul" or anything like that. She explained that she kept the law of chastity and the Word of Wisdom. She said she loved her parents, and had a growing testimony. "But sometimes," she said, "it's just hard."

At times it may seem like the lessons you hear are prepared for those who need a "spiritual overhaul." And there are times when teachers and leaders do have to leave the "ninety and nine" and try to reach the "one." But, of course, some people don't need a complete overhaul. Maybe they need only a quick battery charge because, well, "it's just hard."

A Book of Mormon prophet named Jacob had this challenge. He knew that many in his audience were pure in heart, and needed only a battery charge. He also knew that some had great sins and needed the spiritual overhaul of deep repentance. Jacob's words to the pure in heart are some of the most comforting I've ever read. See if you agree.

> But behold, I, Jacob, would speak unto you that are pure in heart. Look unto God with firmness of mind, and pray unto him with exceeding faith, and he will console you in your afflictions, and he will plead your cause, and send down justice upon those who seek your destruction.
>
> O all ye that are pure in heart, lift up your heads and receive the pleasing word of God, and feast upon his love; for ye may, if your minds are firm, forever.
>
> But, wo, wo, unto you that are not pure in heart, that are filthy this day before God. (Jacob 3:1–3)

Jacob goes on for another eleven verses talking to the second group. (Look it up, he doesn't hold back—prophets rarely do.) When I wrote back to this young woman, I told her about this scripture. And what does it say to the pure in heart? The same thing prophets and teachers always say: pray and read your scriptures (the way Jacob says "read your scriptures" is "receive the pleasing word of God"). Whether you need a spiritual overhaul or just a daily battery charge, the Book of Mormon is for you.

YOU WILL MEET NEPHI

There are a lot of things in heaven to look forward to. One of them is that you're going to meet all the prophets whose words you've read. Yes, you'll meet Nephi. And you'll meet Jacob and Moroni too. Guaranteed. It's in the Book!

Nephi testifies to the whole world as he closes the book of Second Nephi. His last words are powerful:

> And now, my beloved brethren, and also Jew, and all ye ends of the earth, hearken unto these words and believe in Christ; and if ye believe not in these words

believe in Christ. And if ye shall believe in Christ ye will believe in these words, for they are the words of Christ, and he hath given them unto me; and they teach all men that they should do good.

And if they are not the words of Christ, judge ye—for Christ will show unto you, with power and great glory, that they are his words, at the last day; *and you and I shall stand face to face before his bar;* and ye shall know that I have been commanded of him to write these things, notwithstanding my weakness. (2 Nephi 33:10–11; emphasis added)

Nephi's younger brother Jacob will be there too.

O be wise; what can I say more?

Finally, I bid you farewell, until *I shall meet you before the pleasing bar of God,* which bar striketh the wicked with awful dread and fear. Amen. (Jacob 6:12–13; emphasis added)

Moroni will be there as well, but he won't be doing the talking.

And I exhort you to remember these things; for the time speedily cometh that ye shall know that I lie not, *for ye shall see me at the bar of God;* and the Lord God will say unto you: Did I not declare my words unto you, which were written by this man, like as one crying from the dead, yea, even as one speaking out of the dust? (Moroni 10:27; emphasis added)

When we're at the judgment bar, looking the authors of the Book of Mormon in the face, that would not be a good time to say, "But it was boring." You probably ought to keep that one inside. Anyone who believes that hasn't read it. I think the Book of Mormon is the most exciting and interesting book in the world! And it's true! Yes, we'll meet Moroni, and I believe that President Gordon B. Hinckley will be there too. What does he have to say about the Book of Mormon?

> I would like to urge every man and woman . . . and every boy and girl who is old enough to read to again read the Book of Mormon during this coming year. This was written for the convincing of the Jew and the Gentile that Jesus is the Christ. There is nothing we could do of greater importance than to have fortified in our individual lives an unshakable conviction that Jesus is the Christ, the living Son of the living God. That is the purpose of the coming forth of this remarkable and wonderful book. May I suggest that you read it again and take a pencil, a red one if you have one, and put a little check mark every time there is a reference to Jesus Christ in that book. And there will come to you a very real conviction as you do so that this is in very deed another witness for the Lord Jesus Christ. (*Teachings of Gordon B. Hinckley* [Salt Lake City: Deseret Book, 1997], 44)

Well, my friends, what are we going to do about President Hinckley's challenge? Why don't you and I, right now, decide that we are going to read the Book of Mormon once through every year, for the rest of our lives! What do you think? The Book of Mormon is 531 pages, and that comes out to a page and a half per day. Piece of cake, right? Let's do it! Now, maybe you have another idea. Maybe you want to read for a certain amount of time each day. That's great! That way, if you want to study a certain verse, you can spend as much time on it as you need. Whatever you decide, write it down right here, and write down the date, too. (You see, if you perform a physical action, such as signing this book, your commitment will be higher.) The point is, *read the book!*

My commitment _____

Date _____

Now, here's some more motivation from President Hinckley:

> Without reservation I promise you that if you will prayerfully read the Book of Mormon, regardless of how many times you previously have read it, there will come into your hearts an added measure of the Spirit of the Lord. There will come a strengthened resolution to walk in obedience to his commandments, and there will come a stronger testimony of the living reality of the Son of God. (*Teachings of Gordon B. Hinckley,* 41)

President Ezra Taft Benson made a similar promise:

> There is a power in the book which will begin to flow into your lives the moment you begin a serious study of the book. You will find greater power to resist temptation. You will find the power to avoid deception. You will find the power to stay on the strait and narrow path. . . .
>
> Our youth ought not to wait until the mission field to get a grasp of the scriptures and a closeness to the Lord. Lehi said that his son Jacob beheld the glory of the Lord in his youth. (See 2 Nephi 2:4.) Imagine what would happen to missionary work if we sent out that kind of young men. (*A Witness and a Warning,* 21–22, 71)

Well, Fourth Period is almost over. If you don't get anything else out of this book, make a commitment to read the Book of Mormon. In the eternal scheme of things, this book doesn't mean much at all. But the Book of Mormon contains the everlasting gospel! Joseph Smith said:

> I told the brethren that the Book of Mormon was the most correct of any book on earth, and the keystone of our religion, and a man would get nearer to God by abiding by its precepts, than by any other book. (*History of the Church,* 4:461)

We may never see the Book of Mormon on the evening news, but the day will come when *everyone* will know that it is true. Joseph Smith declared:

> The standard of truth has been erected. No unhallowed hand can stop the work from progressing; persecutions may rage, mobs may combine, armies may assemble, calumny may defame, but the truth of God will go forth boldly, nobly, and independent, till it has penetrated *every* continent, visited *every* clime, swept *every* country, and sounded in *every* ear, till the purposes of God shall be accomplished, and the Great Jehovah shall say the work is done. (*History of the Church,* 4:540)

I can think of no better way to end this chapter than with the words of President Gordon B. Hinckley:

> This work is true. You know that, as do I. It is God's work. You know that also. It is the restored gospel of Jesus Christ. It is the way to happiness, the plan for peace and righteousness.
>
> God our Eternal Father lives. His Son, our Redeemer, the resurrected Savior of the world, lives. They appeared to the boy Joseph Smith to part the curtains in opening a great work of restoration, ushering in the dispensation of the fulness of times. The Book of Mormon is true. It speaks as a voice from the dust in testimony of the divinity of the Lord. The priesthood with its keys, its authority, and all of its blessings is upon the earth. (*Ensign,* November 1999, 91)

Thanks for reading! See you in Fifth Period, and don't forget to read your scriptures!

HOMEWORK

The Book of Mormon: Another Testament of Jesus Christ

EXTRA CREDIT

A Witness and a Warning, Ezra Taft Benson (Salt Lake City: Deseret Book, 1988).

Fifth Period: Media Influence 101

TV or Not TV? That Is the Challenge

If the television craze continues with the present level of programs, we are destined to have a nation of morons.
—*Daniel Marsh, President, Boston University*

Ooh, isn't that a good quote? " . . . Destined to have a nation of morons." (If we insert one letter into the middle of the word we get, " . . . we are destined to have a nation of *Mormons.*" That would be nice. Oh well.) Daniel Marsh made that comment in 1950, and the "level of programs" has changed dramatically since then. They're much worse than they used to be. There's more trash than ever before, and there's more to come! Have you ever filled a pot with hot water, then tried to drop a frog in it? Or have you ever put a frog in cold water and heated it up? Me neither. Sounds kind of rude. But it makes a great analogy. If you *did* drop a frog in a pot of hot water, what would happen? He would jump out! What if you put a frog in cool water, and heated it up slowly? The frog wouldn't notice the gradual change, he would get comfortable and, before he knew it, he'd be cooked! Hi, ho, Kermit the soup here.

Like that frog, we are all in "hot water." Television has changed over the years, but the changes have been so gradual that they've gone largely unnoticed. Meanwhile, we're getting cooked. When I was younger, one of my favorite shows was about a small-town sheriff, his deputy, his little boy, and his aunt who made great apple pies. They led a simple life, ate lunch at the diner, sang in the church choir, and went fishing. They also taught a good lesson in every show, while at the same time making us laugh. But times have changed, and television has changed too. It's getting hot in this pot, and people are beginning to notice. It's in all the papers. Let's read all about it, shall we?

Headline: Pediatric group suggests cutting TV viewing in half.

The scoop: Long-term television viewing is one cause of violent or aggressive behavior in children and contributes substantially to childhood obesity, the American Academy of Pediatrics said Monday. (Associated Press story appearing in the *Daily Universe,* 17 April 1990)

Headline: Turn on the TV and bingo: You're brain dead.

The scoop: Watching television is like doing nothing at all, only more so. That's essentially the conclusion Memphis psychologists came to after they wired up 31 kids, stuck them in front of a television set, turned on "The Wonder Years" and watched their vital signs plunge. "The metabolic rate during television viewing was even lower than it was during rest," the psychologists reported. (As cited in *Deseret News,* 28 February 1993, A2)

Headline: TV taking its bite out of academics.

The scoop: More than 40 percent of Utah County's school children spend more time watching TV than studying, according to their parents. Many experts say this has an adverse effect on the kids' mental ability and performance. (Michael Morris, *Utah County Journal,* 16 February 1993, A1, A3)

Television has become a part of our lives. Chances are, the most worn-out furniture in the house is facing the television. Unfortunately, the TV has replaced the library as the center of learning. We watch it, we plan our evenings around it, and we talk about it at school. How many times a day does someone say, "Hey, did you see _____ last night?" And we hope we saw _____ last night, because we want to fit in.

The question is this: Is there any nutrition in this mental diet that we call television? And who's in charge of the menu? What's cooking in Hollywood for us to swallow tonight? Suppose you walked into your favorite restaurant and saw the cook putting floor sweepings in your spaghetti. Would you eat it? Yuck! If you did, you'd throw up! What about the stuff you put in your brain? Your brain can't throw up. If you see something gross on TV, it's yours forever. Elder Dallin H. Oaks said:

> The body has defenses to rid itself of unwholesome food, but the brain won't vomit back filth. Once recorded it will always remain subject to recall, flashing its perverted images across your mind, and drawing you away from the wholesome things in life. (As cited by N. Eldon Tanner, *Ensign,* January 1974, 8)

Yes indeed, if television is food for our brains, we'd better talk to the cooks, and see what's happening in the kitchen! *Newsweek* magazine talked to the cooks almost ten years ago, and here's what they found out:

> Hollywood really is different from the rest of the country. A survey of 104 top television writers and executives found that their attitudes toward moral and religious questions aren't shared by their audience.
>
> **Believe adultery is wrong:** Hollywood 49% Everyone else 85%
>
> **Have no religious affiliation:** Hollywood 45% Everyone else 4%
>
> **Believe homosexual acts are wrong:** Hollywood 20% Everyone else 76%

> Believe in a woman's right to an abortion: Hollywood 97% Everyone else 59% (Kenneth L. Woodward, "The Elite and How to Avoid It," *Newsweek,* 20 July 1992, 55)

The problem with the restaurant of television—or rather, the problem with us—is that we'll eat whatever they give us, whether we ordered it or not. Most of us don't plan what we're going to watch. We just plop down on the couch to "watch TV" and let it feed us whatever's on the menu.

What would the cooks, the television writers, say about this? They would argue, "Hey, we're only giving you what you want! Don't blame us. We only serve the public what they order." Oh, really? We're going to read an interview with one of the cooks. As you read, ask yourself—is he really concerned with what people want, or does he have his own plans for the menu? This interview, with television producer Steven Bochco, appeared in *American Film* magazine in the July/August 1988 issue.

> Question: With "Hill Street" and "L.A. Law," you have really pushed the line as far as what you can do on network television.
>
> Bochco: We're going to go further.
>
> Question: You don't think that you've already gone further than any other shows?
>
> Bochco: Yeah, but not enough. I want more.
>
> Question: A lot of the dialogue is stuff that you would never have heard five years ago.
>
> Bochco: That's true. It's actually beginning to sound like how grown-ups really talk. If you give me five more years [laughs], I think we'll get the rest of the way. I'll tell you what I'd love to be able to do on television: I'd love to have characters speak the way you and I do. And use language that you and I use. You know, your vast array of four-letter words that are common usage in

virtually every venue of life, whether you're checking your groceries or in a college classroom. And I'd like us to be able to be sexier, legitimately sexier. I think you're going to see all kinds of things in the next half-dozen years that you can't even imagine today.

Did you catch all that? "*I* want more . . . *I'll* tell you what *I'd* love to be able to do on television." We didn't hear a lot of concern about what the public wants in that interview, did we? There's more:

> Question: Do you take audience demographics into consideration when deciding what story to tell, and how?
> Bochco: Quite frankly, I've always tried to avoid figuring out an audience, and I've never tried to structure a story to accommodate an audience.

So much for getting what *we* want. But there's something else even more interesting in that 1988 interview. Bochco said, "If you give me about five more years, I think we'll get the rest of the way." Hmmm, five years. Let's pick up another newspaper, this one from exactly five years later: Deseret News, 28 July 1993, page C6.

Headline: Despite flinching just a bit, ABC chief will air 'NYPD Blue'

> UNIVERSAL CITY, Calif.—The President of ABC Entertainment admits he's not entirely comfortable with the contents of his network's upcoming "NYPD Blue," but he still plans to let producer Steven Bochco do what he wants with the series.

See that? "Do what *he* wants." He wanted it, he set a goal, and he got it. Gee, they're just falling all over themselves to give the public what they want, aren't they!

Here's a more recent story:

Headline: Bochco spreads the *Philly* cheese this fall on ABC

This latest story talks about a new series Steven Bochco is pushing called "Philly," which "aims to be bluer than blue" by expanding the meaning of "partial nudity" (*TV Guide,* 10–16 February 2001, 34).

He's at it again, folks.

PROVE IT TO YOURSELF

All of this is really beside the point, isn't it? We're probably not going to change things in Hollywood. The point is, "we are what we eat," and perhaps we ought to pay more attention to our spiritual diets. Sometimes we're like the frog that is slowly being cooked; in the comfort of the warm water, we go a little crazy. We think the thirteenth Article of Faith says, "If there is anything virtuous, lovely, or of good report or praiseworthy, we seek after these things, unless our favorite show is on." Or we think Moroni said, "Deny yourselves of all ungodliness; and fast forward the bad parts" (see Moroni 10:32).

We must not allow Hollywood to make us hypocrites! We say, "We believe" when we repeat the Articles of Faith. Well, do we? Do we really believe what they say? Moroni gives hard counsel when he says, "deny yourselves of *all* ungodliness." Is "all" a pretty high percentage? When Hollywood is criticized for its programming, the usual response is, "If you don't like it, turn it off." Hmmm, that's a new thought: Turn it off. What would happen to your life if you did? Here's another headline:

Headline: **Turning off the tube may be 1st step toward turning on life**

The scoop: People sometimes ask why I, a professor of communication, do not have a television in my home.

... Television presents a dilemma: Many of us find that it does not represent a productive or enriching use of time, but we nevertheless find it attractive as a source of entertainment and information. ... Television seeks audiences for only one reason—to sell those audiences to advertisers. When I watch television, I am investing uncompensated time as a "commercials viewer" and my time is being sold to an advertiser by a network. No, thanks. I've got better things to do. ... Television robs relationships of time. Relationships among friends and family members take time to develop—quantity time. ... Television steals the time it takes to build and enjoy relationships, which are to my mind a lot more satisfying than sitcoms. (James A. Herrick, *Deseret News* Opinion/Editorial page, 16 March 1994)

I agree; we've got better things to do. We have our own goals and dreams to pursue! What do you think, my friend? Do you think you could turn the TV off for a week? Two weeks? A month? Elder H. Burke Peterson counseled:

Stay away from any movie, video, publication, or music—*regardless of its rating*—where illicit behavior and expressions are a part of the action. Have the courage to turn it off in your living room. Throw the tapes and the publications in the garbage can, for that is where we keep garbage. ... Again I say, leave it alone. *Turn it off,* walk away from it, burn it, erase it, destroy it. I know it is hard counsel we give when we say movies that are R-rated, and many with PG-13 ratings, are produced by satanic influences. Our standards should not be dictated by the rating system. (*Ensign,* November 1993, 43; emphasis added)

TV or not TV; that is the challenge. We could look at more headlines, but maybe we ought to bag all that and prove to ourselves what effect TV has on us. When Moroni wrote his last words in the Book of Mormon, he didn't try to prove it was true. He simply said, in effect, "read it for yourself, and ask God." Maybe that's the best way to come to a conclusion on this media-influence issue.

Would you like to try a little experiment? Do you have the courage? I'm going to make a challenge here—are you sure you want to keep reading? Here it comes. Ladies and gentlemen (please imagine a drum roll somewhere in the distance), I challenge you . . . wait . . . I challenge *thee* (it sounds more, you know, like a commandment), I challenge thee to fast from TV for a month! No TV, no movies, no videos! (Okay, end the drum roll and imagine a cymbal crash.)

Well, what do you think? Are you saying, "You've *got* to be kidding"? If so, I'll answer you. No, I'm not kidding. I did it myself—I fasted from TV for a whole month. It wasn't that bad. In fact, it was great. I had no idea it would affect me the way it did. If you feel you can't do it, I'll understand. I won't judge you unrighteously or anything. I'll still think you're great. Just write your pathetic, miserable excuse in the space below, you big party pooper.

Lame excuse

_____

One excuse you can't use is, "I don't have time," because television *takes* time. As for those of you who didn't write an excuse, who have decided to accept the challenge, may I offer you literary high-fives? And may I take a moment to express a few thoughts? I think you're wonderful, heroic, courageous, stupendous, marvelous, intelligent, terrific, outrageous, sensational, superb, splendid, fabulous, remarkable, fantastic, phenomenal, incredible, amazing, magnificent, miraculous, glorious, and nifty.

I'd like to make a few predictions. I did this little experiment myself a few years ago in February (okay, I picked the shortest month, but it's still a month), and I think I know what will happen to you.

Day One. You won't know what to do with yourself. You'll think, "Is Nintendo allowed?" (It isn't.) You'll say, "Mom, there's nothing to do," and she'll give you a list, starting with "Clean up your room." You'll never complain to her again.

Day Four. You'll begin to notice how much time you have, and it will be exciting. You'll compile a list of things to do during your TV fast: books to read, places to go, projects to complete, and so on.

Day Ten. You'll notice you're having a much easier time controlling your thoughts. You'll realize that the main place where "the truth and values we embrace are mocked on every hand" is on television. You won't be hearing the crass jokes and witnessing the illicit situations on prime time. You'll remember a scripture you once read: "For our words will condemn us, yea, all our works will condemn us; we shall not be found spotless; and our thoughts will also condemn us; and in this awful state we shall not dare to look up to our God" (Alma 12:14).

Day Fourteen. You'll find it's hard not to judge other TV watchers around you. It will seem like that's all everyone else ever does. You'll say to yourself, "Everyone seems so lazy all of a sudden—did I used to waste time like that?"

Day Sixteen. You'll find it much easier to concentrate when you read your scriptures or pray. You'll notice you don't have to take a minute and clean out your brain before such activities. You'll realize that the bad stuff in your head blocks out the good stuff. Listen to Elder H. Burke Peterson:

> When we see or hear anything filthy or vulgar, whatever the source, our mind records it, and as it makes the filthy record, beauty and clean thoughts are pushed into

the background. Hope and faith in Christ begin to fade, and more and more, turmoil and discontent become our companions. (*Ensign,* November 1993, 43)

Day Twenty. You'll say, "Why didn't I try this before?" You'll be getting your homework done, you'll read good books, you'll exercise, you'll even have a cleaner room! (Mom will love that.)

Day Thirty. You'll think a lot on this day. You'll ask yourself, "Do I really want to start watching again?" You'll think about how we try to protect ourselves from things: We put dead-bolt locks on the doors, motion-sensor lights in the yard, and burglar alarms in the entrances to the house. To keep things warm inside, we buy double-paned glass, insulation, and weather stripping. Then we kneel down as a family and say "protect us from harm or accident."

But Satan is clever. He can find a way into our house. He can come right through the antenna (or the cable). Or we can actually pay money to rent his influence at the video store.

A month has passed, and now your experiment is over. If you start watching again, you'll notice that your vacation from television has increased your sensitivity. You'll realize that you used to be accustomed to the language of television, but now it will bug you. You'll hear the Lord's name taken in vain, and other crude language, and your mental taste buds will say, "Yuck, this is sick." Listen to Elder Boyd K. Packer:

> Profanity is more than just untidy language, for when we profane we relate to low and vulgar words, the most sacred of all names. I wince when I hear the name of the Lord so used, called upon in anger, in frustration, in hatred. (In Conference Report, October 1967, 128)

Now it's time for some intense honesty. Elder Robert D. Hales said:

Do you know how to recognize a true friend? A real friend loves us and protects us.

In recognizing a true friend we must look for two important elements in that friendship:

A true friend makes it easier for us to live the gospel by being around him.

Similarly, a true friend does not make us choose between his way and the Lord's way. (*Ensign,* May 1990, 40)

Elder Hales has given us an excellent tool to test our friendships. Let's take the words *true friend* and replace them with some other phrases to see if they work.

"_____ makes it easier to live the gospel."

How about "the Book of Mormon"? (Put that in the blank and try it.) Yes, that works. How about your best friend? Put his or her name there. Hopefully that works too. Now take the word *television* and put it in there.

"Television makes it easier to live the gospel."

How did that feel? I don't know about you, but I could not say that television is a true friend. There is no way I could honestly say that television has made it *easier* for me to live the gospel.

I hope you will take the TV or not TV challenge. I know you can do it because I did it. Try it! Prove it to yourself and see what happens. Keep a journal and take note of what abstaining from television does for your spirit. I have some friends who took the TV challenge, and wrote me about it. Listen to Lindsay from Clayton, California:

Dear John [story of my life],

I liked what you had to say about TV and I decided to take the challenge not to watch TV for one whole month . . . and well, to make a short story shorter, my whole family decided to go without TV. I think it was the hardest on my mother because she doesn't have a job and is home all the time, but she took up canning. So now we have every kind of jam and jelly you can think of. Name it and we've got it in our freezer. My dad has suddenly found time to figure out our new computer system, and all of us have been able to work on and develop our own talents. It's incredible to think back and realize how much we were letting television monopolize our lives. Our home is much quieter and peaceful now.

. . . But I think the neatest thing is that the Spirit can be in our home all the time. . . . I'd like to thank you for giving us that challenge. My family and I have really benefited from it and we've liked it so much that we're going to try to go for a whole year.

Here's another—meet Laura from Delta, Utah!

Dear John [see what I mean?],

I don't know how I can thank you for this wonderful experience of the "TV Blackout." It has changed my life greatly for the better. I have gained a stronger testimony by using time to read the scriptures. . . . I found that I had uplifting thoughts and it was easy for me because the garbage that is on TV didn't come into my mind. I earned a 3.994 this term because I found I had more time in the evening to study instead of watching TV. . . . I have lost 15 pounds because I have been going to the Recreation Center instead of watching TV. . . . I have decided that I should only watch the three shows that I really like. TV can be such a time waster. Because I have seen how much I can accomplish, and what a great effect this has had on me, I simply refuse to sit in front of the TV and do nothing.

Now, I don't know if you'll lose fifteen pounds, but I think I can promise you four things: *First,* you'll have much more time. (They say the average daily television viewing per household is seven hours four minutes per day!). *Second,* you'll have an easier time controlling your thoughts. (You know what they say in the computer-programming business: "Garbage in, garbage out!"). *Third,* your spiritual sensitivity will increase. As you "deny yourself of all ungodliness" (see Moroni 10:32), you'll feel closer to the Lord. *Fourth,* you'll be more selective in the future. You won't just sit down to "watch TV." You'll choose carefully what you watch instead of punching the remote from a slouched position for three hours.

President Gordon B. Hinckley taught:

> I am suggesting that we spend a little less time in idleness, in the fruitless pursuit of watching inane and empty television programs. Time so utilized can be put to better advantage, and the consequences will be wonderful. (*Teachings of Gordon B. Hinckley* [Salt Lake City: Deseret Book, 1997], 621)

Any powerful tool can be used as an awful weapon. Of course, there are excellent programs on TV, programs that can lift and inspire. Watch that kind of program when you choose to watch. But remember that Satan has found a way to use the media as a weapon as well. So, fellow frogs, maybe now would be a good time to jump out of the pot, because something's cooking, and I think it's us! Good luck with your experiment, thanks for reading, and I'll see you in Sixth Period!

EXTRA CREDIT

Protecting Your Family in an X-rated World, Randal A. Wright (Salt Lake City: Deseret Book, 1988).

"The Effects of Television," M. Russell Ballard, *Ensign,* May 1989, 78–81.

"TV Free: Giving Up the Daytime Habit," Kelly Strong Thacker, *Ensign,* July 1991, 29–31.

Sixth Period: Religions 101

Why Are There So Many Churches?

*Obtain a knowledge of history, and of countries,
and of kingdoms, of laws of God and man, and all
this for the salvation of Zion.*
—D&C 93:53

'm not afraid to admit it. When I was in eighth grade I took a Home Economics class. Yup. A class about sewing and cooking. Some friends of mine wanted to take it, and when I asked them why, they said, "Because you get to eat." That did it for me. I love to eat. The only problem was that we had to eat our own cooking. Sick.

Eighth grade Home Economics stands out in my memory not because of our gourmet dishes, but because of the friendly but spirited discussions we always had at our table as we sat down to consume our "burnt offerings." There were four of us, three Latter-day Saints and a Presbyterian. We were good friends and remained good friends throughout high school. My Presbyterian friend knew so much. Sometimes I felt like he knew more about my church than I did. When he would ask about our beliefs on certain things, I was forced to rely on the vast knowledge in my eighth-grade brain. I knew many answers, but I really became curious about the larger picture. Why are there so many churches, anyway? Where did they all come from? I didn't know. Who was Martin Luther? Who was John Calvin? I didn't know. What about Catholics, or Methodists, or Baptists, or Lutherans? When did all those churches start, and how do they fit into the overall picture? I didn't know. In fact, I didn't have a clue.

As we discussed earlier, knowledge is power, and I was powerless. Answers to all these questions were available without charge from my Dad's own library, but they required an action that causes many people great physical and emotional discomfort—turning off the TV, and opening up a book. (Fortunately for you, this is no problem; you're already reading a book.) I knew that the scriptures would increase my testimony, but I had no idea that my testimony could grow by leaps and bounds if I studied a not-so-popular school subject . . . can I say it? . . . *History*. Yes, HISTORY!

Well, I studied, and boy, did I learn. Would you like to know what I found out? Because I'd love to tell you. Get comfortable in your chair and enjoy. And if you have a friendly discussion group like I had in eighth grade Home Economics, now you'll have a little more power to answer! I'm excited to share this information with you, because I can almost guarantee that you will say to yourself "I didn't know that" about fifteen times. Isn't it exciting to know that in a few more minutes (the time it will take to read this chapter), you'll know fifteen things you didn't know before? That is the unique thrill of discovery. May it be a lifelong pursuit for you, my friend.

Okay, let's get to work. We're going to have to review a few basics, but you'll see later on why it's important. Get your scriptures, and accompany me through the New Testament church, the Great Apostasy, the Dark Ages, the Reformation, and the Restoration.

THE NEW TESTAMENT CHURCH: 30 A.D. to 325 A.D.

Jesus came to earth, organized his church, and ordained twelve apostles. What would happen if one of the apostles was killed? Would they replace him? As you know, in about 30 A.D. Jesus was crucified, then was resurrected three days later. He stayed with the apostles for a time and then ascended to heaven. Judas, who had betrayed Jesus, committed suicide. This left only eleven apostles. The remaining apostles met to fill the vacancy:

> And they prayed, and said, Thou, Lord, which knowest the hearts of all men, shew whether of these two thou hast chosen,
> That he may take part of this ministry and apostleship, from which Judas by transgression fell, that he might go to his own place.
> And they gave forth their lots; and the lot fell upon Matthias; and he was numbered with the eleven apostles. (Acts 1:24–26)

Apparently, the Lord wanted the organization to continue with twelve apostles, not eleven. Notice also that the apostles did not choose a new apostle without the Lord's help, but they prayed for inspiration to ensure that the new member would be called of God, as they were. Hebrews 5:4 states, "And no man taketh this honour unto himself, but he that is called of God, as was Aaron" (see also John 15:16).

Since Old Testament times, prophets had known that the day would come when the true gospel would not be on the earth. There would be a "falling away," or an "apostasy."

> Behold, the days come, saith the Lord God, that I will send a famine in the land, not a famine of bread, nor a thirst for water, but of hearing the words of the Lord:
> And they shall wander from sea to sea, and from the north even to the east, they shall run to and fro to seek the word of the Lord, and shall not find it. (Amos 8:11–12; see also Isaiah 24:1–6; 1 Timothy 4:1–3; Matthew 24:9–12; Acts 20:29–30; 2 Timothy 3:1–5; 2 Peter 2:1–3; 1 Nephi 13:24–29. See also scriptures listed in *Topical Guide,* "Apostasy of the Early Christian Church")

God knew that this apostasy would take place, and had prepared for the gospel to be restored. Peter told the Jews:

> He shall send Jesus Christ, . . . whom the heaven must receive until the times of *restitution of all things,* which God hath spoken by the mouth of all his holy prophets since the world began. (Acts 3:20–21; emphasis added)

Restitution means "restoration" (of course, something must be lost before it can be restored). Many believed that the second coming of Jesus Christ would be very soon after his resurrection and ascension. Paul wrote to them and said:

> Be not soon shaken in mind, or be troubled, neither by spirit, nor by word, nor by letter as from us, as that the day of Christ is at hand.
>
> Let no man deceive you by any means: for that day shall not come, except there come *a falling away first.* (2 Thessalonians 2:2–3; emphasis added)

After Jesus was resurrected, he told the apostles, "Go ye into all the world, and preach the gospel to every creature" (Mark 16:15). This the apostles did, and except for John they were all killed. John Foxe's *Book of Martyrs* accounts for the death of the apostles as follows: Peter was crucified head downward at Rome; James (the son of Zebedee) was beheaded; John was banished to the Isle of Patmos; Bartholomew was beaten, crucified, and then beheaded. James (the son of Alphaeus) was stoned and beaten to death. Matthew was slain with a halberd. Andrew, Simon (Zelotes), Thaddeus, and Philip were crucified. Thomas was killed with a spear. Matthias was stoned and then beheaded. Paul was beheaded in Rome by Nero (see John Foxe, *Book of Martyrs,* ed. G.A. Williamson, Boston: Little, Brown, 1965).

The apostle John was taken out of the ministry, and

nothing is heard of him after about 101 A.D. Elder Mark E. Petersen explains that John was not permitted to remain in Patmos because wickedness had nearly taken over the church. Doctrines and ordinances were changed, authority was ignored, and sin became rampant, even among the members of the church (see Mark E. Petersen, *Which Church Is Right?* [Salt Lake City: The Church of Jesus Christ of Latter-day Saints, 1974], 12).

The apostles were unable to meet in order to fill the vacancies in the twelve, as they had done before. Bishops (*local* authorities) of the many cities were left without the priesthood supervision of the apostles (*general* authorities). False teachers and false doctrines arose. This is confirmed in the writings of Eusebius, an ancient historian who lived about 260–339 A.D.

> The Church continued until then [close of the first century] as a pure and uncorrupt virgin, whilst if there were any at all that attempted to pervert the sound doctrine of the saving gospel, they were yet skulking in dark retreats: but *when the sacred choir of Apostles became extinct* and the generation of those that had been privileged to hear their inspired wisdom had passed away, then also the *combinations of impious errors* arose by the fraud and delusions of false teachers. These also as there were none of the apostles left, henceforth attempted without shame, to preach their *false doctrines against the gospel truth.* (Eusebius is quoting Hegesippus, as cited in B.H. Roberts, *The Falling Away* [Salt Lake City: Deseret Book, 1931], 29; emphasis added)

A modern historian (non-LDS) agrees with Eusebius that the death of the apostles marked the beginning of the apostasy:

> With the close of the New Testament records, and the death of the last surviving apostle, the history of the

church passes from its sacred to its purely human phase. The miraculous gifts which attested the Divine mission of the apostles ceased; not indeed by any formal record of their withdrawal, but by the *clear evidence that they were possessed no longer.* (Dr. Phillip Smith, *Students Ecclesiastical History,* 1:6, as cited in Roberts, *The Falling Away,* 83; emphasis added)

During the next two centuries, the church drifted without direction. Horrible government-sponsored persecutions were inflicted on the Christians, and they were forced underground (literally underground, into the catacombs beneath Rome!). The simple and pure doctrines of the gospel were changed and mixed with pagan religions and the philosophies of men.

During the second century, Greek philosophy, particularly the writings of Plato, were the accepted belief among the ruling class. The Christians were persecuted and criticized, in part because their teachings were not enough like Plato's teachings. Plato taught that God was incomprehensible to men, and completely unlike man in every way, while the Christians (at least the ancient Christians), believed the words of the prophets, who taught that God has a body, and that we were created in his image. In order to win respect and acceptance from those in the Greco-Roman world, some Christians sought to defend Christianity using Greek Philosophy. The ideas that Plato held about God suddenly became more important than what the Son of God taught! As one scholar put it, "it may well be said of Plato that he had a greater influence in forming the traditional concept of God than Christ himself" (Joseph Fielding McConkie, *Sons and Daughters of God* [Salt Lake City: Bookcraft, 1994], 237).

In the middle of the third century, a man named Cyprian, who was the Bishop of Carthage, baptized by sprinkling instead of immersion when the person being baptized had some physical weakness (Eusebius, *History of the Church from Christ to Constantine,* tr. G.A. Williamson [New York: Dorset Press, 1984], 4:282–83). Sprinkling baptism caught on and became a widely accepted practice. A few centuries later, the practice of baptizing infants began. (See James E. Talmage, *The Great Apostasy* [Salt Lake City: Deseret Book, 1968], 118–19; see also B.H. Roberts, *Outlines of Ecclesiastical History* [Salt Lake City: The Church of Jesus Christ of Latter-day Saints, 1950], 141; Eusebius, *From Christ to Constantine,* 4:282–83.)

THE GREAT APOSTASY: 325 A.D. to 1045 A.D.

Persecutions continued, but Christianity would not go away. The emperor of Rome at the time, Constantine, decided to support Christianity. He thought he could unite his empire by uniting the Christians and making Christianity the state religion. Constantine called a council for all the Bishops in the world in 325 A.D. to resolve several issues, including a disagreement about the nature of God. Some argued that the Father and the Son were of the same substance (or "consubstantial"), and others believed they were separate individuals (that the Father existed before the Son). The council, which was convened in a place called Nicaea, came up with a statement of beliefs that became known as the Nicene Creed. By vote, and with some pressure from Constantine, the doctrine of the Trinity emerged. That doctrine states that there are three persons in the Godhead who make up one God; and that God the Father and Jesus Christ are not only one in *purpose,* but one in *person.* (For more information, see Bruce R. McConkie, "Nicene Creed," in *Mormon Doctrine,* 2d. ed. [Salt Lake City: Bookcraft, 1979], 535–37.) The doctrine of the Trinity was basically a product of debate and compromise.

There was no revelation, no authority, no attempt at inspiration. This council was also the first step toward making the church a department of the Roman Empire.

Thus we can see that only a few centuries after Christ, the apostasy was essentially complete. Priesthood leadership and authority were lost, the nature of God was changed by vote, the mode of baptism was altered, and Constantine, an "uninspired, unbaptized sun-worshiper who committed murder within his own family," was appointing new Bishops (Petersen, *Which Church Is Right?* 12). Constantine's plan to unite the empire was successful, and the new state-sponsored church would eventually be called the "universal" or "Catholic" church.

That was essentially the only Christian church in existence for several centuries, its history characterized by power struggles, rivalries, and corruption. A historian describing these years said:

> It seemed impossible that things could become worse; yet Rome had still to see Benedict IX, A.D. 1033, a boy of less than twelve years, raised to the apostolic throne. Of this pontiff, one of his successors, Victor III, declared that his life was so shameful, so foul, so execrable, that he shuddered to describe it. He ruled like a captain of banditti rather than a prelate. The people at last, unable to bear his adulteries, homicides and abominations any longer, rose up against him. In despair of maintaining his position, he put up the papacy to auction. It was bought by a presbyter named John, who became Gregory VI, A.D. 1045. (John William Draper, *Intellectual Development of Europe,* 1:378–82, as cited in Roberts, *The Falling Away,* 125. See also Sir Nicolas Cheetham, *A History of the Popes* [New York: Dorset Press, 1982], 84)

THE DARK AGES: 1045 A.D. to 1440 A.D.

The church had changed from a persecut*ed* church to a persecut*ing* church. More basic doctrines were altered. Instead of a worship service where the members participated, the Mass became more of a performance with much mystery and ceremony. In the year 1054, centuries-old rivalries concerning the city from which the church should be governed resulted in the split of the church into the Roman Catholic Church, with headquarters in Rome, and the Greek Orthodox Church, with headquarters in Constantinople, Greece.

The western church developed faster than the eastern church. The Roman church filled Europe but was ruled from Rome. Those who disagreed with the doctrines or practices of the church were called heretics and were usually tortured and killed. Not surprisingly, these many centuries when the "Light of the World" was gone are referred to by almost all historians as the "Dark Ages."

Very few copies of the scriptures were in existence. Books had to be copied by hand and were very expensive. The church actually discouraged reading the scriptures, reserving that right for the clergy only. In about 1440, the printing press was invented. This meant that copies of the scriptures would be more available. You would think that this advance would be welcomed by the clergy, but interestingly enough, the church was violently opposed to the development of printing. Elder Bruce R. McConkie states:

> Few tools were more effective than printing in paving the way for the great revival of learning, for the religious reformation, and for the breaking away of peoples and nations from religious domination. Without the discovery of movable type in about 1440 A.D. the barrier of gross darkness covering the apostate world could scarce

have been pierced. One of the first books published was the Gutenberg Bible in 1456 A.D.

Perhaps no important discovery in world history ever faced such intense and bitter opposition as arose over the use and spread of printing. Civil and ecclesiastical tyrants feared the loss of their ill-held and evilly-exercised powers should knowledge and truth be made available to people generally. "We must root out printing," said the Vicar of Croydon from his pulpit, "or printing will root us out." (*Mormon Doctrine*, 716)

THE REFORMATION: 1440 A.D. to 1830 A.D.

Despite the opposition, printing flourished, and the scriptures were read by an ever-increasing number of people during the Reformation. There was a great revival of learning and of the arts. This period marks the end of the Dark Ages and is often called the renaissance (meaning "rebirth").

At this point we begin to see the hand of the Lord preparing the world for the "restitution of all things" spoken of by Peter. In 1492, Christopher Columbus set off to find a shorter route to India. This event is prophesied in the Book of Mormon:

> And I looked and beheld a man among the Gentiles, who was separated from the seed of my brethren by the many waters; and I beheld the Spirit of God, that it came down and wrought upon the man; and he went forth upon the many waters, even unto the seed of my brethren, who were in the promised land. (1 Nephi 13:12)

Did Christopher Columbus know that the Spirit was working on him? Let's see what he says:

> Our Lord unlocked my mind, sent me upon the sea, and gave me fire for the deed. Those who heard of my enterprise called it foolish, mocked me, and laughed. But

who can doubt but that the Holy Ghost inspired me? (In Jacob Wasserman, *Columbus, Don Quixote of the Seas,* 19–20, as cited in *The Teachings of Ezra Taft Benson* [Salt Lake City: Bookcraft, 1988], 577)

As time passed, more and more people were studying the scriptures, and more and more people were asking questions. (Isn't it interesting what happens when people read their scriptures?) A monk and university professor named Martin Luther became concerned about certain abuses and practices in the church. In 1517, he prepared a list of 95 theses (subjects for debate) and nailed it to the door of the All Saints Church in Wittenberg, Germany.

The Catholic church did not appreciate Luther's complaining, and eventually he was forced into hiding. If Luther had not had friends in high places, he probably would have been killed, as were many others who protested against the church. Luther hid himself away and continued to write. Some agreed with Luther; others opposed him. King Henry VIII of England published a book in defense of the church for which he was awarded the title "Defender of the Faith," a title still carried by British kings. Luther gained a following, and his movement eventually resulted in the formation of a "new" church called the Lutheran Church. Martin Luther "protested," and is recognized as the first "protestant." His movement marks the beginning of the Reformation. Actually, it was not Luther's original intent to form a new church; he just wanted to reform the old one. He said:

> I have sought nothing beyond reforming the Church in conformity with the Holy Scriptures. The spiritual powers have been not only corrupted by sin, but absolutely destroyed; so that there is now nothing in them but a depraved reason and a will that is the enemy and opponent of God. I simply say that Christianity has

ceased to exist among those who should have preserved it. (As cited in *The Falling Away and Restoration of the Gospel of Jesus Christ Foretold* [pamphlet] Salt Lake City: The Church of Jesus Christ of Latter-day Saints)

Tension had been mounting for some time between the church in Rome and the governments of some European nations. Some of the taxes collected by these governments were sent to Rome. Tensions reached a peak in England when, in 1529, King Henry VIII wanted a divorce from his wife, Catherine of Aragon. The pope would not give Henry a divorce. So, in 1535, parliament declared Henry VIII the supreme head of the church in England. Thus, Henry VIII became head of both church and state in England, giving him the authority to grant his own divorce. Some in the church in England refused to recognize this action, and Henry had many of them executed. Ties with the Roman church were formally broken, and the Church of England—also called the Anglican church, and in America the Episcopalian church—was born.

Another group, observing that in the scriptures baptism was performed only for those capable of repenting, was eventually formed into a church by John Smyth in 1609. This group performed baptisms first by pouring and later by immersion. Others referred to them as "Anabaptists" or re-baptizers. Persecutions raged against them, and many Anabaptists were publicly drowned. The Anabaptists were the beginning of the Baptist movement.

Just eleven years later, in 1620, the *Mayflower* set sail for America, its passengers in search of religious freedom. Seven ancestors of Joseph Smith were on board.

In 1639, in Providence, Rhode Island, a Puritan minister named Roger Williams founded the first Baptist church in America. Eventually, he refused to continue as a pastor on the grounds that there was "no regularly constituted church on earth, nor any person authorized to administer any Church ordinance; nor could there be until, *new apostles are sent* by the Great Head of the Church for whose coming he is seeking" (*Picturesque America, or the Land We Live In,* ed. William Cullen Bryant [New York: D. Appleton and Co., 1872], 1:502, as cited in LeGrand Richards, *A Marvelous Work and a Wonder* [Salt Lake City: Deseret Book, 1976], 27).

John Calvin and John Knox were the forces behind the protestant movement called Presbyterianism, which was formed about 1649. The word *Presbyterian* refers to a representative form of church government. In Greek, *presbyteros* means elder (see Leo Rosten, ed., *Religions of America* [New York: Simon and Schuster, 1975], 200–201). Calvin and Knox formed a church government similar to that which had been practiced in the first century. That is how the Presbyterian church came into existence.

John and Charles Wesley were brothers who attended Oxford University in England. They formed the "Holy Club," but were nicknamed "methodists" by the student body because of their strict and methodical rules of conduct in their club meetings. John Wesley did not intend to organize a new church, but gained many followers after he began to preach in about 1738. The first Methodist church in America was formally established in 1784 (see Rosten, ed., *Religions of America,* 172–173). How did John Wesley feel about traditional Christianity? He explains:

> It does not appear that these extraordinary gifts of the Holy Ghost were common in the Church for more than two or three centuries. We seldom hear of them after that fatal period when the Emperor Constantine called himself a Christian. . . . From this time they almost totally ceased. . . . The Christians had no more of the

Spirit of Christ than the other heathens. . . . This was the real cause why the extraordinary gifts of the Holy Ghost were no longer to be found in the Christian Church; because the Christians were turned Heathen again, and had only a dead form left. (*Wesley's Works,* vol. 7, sermon 89, 26–27, as cited in *The Falling Away and Restoration . . . Foretold*)

In 1776 the Declaration of Independence was signed, starting the wheels in motion for America to become a self-governing country. The writer of the Declaration was Thomas Jefferson. (His face is on the nickel in your pocket—unless you're from Canada.) Read what Jefferson has to say and ask yourself if he was inspired:

The religion builders have so distorted and deformed the doctrines of Jesus, so muffled them in mysticisms, fancies and falsehoods, have caricatured them into forms so inconceivable, as to shock reasonable thinkers. . . . *Happy in the prospect of a restoration of primitive Christianity,* I must leave to younger persons to encounter and lop off the false branches which have been engrafted into it by the mythologists of the middle and modern ages. (*Jefferson's Complete Works,* 7:210, 257, as cited in *The Falling Away and Restoration . . . Foretold;* emphasis added)

Men like Luther, Calvin, and Wesley all had a portion of the Spirit of God. We remember the reformers as noble men who sought to benefit mankind. Their efforts put the scriptures into the hands of common people, and people who read the scriptures do uncommon things. William Tyndale, who translated the Bible into English in 1526, said to those who opposed his work, "If God spare my life, . . . I will cause a boy that driveth the plough shall know more of the scripture than thou dost" (as cited in Thomas S. Monson, *Ensign,* May 1975, 16).

Speaking of the reformers, President Thomas S. Monson said:

> Such were the teachings and lives of the great reformers. Their deeds were heroic, their contributions many, their sacrifices great—but they did not restore the gospel of Jesus Christ.
>
> Of the reformers one could ask, "Was their sacrifice in vain? Was their struggle futile?" I answer with a resounding "No!" The Holy Bible was now within the grasp of the people. Each man could better find his way. Oh, if only all could read and all could understand. But some could read, and others could hear; and every man had access to God through prayer. (*Ensign,* May 1975, 16)

THE RESTORATION: 1820 TO THE PRESENT

Only fourteen years after the Bill of Rights was ratified in the newly independent United States, guaranteeing religious freedom, a boy was born in Sharon, Vermont. There is not room to retell the story here; please put this book down and read it for yourself in Joseph Smith—History in the Pearl of Great Price.

In short, young Joseph, a "boy that driveth the plough," became confused by the many religions that argued and contended one with another. After reading and pondering the fifth verse in the first chapter of James, he decided to "ask of God." His question was *not,* "Is there a true church?" Apparently, he thought one of them might be true. His question was, "Which one should I join?" In response to Joseph's prayer, the heavens were opened and Father in Heaven once again spoke to his children on the earth. Later, other heavenly messengers visited the earth, including John the Baptist and Peter, James, and John. The true nature of God as a literal Father in Heaven was revealed, priesthood power with the authority to baptize was restored, and a "voice from the dust," the Book of Mormon, containing the "everlasting gospel," was brought forth by an angel (see Revelation 14:6). All things that had been altered or lost were restored.

The excitement of the Restoration is captured in the words of a favorite Latter-day Saint hymn:

> The Spirit of God like a fire is burning,
> The latter-day glory begins to come forth.
> The visions and blessings of old are returning,
> And angels are coming to visit the earth!
> (*Hymns,* no. 2)

You, my friend, as you've been told so many times, are part of the Restoration. This is your great spiritual heritage and mission! But we'll come back to that later. Let's get back to our original question.

WHY ARE THERE SO MANY CHURCHES?

Originally, there was the church of Jesus Christ. But, as prophesied, the church was taken from the earth. People were left to interpret the scriptures without the aid of a prophet. The philosophies of men corrupted the pure doctrines of Christ, and the church fell into apostasy and into the Dark Ages. At the close of the Dark Ages, "the spirit of inspiration rested upon [the reformers]," said Elder Bruce R. McConkie, "causing them to rebel against the religious evils of the day and seek to make the Bible and other truth available to all who would receive such" (*Mormon Doctrine,* 717). The Reformation resulted in many different churches all trying to return to the pure doctrine of Christ. However, none of them had the proper authority, and most of them retained ideas and philosophies from the Roman church, which had been corrupted centuries earlier.

WHY DO WE SAY WE ARE THE ONLY TRUE CHURCH?

Because that's what Jesus Christ called us: "the only true and living church upon the face of the whole earth" (D&C 1:30). Not only the true church, but the only true and *living* church. It is living because he lives, and he is the head of it. Under his guidance and direction, his church was re-established on the earth. A reformation wasn't enough. A restoration was needed.

Many of our friends are offended by the idea of only one true church, and we need to be sensitive as we share our message. President Gordon B. Hinckley taught:

> The Lord said that this is the only true and living Church upon the face of the earth with which He is well-pleased. I didn't say that. Those are His words. The Prophet Joseph was told that the other sects were wrong. Those are not my words. Those are the Lord's words. But they are hard words for those of other faiths. We don't need to exploit them. We just need to be kind and good and gracious people to others, showing by our example the great truth of that which we believe, and leading them in the direction which we would like to see them go. ("Messages of Inspiration from President Hinckley," *Church News,* 3 June 2000)

We must always recognize that there are wonderful people who are honest in heart who are members of other churches, or not members of any church at all. "We claim the privilege of worshiping Almighty God according to the dictates of our own conscience, and allow all men the same privilege, let them worship how, where, or what they may" (Article of Faith 11). Coupled with this belief, however, is the charge given to the original apostles and repeated in our day: "Go ye into all the world, preach the gospel to every creature, acting in the authority which I have given you, baptizing in the name of the Father, and of the Son, and of the Holy Ghost" (D&C 68:8). President George Albert Smith helps us understand the attitude we should have toward our friends of other faiths:

> Today as I stand here, I realize that in this city, in the Catholic Church, the Presbyterian Church, the Methodist, the Baptist, the Episcopalian, and the other churches, I have brothers and sisters that I love. They are all my Father's children. He loves them and he expects me and he expects you, to let our lights so shine that these other sons and daughters of his, seeing our good works, will be constrained to accept all the truth of the Gospel of Jesus Christ our Lord. (*Sharing the Gospel with Others,* comp. Preston Nibley [Salt Lake City: Deseret Book, 1948], 4)

How have others reacted to our claim of being the only true church? Some of the responses are quite interesting. Orson F. Whitney relates this experience:

> Many years ago a learned man, a member of the Roman Catholic Church, came to Utah and spoke from the stand of the Salt Lake Tabernacle. I became well-acquainted with him, and we conversed freely and frankly. A great scholar, with perhaps a dozen languages at his tongue's end, he seemed to know all about theology, law, literature, science and philosophy. One day he said to me: "You Mormons are all ignoramuses. You don't even know the strength of your own position. It is so strong that there is only one other tenable in the whole Christian world, and that is the position of the Catholic Church. The issue is between Catholicism and Mormonism. If we are right, you are wrong; if you are right, we are wrong; and that's all there is to it. The Protestants haven't a leg to stand on. For, if we are wrong, they are wrong with us, since they were a part

of us and went out from us; while if we are right, they are apostates whom we cut off long ago. If we have the apostolic succession from St. Peter, as we claim, there is no need of Joseph Smith and Mormonism; but if we have not that succession, then such a man as Joseph Smith was necessary, and Mormonism's attitude is the only consistent one. It is either the perpetuation of the gospel from ancient times, or the restoration of the gospel in latter days." (As cited in LeGrand Richards, *A Marvelous Work and a Wonder* [Salt Lake City: Deseret Book, 1976], 3–4)

From what we have already seen, many of the reformers were convinced of the apostasy, at least to some degree. How would they respond to the message of the Restoration? How would the Founding Fathers respond? The Founding Fathers *did* respond! Wilford Woodruff reports:

I will here say, before closing, that two weeks before I left St. George, the spirits of the dead gathered around me, wanting to know why we did not redeem them. Said they, "You have had the use of the Endowment House for a number of years, and yet nothing has ever been done for us. We laid the foundation of the government you now enjoy, and we never apostatized from it, but we remained true to it and were faithful to God." These were the signers of the Declaration of Independence, and they waited on me for two days and two nights. I thought it very singular, that notwithstanding so much work had been done, and yet nothing had been done for them. The thought never entered my heart, from the fact, I suppose, that heretofore our minds were reaching after our more immediate friends and relatives. *I straightway went into the baptismal font and called upon Brother McCallister to baptize me for the signers of the Declaration of Independence, and fifty other eminent men, making one hundred in all, including John Wesley, Columbus, and others;* I then baptized him for every President of the United States, except three; and when their cause is just, somebody will do the work for them. (*Journal of Discourses,* 19:229; emphasis added)

WOULD YOU HAVE ACCEPTED JESUS?

At times I have pondered about living in the days of Jesus. I've wondered if I would have been open-minded enough to believe in him, or if I would have been skeptical and hard-hearted like the scribes and Pharisees. I find great comfort in this statement of Elder Bruce R. McConkie:

> Who will honor the name of Joseph Smith and accept the gospel restored through his instrumentality?
>
> We answer: The same people who would have believed the words of the Lord Jesus and the ancient Apostles and prophets had they lived in their day.
>
> If you believe the words of Joseph Smith, you would have believed what Jesus and the ancients said.
>
> If you reject Joseph Smith and his message, you would have rejected Peter and Paul and their message. (*Ensign,* November 1981, 48)

Yes, you would have accepted Jesus because you have believed Joseph Smith. Moroni told the Prophet Joseph that his "name should be had for good and evil among all nations, kindreds, and tongues" (Joseph Smith—History 1:33). Although not everyone has accepted Joseph Smith as a prophet, many have marveled at his influence. A writer from the New York *Herald* visited Joseph Smith and published this in 1842:

> Joe Smith is undoubtedly one of the greatest characters of the age. He indicates as much talent, originality and moral courage as Mahomet, Odin or any of the great

spirits that have hitherto produced revolutions of past ages. . . . While modern philosophy, which believes in nothing but what you can touch, is overspreading the Atlantic States, Joe Smith is creating a spiritual system, combined also with morals and industry, that may change the destiny of the race. (As cited in *Times and Seasons,* 4:773)

The London *Morning Chronicle* published this in 1851:

It cannot be denied that Joseph Smith was one of the most extraordinary persons of his time, a man of rude genius, who accomplished a much greater work than he knew; and whose name, whatever he may have been whilst living, will take its place among the notabilities of the world. (As cited in B. H. Roberts, *A Comprehensive History of the Church,* 6 vols. [Salt Lake City: Deseret News Press, 1930], 2:349)

The Count Leo Tolstoy once said, "If Mormonism is able to endure unmodified until it reaches the third and fourth generation, it is destined to become the greatest power the world has ever known." (As cited in *Messages of the First Presidency,* 6 vols., comp. James R. Clark [Salt Lake City: Bookcraft, 1965–1975], 6:265–66)

Wow. My "academic" testimony continues to grow as I study the Apostasy and the Restoration. An academic testimony is based on things you believe because they make sense—because they're logical. Once you learn about those things, you can pray about them and gain a spiritual testimony. And here's the exciting part: the more you learn (academic), the more the Spirit can confirm to your heart (spiritual). Or, you can sit around, watch TV and read comics, and wonder if you have a testimony. I know you won't do that, because you're reading a book right now! Read on, my friend, read on!

I give my witness of the Restoration. The gospel is true. The Holy Ghost testifies of it, and so does history. We are privileged to be here during this time. We are part of the Restoration, and we're not here by accident! This means we have a great responsibility. President Ezra Taft Benson told us of our task: (I've already used this quote in this book, but notice the italicized part this time.)

> For nearly six thousand years, God has held you in reserve to make your appearance in the final days before the Second Coming. *Every previous gospel dispensation has drifted into apostasy, but ours will not.* . . . God has saved for the final inning some of his strongest children, who will help bear off the kingdom triumphant. And that is where you come in, for you are the generation that must be prepared to meet your God. ("In His Steps," *1979 Devotional Speeches of the Year* [Provo, Utah: Brigham Young University Press, 1980], 59)

I hope this chapter has helped to answer some of your questions. I wish I had known more about these things when I was in high school! The scriptures tell us to "obtain a knowledge of history, and of countries, and of kingdoms, of laws of God and man, and all this for the salvation of Zion" (D&C 93:53). Knowledge is power, and there is so much to learn! Dare to be different, turn off the TV, get into the "best books," especially the scriptures and the writings of the living prophets, and prepare for your role in the final days before the Second Coming (see D&C 88:79, 118; 90:15).

EXTRA CREDIT

Truth Restored, Gordon B. Hinckley (Salt Lake City: The Church of Jesus Christ of Latter-day Saints, 1979).

A Marvelous Work and a Wonder, LeGrand Richards (Salt Lake City: Deseret Book, 1976).

"The Way Home," Thomas S. Monson, *Ensign,* May 1975, 15–17.

"Comparing LDS Beliefs with First-Century Christianity," Daniel C. Peterson and Stephen D. Ricks, *Ensign,* March 1988, 6–11.

"Columbus and the Hand of God," De Lamar Jensen, *Ensign,* October 1992, 7–13.

"A Bible, A Bible," Robert J. Matthews, *Ensign,* January 1987, 22–27.

Seventh Period: Gratitude 101

We've Got It Good

*I believe that one of the greatest sins of which
the inhabitants of the earth are guilty today
is the sin of ingratitude.*
—Joseph F. Smith

If you asked students at your school, "What are the greatest challenges facing young people today?" what would they say? Probably things like drugs, crime, gangs, alcohol abuse, and so on. Do you think anyone would say "wealth" or "high standard of living" or "too much free time? Probably not. But, believe it or not, our comfortable lifestyle is a *major* problem facing us today.

If we were to ask Brigham Young what his greatest fears were about the church, what would he say? Mobs? Persecutions? Trials? Cold winters? Anti-Mormons? Here's his answer:

> The worst fear I have about this people is that they will get rich in this country, forget God and His people, wax fat, and kick themselves out of the Church and go to hell. This people will stand mobbing, robbing, poverty, and all manner of persecution and be true. But my greatest fear is that they cannot stand wealth. (As cited in Spencer W. Kimball, *The Miracle of Forgiveness* [Salt Lake City: Bookcraft, 1969], 48)

So, how many of you lost sleep last night worrying that you might become rich? The truth is, we *are* rich. Our standard of living is very high—it's a fact, we have a lot! Perhaps you're thinking, "I don't know who he's talking to, but it's not me. Maybe some readers of this book are rich, but not me."

If you could spend some time traveling the world, and see

how *most* people on this planet live, you would come home, look in the mirror, and say to yourself, "Wow. I'm rich." Is being rich a problem? President Spencer W. Kimball pointed out, "The possession of riches does not necessarily constitute sin. But sin may arise in the acquisition and use of wealth." He continued:

> Book of Mormon history eloquently reveals the corrosive effect of the passion for wealth. Each time the people became righteous, they prospered. Then followed the transition from prosperity to wealth, wealth to the love of wealth, then to the love of ease and luxury. They moved then into spiritual inactivity, then to gross sin and wickedness, then on to near destruction by their enemies. (*The Miracle of Forgiveness,* 47)

Many great dangers accompany the pursuit of wealth, but the one we're going to focus on is *ingratitude.* Since we got rather excited about the scriptures in Fourth Period, and since we're still excited about the scriptures, we'll begin with a few verses:

> Ye are cursed because of your riches, and also are your riches cursed because ye have set your hearts upon them, and have not hearkened unto the words of him who gave them unto you.
>
> Ye do not remember the Lord your God in the things with which he hath blessed you, but ye do always remember your riches, not to thank the Lord your God for them; yea, your hearts are not drawn out unto the Lord, but they do swell with great pride, unto boasting, and unto great swelling, envyings, strifes, malice, persecutions, and murders, and all manner of iniquities. (Helaman 13:21–22)
>
> And in nothing doth man offend God, or against none is his wrath kindled, save those who confess not

his hand in all things, and obey not his commandments. (D&C 59:21)

Thou shalt thank the Lord thy God in all things. (D&C 59:7)

The younger generation has only recently arrived on the scene; but your parents and grandparents have seen enormous changes. Many in my generation, and in yours, have had it rather easy. Think about it for a minute: We haven't lived through a depression or a major war. Most of us are hip-deep in toys and gadgets like video games, scooters, computers, TVs, and DVDs. We have spare time to do things like play Little League, take music lessons, go snowboarding, or hang out at the mall. In many countries around the world, people do nothing but work all day long just to be able to feed their families. Meanwhile, we're getting soft! Are we ready for what's ahead? Here's a quote we heard before, in Second Period:

> This generation will face trials and troubles that will exceed those of their pioneer forebears. Our generation has had some periods of respite from the foe. The future generation will have none. (Vaughn J. Featherstone, *Ensign,* November 1987, 28)

We learned earlier that wise people learn from experience, and superwise people learn from others' experience—or in other words, from history. Recently, after giving a little presentation at an elementary school, I had one of the kids ask me what my favorite subject was. I replied "history." As if on cue, the entire group said "Eeeew!" You'd think I had force-fed them creamed spinach. Why do I like history? Because it increases my testimony, and it also increases my gratitude.

When an older person begins retelling one of those "when I was a boy" stories, we often roll our eyes, tune out, or leave the room. We're missing out on some interesting stuff. Sit down with your grandparents or someone else who's "been around," and listen to their history. I interviewed my grandma once for a school project. It was amazing! I had no idea all the things she'd done! And what she'd been through!

My grandpa told me some interesting things too. One Christmas morning, he peeked into the front room and saw his mother filling the children's stockings. She wept as she put an orange in his stocking—his one and only Christmas present. Maybe that's why whenever someone would say "I don't like this" at the dinner table, Grandpa would always say, "Eat whatsoever is placed before you, asking no questions."

I don't remember a lot of trauma in my life as a four-year-old. But I know someone who was four years old during the Depression. Here's an excerpt from his journal:

> I was born in January, 1926. When I was four years old the Depression began to deepen. I remember my father was out of work and we were very, very poor. He went looking for work day after day and worried himself into the hospital. After a brief stay he resumed looking and took a part-time job at Hogle Zoo cleaning out animal cages. I remember eating cornmeal mush for breakfast, lunch and dinner day after day. Many days I went to bed hungry. I had two older brothers and two older sisters. Our school clothes were well worn but clean. Most of the time I wore bib overalls and went barefoot to save my one pair of shoes. Mother worried along with my father as money was so scarce. If ever there was any to spare I might get a dime for myself. My mother took a job in the early thirties serving in the school cafeteria at South High School. We lived in a rented house at 352 Westminster Ave. My dad was several months behind in rent but the landlord let us stay. I shared a bed with my two brothers and often one of us would end up on the

floor. Most of the time the one on the floor was me. Even with both incomes it was a struggle to pay the rent, other household expenses, and clothe and feed five children. Whatever money now came in was very frugally spent. Ten cents worth of hamburger and a loaf of bread was a good supper. Through the years 1928 to about 1934 we lived in severe poverty. We didn't own a car until the late thirties.

That journal entry really touches me, because it was written by my dad!

I remember standing on the *USS Arizona* Memorial in Pearl Harbor, and looking at the names of the eleven hundred men who were entombed beneath my feet. I had no idea it would affect me the way it did! It was one of the most sobering, humbling experiences of my life. These eleven hundred sailors were young men, many who were only eighteen and nineteen years old, who had their whole lives ahead of them. But they chose to serve their country, and because of a surprise attack, they are now entombed in a sunken battleship. "They are still serving," a Navy veteran told me. And he was right. They served *me* by filling me with gratitude. Dick Cheney, Vice President of the United States and a former Secretary of Defense, said, "It is easy to take liberty for granted when you have never had it taken from you." I was inspired and humbled as I heard of the inscription over an American World War II cemetery in the Philippines which states, "We gave our todays, in order that you might have your tomorrows." What sacrifice! What commitment!

> Greater love hath no man than this, that a man lay down his life for his friends. (John 15:13)

In the early history of this country, Patrick Henry said, "Give me liberty or give me death." We get all bent out of shape if Mom asks us to clean our room or get a can of beans from the basement. (Well, maybe you don't get bent out of shape, but I'm embarrassed to say I used to.) What a slap in the face to all who have gone before us, if all we do is complain, protest, and gripe rather than serve, sacrifice, and thank the Lord for our blessings! One day, on the other side of the veil, we will meet those men and women who served when their country called. For now, we can remember them and be grateful to them.

If I make it to heaven, I will be looking for three guys who accomplished a major feat when they were not much older than you guys. I hope I'll be there, 'cause I know they will. I can't wait to meet them and shake their hands. When I do, I will be in the presence of true heroes. Not the kind of heroes who play sports on national television, make millions advertising light beer and shoes, and get fined for slugging each other on the court. But the real kind of heroes, who have honor, courage, and faith in God. Can you guess who the three teenagers are? Good, because I can't wait to tell you.

Captain Edward Martin was leading a handcart company of Saints across the plains. They were stuck in Wyoming in a place called Devil's Gate. So many of their group were sick and dying that they stopped for a while to regain some strength. When the handcarts started to move again with the help of a rescue party in early November, they reached a river filled with floating ice.

> To cross would require more courage and fortitude, it seemed, than human nature could muster. Women shrank back and men wept. Some pushed through, but others were unequal to the ordeal.
>
> Three eighteen-year-old boys belonging to the relief party, came to the rescue; and to the astonishment of all who saw, carried nearly every member of the ill-fated handcart company across the snow-bound stream. The strain was so terrible, and the exposure so great, that in

later years all the boys died from the effects of it. When President Brigham Young heard of this heroic act, he wept like a child, and later declared publicly, "That act alone will ensure C. Allen Huntington, George W. Grant, and David P. Kimball an everlasting salvation in the Celestial Kingdom of God, worlds without end." (In LeRoy R. Hafen and Ann W. Hafen, *Handcarts to Zion* [Glendale, Calif.: Arthur H. Clark Co., 1960], 132–33)

Wow. And sometimes we moan when we have to go to a service project.

Why don't we try a little exercise in gratitude and see how lucky we are? If you ever need to do an activity for a Young Men or Young Women group, this one would be fun. First, look over the following list of blessings:

___ Electricity
___ Telephone
___ Microwave Oven
___ Furnace
___ Refrigerator
___ Car
___ Stereo
___ Water Heater

If you had to give up one of these, which would it be? Put a number 1 next to the thing you'd do without. Which one did you pick?

Electricity. Good thing you didn't pick this one, huh. Without it, you couldn't use the fridge, the microwave, or the stereo. And how would you get ready in the morning? Curling irons and blow dryers are out, and so are electric shavers. No television, no dishwasher, no trash compactor, vacuum cleaner, computer, Play Station, washer, dryer, etc. You couldn't listen to music in the morning unless you bought a lot of batteries. Hey, how would you wake up in the

first place? You'd have to get one of those old-fashioned wind-
ing clocks whose alarms are so loud they can be heard by
orbiting space shuttles.

Refrigerator. Good thing you didn't pick this one either.
What would you do? If you like cold cereal, you'd have to mix
powdered milk each day, or else use canned milk. Maybe you
could get a cow of your own. Of course, you'd have to feed it
every day, and shovel manure on occasion. Better get a pair
of shoes just for that, and don't wear them to prom. What
about the freezer? What about ice! No more of that in your
Kool-aid. I guess you'd have to buy fresh food every day,
because everything would spoil.

Telephone. Good thing you didn't pick this one. How would
you communicate with the outside world? Instead of calling
your friend and saying, "Can I come over?" you'd have to go
all the way over to find out if you could come over. How
would you get a date? Ask someone face to face? Oh my
blushing festival! How would you let someone know you
needed a ride? How would you know when a store was going
to close? And what about emergencies? No more 911 when
something went wrong. You'd have to learn first aid, and
CPR, and the Heimlich maneuver, and more importantly,
how would you order pizza?

Car. Oh, sure, like anyone would pick this one. Every
fifteen-year-old I've ever met says, "I'm almost sixteen,"
when asked their age. Why? Because sixteen-year-olds can
date and drive. I guess you'd have to walk to school, and
home, and to the mall, and to church, and to your dates. Have
you ever ridden the bus to prom? It's so romantic. And all the
passengers compliment you on your corsage.

Microwave oven. Good thing you didn't pick this one. Who
wants to wait for thirty minutes to cook a bean-and-cheese
burrito! I mean, we have things to do, you know? No more

sixty-second hot-pockets, and . . . hey, no more microwave popcorn! How do you make popcorn without a microwave? Don't you have to pour a bunch of hot oil into some contraption? And then you have to clean the stupid thing afterwards! Oh well, at least we wouldn't have to worry about that "don't put aluminum foil in here" rule anymore.

Stereo. Whoa, good thing you didn't pick this one! Seriously, go count up all the CDs you own! What would you do with them, recycle? What would life be like without your music? (Try going without it for a day.) What would you listen to when you woke up? What would you listen to as you: Got dressed? Drove to school? Drove home from school? Went inside after school? Went jogging? Got ready for bed?

Furnace. Oh, brilliant. Who would pick the furnace? Only those who live in a place where they don't need one. (If that's you, replace "furnace" with "air conditioner." And why aren't you at the pool or the beach?) I guess you might do without the furnace if you love chopping firewood, or if you have an electric blanket, electric couch, electric carpet, etc. (My brother served his mission in northern Japan where they had no central heating. They had to chip the ice off the shower walls. Brrrr.) Oh well. I suppose Christmas would be more festive. You know, "Jack Frost nipping at your nose" and all.

Water heater. Another brilliant choice. Try a totally cold shower just once if you picked this one. You'd come out of the bathroom wearing icicles. Hey, you could wear your own Christmas decorations! I guess you could heat water by the fireplace if you wanted, or heat a quart at a time in the microwave.

Okay, stop, pencils down, exercise over. Why did we use those eight items? Because I served a mission to the Philippines, and I worked with people who didn't have any of them. And some of my friends in the Philippines are happier *without any* of them than we are *with all* of them. So what's the point? The point is, *none* of those things are necessities. We could live without them. They are all *blessings.* And what do we do with blessings? We thank our Father in Heaven for them. If we don't, we're guilty of the sin of ingratitude.

The danger is that we often end up complaining about our blessings! The very things we should be thankful for! If my Filipino friends had heard the way I complained in high school, they wouldn't have believed it.

> Me: "C'mon, Dad, that's a Grandma car. Can't I take the Honda?"
>
> My friends: "No way, you have *two* cars?"
>
> Me: "I don't like this casserole, Mom."
>
> My friends: "You mean, you're not going to eat it? You're going to throw it away?"
>
> Me: "Mom, I need a check for Little League baseball— it's fifty bucks plus a uniform."
>
> My friends: "Little League? You have *time* for that? Who works in the fields?"
>
> Me: "Dad, can I get a phone in my room so I can have some privacy?"
>
> My friends: "Wow, you have a phone in your *house?* We don't even have a phone in our town."

Please don't misunderstand. Is there anything wrong with having two cars, Little League, and phones? Yes, if we're not grateful and haven't learned to share! We ought to be filled with gratitude every day! Instead, it seems that the wealthiest people in the world (us) do most of the whining. And what is more annoying than a wealthy whiner?

We should be thankful for our temporal blessings, and perhaps even more thankful for our spiritual blessings. We have the scriptures, the prophets, the general conference issues of the *Ensign!* Think how many church leaders have been quoted just in this book! We should be grateful for them, and never take them for granted. President Harold B. Lee told this story:

> A man came in to see me and said that he had heard that some man appeared mysteriously to a group of temple workers and told them, "You had better hurry up and store for a year or two, or three, because there will come a season when there won't be any production." He asked me what I thought about it and I said, "Well, were you in the April Conference of 1936?" He replied, "No, I couldn't be there." And I said, "Well, you surely read the report of what was said by the Brethren in that Conference?" No, he hadn't. "Well," I said, "at that Conference the Lord did give revelation about the storage of food. How in the world is the Lord going to get over to you what he wants you to do if you are not there when he says it, and you do not take the time to read it after it has been said?"
>
> Well, that is it. It is a changing situation. The Lord is going to keep his people informed, if they will listen. As President Clark said in a classic talk that he gave, *"What we need today is not more prophets. We have prophets. But what we need is more people with listening ears."* (From an address to Seminaries and Institutes of Religion personnel, Brigham Young University, 8 July 1964, as cited in *Lay Hold upon the Word of God: Melchizedek Priesthood Personal Study Guide* 1, 33–34; emphasis added)

Perhaps the classic story of ingratitude involves the Savior, and how some people received his remarkable gifts. Let's read from the book of Luke:

And as he entered into a certain village, there met him ten men that were lepers, which stood afar off:

And they lifted up their voices, and said, Jesus, Master, have mercy on us.

And when he saw them, he said unto them, Go shew yourselves unto the priests. And it came to pass, that, as they went, they were cleansed.

And one of them, when he saw that he was healed, turned back, and with a loud voice glorified God,

And fell down on his face at his feet, giving him thanks: and he was a Samaritan.

And Jesus answering said, Were there not ten cleansed? but where are the nine?

There are not found that returned to give glory to God, save this stranger.

And he said unto him, Arise, go thy way: thy faith hath made thee whole. (Luke 17:12–19)

I love this story, because it forces me to ask myself, "Am I one of the 10 percent or one of the 90 percent?" If those numbers are right, only around 10 percent of us remember to say thank you. You and I ought to be in that 10 percent, because we're rich. Remembering to express our thanks isn't just polite, it's required; when we aren't grateful, it's a sin. President Brigham Young said, "I do not know of [any], excepting the unpardonable sin, that is greater than the sin of ingratitude" (*Journal of Discourses,* 14:277).

Wow. *Thank you* for being here! And be *thankful* that you can read. See you in Summer School!

EXTRA CREDIT

"Think to Thank," Thomas S. Monson, *Ensign,* November 1998, 17–20.

"Gratitude," Lloyd P. George, *Ensign,* May 1994, 27–28.

Relationships 101

Why Don't I Have Any Friends?

The Lord will never forsake or abandon anyone. You may
abandon him, but he will not abandon you. You never
need to feel that you are alone.
—Joseph B. Wirthlin

One summer afternoon, at the close of a wonderful youth conference, a young man approached me and asked, "What can I do to make people like me?" The tears in his eyes were evidence that he often felt alone and friendless. I've thought a lot about his question, not only for him, but for any young person who has a hard time fitting in.

Not all of us can be the homecoming queen, the class president, or the starting quarterback. High School honors seem to come with a set of friends as standard equipment. Everyone seems to make a big deal out of these positions, leaving a lot of us, in the world's view, in the "average" category. However, if you're reading this chapter right now, you've already shown that you're anything but average.

One of the hard lessons to learn in life is that there are some things you can control and some things you can't. If you want a short recipe for being frustrated and miserable, this is it: focus on things you can't control. While you may not be able to "make" someone like you, it is possible to make yourself more "likable." The way to do that is to focus on what you can control (see D&C 123:17). Here are three things you can do, even when you feel like there isn't a friend in sight. You can be curious, you can be clean, and you can be Christlike.

YOU CAN BE CURIOUS

Our world is drowning in a sea of self-centeredness. You can make yourself quite unique right away by leaving this ocean of selfishness and choosing to be curious about other people. Some well-meaning teenagers spoil the chances for successful friendships by talking too much about their own interests and activities. They may even act loud or obnoxious in an effort to convince others that they feel good about themselves. Usually, the result is just the opposite. It reminds me of a verse in Proverbs: "A fool uttereth all his mind: but a wise man keepeth it in till afterwards" (29:11).

Instead, calm down and be quiet. Be a listener. Ask questions. Be interested in others, and more people will be interested in you. Someone once said, "A good listener is not only popular everywhere, but after a while he knows something."

People who are curious spend a lot of time observing. Watch the people in your school that you most respect. (Not the most popular, but the most respected.) What do they do? How do they take care of themselves? How do they treat others? Perhaps you could try to adopt some of these qualities as your own. If you do, you will eventually become and attract that type of person. Remember, the goal is not just to have more friends but to have friends of high standards. Elder Robert D. Hales once said:

> A true friend makes it easier for us to live the gospel by being around him. (*Ensign,* May 1990, 40)

Look for friends who make you want to be better, and be that kind of friend too.

YOU CAN BE CLEAN

We often use the word *clean* in a gospel context to mean purity. In this case, we are using it to mean physically clean as well. This is another thing you can easily do. I remember one young man in my high school who would have avoided a considerable amount of teasing if he had simply washed his hair regularly. This was something he could easily control!

But he didn't. Most of us can shower and practice basic hygiene by using deodorant, brushing our teeth, and combing our hair. We can be sure our clothes are clean and smell fresh. You should always strive to be clean.

President Spencer W. Kimball suggested we take a close look at ourselves:

> You might take a careful inventory of your habits, your speech, your appearance, your weight, . . . and your eccentricities. . . . Take each item and analyze it. What do you like in others? What personality traits please you in others? Are your dresses too short, too long, too revealing, too old-fashioned? Does your weight drive off possible suitors? Do you laugh raucously? Are you too selfish? Are you interested only in your own interests or do you project yourself into the lives of others? . . . What do you do to make yourself desirable? Do you overdo or underdo? Too much makeup or too little? Scrupulously clean both physically and morally? . . . What are your eccentricities, if any? I think nearly all people have some. If so, then go to work. Classify them, weigh them, corral them, and eliminate one at a time. (*The Teachings of Spencer W. Kimball* [Salt Lake City: Bookcraft, 1982], 295–96)

In driver's education classes, students are constantly warned about "blind spots"—places where other cars may be hiding that you can't see, even with your rearview and side mirrors! It might be a good idea for each of us to find an adult we trust and ask for help in identifying our personal "blind spots." It could be your parents, your bishop, or your Young Men or Young Women adviser. Simply ask, "If you ever notice anything that I'm doing that might make it harder for me to make friends, would you please tell me about it?" It might take some humility, but it might also help you see some things that will help you. I value the people who will love me enough to be honest with me about the faults I can't see and with kindness and sensitivity let me know how I could work on them to become a better person.

YOU CAN BE CHRISTLIKE

Regardless of how others treat you, you can always treat others with kindness and dignity (see *For the Strength of Youth,* 9). Of course, compromising your standards to make friends or to be accepted by another group should never be an option. This will cause you to lose self-respect and the respect of others. Be alone temporarily if you have to, but be Christlike. Remember the words of the prophet Enoch, after the Lord called him to be a prophet:

> Why is it that I have found favor in thy sight, and am but a lad, and all the people hate me; for I am slow of speech; wherefore am I thy servant? (Moses 6:31)

Enoch was worthy of his calling even though he was not accepted by the people. If gaining friends ever means abandoning your standards, then it's definitely not what you want. Sister Ardeth G. Kapp, former General Young Women President, said:

> Never before in the history of the Church has there been such a need for young women who are willing to sacrifice popularity if necessary, suffer loneliness if required, even be rejected if needed, to defend the gospel of Jesus Christ. (*Ensign,* November 1988, 94)

Being Christlike guarantees that you'll have the most important friend of all: the Savior. He knows what it's like to be misunderstood, lonely, and rejected. And that means he knows how to help us when we feel that way. Alma tells us that Jesus suffered "pains and afflictions and temptations of every kind" so that he would know how to take care of us in our infirmities (see Alma 7:11–12). President Ezra Taft Benson gave us a list of the benefits of turning our lives over to God (I know you've seen this before, but this time look closely at the ninth item):

Men and women who turn their lives over to God will discover that He can make a lot more out of their lives than they can. He will deepen their joys, expand their vision, quicken their minds, strengthen their muscles, lift their spirits, multiply their blessings, increase their opportunities, comfort their souls, *raise up friends,* and pour out peace. Whoever will lose his life in the service of God will find eternal life (see Matt. 10:39). (*New Era,* May 1975, 20; emphasis added)

Jesus was the most selfless person who ever lived on the earth. And if we're going to be Christlike, we'll need to adopt that trait too. Once you've worked on being curious, clean, and Christlike, then forget about yourself and think of others and their needs. Somewhere out there, you'll find yourself— and you might just find a few friends as well.

EXTRA CREDIT

1. Next time you're in a conversation with people, listen! Ask yourself, am I talking too much about me? How much time am I spending listening to others? Am I curious about other people's interests and activities?

2. Do what President Kimball suggested, "take a careful inventory of your habits, your speech, your appearance . . . and your eccentricities." Write them down and see if there's anything you could do to change for the better.

3. Who do you most respect in your school or seminary? Watch this person and write down the Christlike traits they

have that you'd like to have. Set some goals about acquiring these traits and put them on the mirror or someplace you will see every day.

Baseball 101

It's Better to Think First Than Think Fast

Young men and young women . . . need to make certain decisions only once. . . . We can make a single decision about certain things that we will incorporate in our lives and then make them ours—without having to brood and redecide a hundred times what it is we will do and what we will not do.
—Spencer W. Kimball

Have you ever had someone throw a ball at you and say, "Think fast!"?

Did you flinch?

It's hard not to when the thrower waits until the ball is six inches from your nose before saying anything.

It reminds me of something that happened to me when I was in sixth grade.

One sunny spring afternoon, I found myself standing in left field, dressed in a baggy white uniform, enjoying the sunshine and the scent of freshly cut grass. *This is the life!* I thought. Little League baseball, with fans in the stands, and hot dogs and drinks for a quarter.

My coach brought me quickly back to the game when he stepped out of the dugout and yelled, "THINK!" *Oh, yeah! I'm in a baseball game.* A good hitter from the opposing team was approaching the plate, and Coach Duran wanted us to be ready. We knew from last week's baseball practice, that when the coach yelled the word *think,* he meant, "Ask yourself, 'What would I do if the ball were hit to me?'"

My eleven-year-old brain went to work—*Let's see, no outs, a runner on second base. If the ball comes to me in the air, I'll catch it, check the runner on second to see if he'll tag-up, and throw to the second baseman. If the ball is on the ground, the runner might advance and I'll probably throw to third.*

Now I knew exactly what to do. With my knees slightly bent, and my eyes fixed on the batter, I was ready for anything.

The pitcher wound up and threw one right over the plate. The batter swung and I heard a loud CRACK as the wood met the ball. He hit a line drive, and it was coming right to me! In a split second, my mental computer judged the baseball's speed and trajectory, and determined it would land just a few yards in front of where I was standing. *If I hustle, I can catch it.* I began running, and out of the corner of my eye I saw the runner leave second base and take off for third. *What was he doing? Didn't he think I could catch it on the fly?* On about my fourth stride, I raised my mitt and felt the ball smack my left hand. In one motion I took the ball out of my mitt and threw it as hard as I could to second base.

I did it! I got the runner out! Or at least I thought I did. Unfortunately, our second baseman forgot to think. He wasn't on his base! He was just standing in the infield watching. The ball bounced on the dirt, but he quickly scooped it up and stepped on the bag just in time to get the runner, who forgot to tag up.

Suddenly, Coach Duran leapt from the dugout and shouted loud enough for all the players and spectators to hear, "Nice job, Bytheway!" A big Boy Scout smile spread across my face as the cheering crowd recognized the little kid in left field who just made a double-play. I owed it all to my coach. He reminded me to think.

Life is going to hit you some line drives, and sometimes you'll have to think fast. However, it's better to think *first* than to think *fast.* If you already know what you're going to do, you're in great shape. If not, your indecision could turn into tragedy.

Some decisions in life you only have to make once. Then you're done. You'll never have to make them again. You won't have to "mull it over," or "kick it around," because you'll already know what you're going to do. President Spencer W. Kimball counselled us to think *first,* by making up our minds:

> I remember that, without being pressured by anyone, I made up my mind while still a little boy that I would never break the Word of Wisdom. . . . I made up my mind firmly and solidly that I would never touch those harmful things. Having made up my mind fully and unequivocally, I found it not too difficult to keep the promise to myself and to my Heavenly Father. . . . If every boy and girl would make up his or her mind, "I will not yield," then no matter what the temptation is: "I made up my mind. That's settled." (*The Teachings of Spencer W. Kimball* [Salt Lake City: Bookcraft, 1982], 205–6)

When you've thought *first,* you can act *fast.* When the batter hit me the ball, I knew what to do and got him out. When Joseph of Egypt was continually invited by Potiphar's wife to break the law of chastity, he fled and "got him out" too.

> And it came to pass about this time, that Joseph went into the house to do his business; and there was none of the men of the house there within.
> And she caught him by his garment, saying, Lie with me: and he left his garment in her hand, and fled, and got him out. (Genesis 39:11–12)

Long before this situation arose, Joseph had made up his mind that he would keep the commandments. He didn't spend any time thinking about the temptation. He didn't weigh the pros and cons in his head. He didn't have to! He knew that if it was wrong before, it would still be wrong now. Joseph simply acted on the decision that he had already made.

Every day, this world sends new batters up to the plate. Think, "What will I do if the temptation comes right to me?" Choose *this day* how you will handle the line drives, pop flies, and ground balls that will come your way (see Joshua 24:15). Decide in your youth to keep the commandments of God (Alma 37:35), and you won't have to think fast, because before the temptation even steps up to bat, you will have made your decision. You were smart enough to think first.

EXTRA CREDIT

"Think First" on these line drives—Come up with the actual words you would say or actions you would take if these temptations were hit right to you:

You are invited to a party where you know there will be drinking. How do you refuse?

Someone asks you out on a date, and you are only fifteen. How do you explain your standards?

You're with a group of friends at someone's house, and someone starts a raunchy movie. How do you get out of the situation without appearing self-righteous?

Perspective 101

When Bad Things Happen

*How different is life when there is no assurance of
eternity. When we know that this earthly estate is but
one station along the road to immortality and eternal life,
things take on an entirely different perspective.*
—Gordon B. Hinckley

had probably the single most intimidating speaking experience of my life back in May of 1999. A seminary teacher friend of mine, Rob Hildebrandt, called and asked if I would be willing to speak to the seminary students in Littleton, Colorado, who had only a few days earlier been through a tragic shooting at Columbine High School.

I spent a couple of sleepless nights wondering what I could possibly say that would help. As I prepared over the next few weeks, my love and appreciation for the scriptures grew and grew and I marveled that the scriptures held so many keys to understanding the evil in the world. I remembered certain passages and stories that had helped me understand why bad things happen—often to good people.

This wonderful story about Albert Einstein helps illustrate the power of the scriptures. He was teaching physics at a large university. After administering a test, Dr. Einstein was walking back to his office with his graduate assistant, who asked, "Hey, Dr. Einstein, isn't this the same test you gave last year?"

"Yes," replied the scientist.

The student was incredulous. "Dr. Einstein," he asked, "how could you give the same test two years in a row?"

"Because," Dr. Einstein said matter-of-factly, "since last year, the answers have changed."

I saved several of my college textbooks from classes I took many years ago. Guess what they're worth now? Nothing!

They're all obsolete. You know why? In only a few years' time, the answers changed. They're not true anymore!

Where can we look where the answers don't change? Is there such a book? Yes, and we have it! It's called the scriptures. My college textbooks were worthless after only a few years, but we can put the scriptures on the shelf, wait a thousand years, (parts of the scriptures are already older than that), and they will still be true.

That idea gave me a great starting point. As I spoke to the Littleton seminary students, I told them that we may never know *all* the answers in this life about why tragedies happen; but we do know several things *for sure*—from a place where the answers don't change.

1. God Loves His Children! (1 Nephi 11:17)

Early in the Book of Mormon, an angel asked Nephi a tough question, "Knowest thou the condescension of God?" Nephi answered, "I know that he loveth his children; nevertheless, I do not know the meaning of all things" (1 Nephi 11:17). Nephi's answer is a perfect statement for us to remember when times are tough for us and our families. We don't know the meaning of all things, but we do *know,* we are *sure,* that God loves his children. Then, instead of asking, "Why did this happen? Doesn't God love me?" we can say, "Well, I know God loves us, so what can I learn from this experience? How does the Lord want me to handle this?" Elder Richard G. Scott taught:

> When you face adversity, you can be led to ask many questions. Some serve a useful purpose; others do not. To ask, Why does this have to happen to me? Why do I have to suffer this, now? What have I done to cause this? will lead you into blind alleys. It really does no good to ask questions that reflect opposition to the will of God. Rather ask, What am I to do? What am I to

learn from this experience? What am I to change? Whom am I to help? How can I remember my many blessings in times of trial? Willing sacrifice of deeply held personal desires in favor of the will of God is very hard to do. Yet, when you pray with real conviction, "Please let me know Thy will" and "May Thy will be done," you are in the strongest position to receive the maximum help from your loving Father. (*Ensign,* November 1995, 16)

One of the mistakes we often make is to believe that all trials come because we did something wrong. That's not always true. Yes, some trials come because of our own disobedience, but many trials are simply part of living on this fallen world. We can think of many examples of righteous people who have suffered: Abraham, Abinadi, Joseph of Egypt, Joseph Smith, and even Jesus. Sometimes bad things happen to good people. But, we know God loves his children! So when tough times come, we can ask him to teach us what can be learned and ask him to help us through.

2. God Allows Evil to Exist in the World (Moses 7:33)

Some of us get confused. When tragedy strikes, we may think, "Well, it must have been God's will." Be careful. God's will is that we choose righteousness! But he has given us a choice. In the Pearl of Great Price (writings which are thousands of years old, but still true!), Enoch sees a frightening vision.

And he beheld Satan; and he had a great chain in his hand, and it veiled the whole face of the earth with darkness; and he looked up and laughed, and his angels rejoiced. (Moses 7:26)

Chains represent bondage in the scriptures, and Enoch sees Satan looking up and laughing at the world in chains. Enoch also sees the Lord, who looks down on the sinful world, and weeps. Enoch seems to be confused, when he sees that a being like God can weep, so he asks:

How is it that the heavens weep, and shed forth their tears as the rain upon the mountains?

And Enoch said unto the Lord: How is it that thou canst weep, seeing thou art holy, and from all eternity to all eternity?

And were it possible that man could number the particles of the earth, yea, millions of earths like this, it would not be a beginning to the number of thy creations; and thy curtains are stretched out still; and yet thou art there, and thy bosom is there; and also thou art just; thou art merciful and kind forever. (Moses 7:28–30)

The Lord answers Enoch, in what I think is one of the saddest passages of scripture in the standard works:

The Lord said unto Enoch: Behold these thy brethren; they are the workmanship of mine own hands, and I gave unto them their knowledge, in the day I created them; and in the Garden of Eden, gave I unto man his agency;

And unto thy brethren have I said, and also given commandment, that they should love one another, and that they should choose me, their Father; but behold, they are without affection, and they hate their own blood. (Moses 7:32–33)

Clearly, the "Lord's will" is that we choose him, our Father. But some do not. They are "without affection, and they hate their own blood." Everyone on earth has agency, and sometimes those who misuse their agency have an impact on many innocent people. I believe that when the Lord views these kinds of tragedies on the earth, he weeps.

President Boyd K. Packer once compared the plan of

salvation to a three-act play. Act I, he said, is the premortal existence. Act II is this life, and is characterized by tests, trials, temptations, and even tragedies. Nowhere, said President Packer, does the phrase "and they lived happily ever after" appear in the second act. That is reserved only for Act III. President Packer also counseled, "Do not suppose that God willfully causes that, which for His own purpose, He permits" ("The Play and the Plan," Church Educational System Fireside, 7 May 1995, 3). You might want to read that again slowly. "Do not suppose that God willfully causes that, which for His own purpose, He permits." Do you see the important difference between causing something to happen and permitting or allowing it to happen? Lehi taught:

> For it must needs be, that there is an opposition in all things. If not so, my first-born in the wilderness, righteousness could not be brought to pass, neither wickedness, neither holiness nor misery, neither good nor bad. (2 Nephi 2:11)

Yes, God allows evil to exist in the world, but one day, there will be an accounting. In this world we have freedom of choice, but we cannot escape accountability for our choices. (That's why the Young Women values stress "Choice *and* Accountability.")

3. Your Work Is Not Yet Finished! (Alma 14:13)

In the Book of Mormon, Alma and Amulek taught the people of Ammonihah. Some of the people were so wicked that they responded to the message by building a bonfire and throwing the believing women and children into the flames. They also threw the scriptural records into the fire, and forced Alma and Amulek to watch the horrible suffering.

> And when Amulek saw the pains of the women and children who were consuming in the fire, he also was pained; and he said unto Alma: How can we witness

this awful scene? Therefore let us stretch forth our hands, and exercise the power of God which is in us, and save them from the flames. (Alma 14:10)

"How can we witness this awful scene?" I wondered if any of the students had similar questions during the tragedy. Alma answered Amulek:

The Spirit constraineth me that I must not stretch forth mine hand; for behold the Lord receiveth them up unto himself, in glory. (Alma 14:11)

These believers in God, went home to be with God. I asked the students to make a footnote next to Alma 14:11 to this comforting passage in the Doctrine and Covenants:

And it shall come to pass that those that die in me shall not taste of death, for it shall be sweet unto them. (D&C 42:46)

Amulek posed to Alma a new possibility: "Perhaps they will burn us also" (Alma 14:12). Alma answered, "Be it according to the will of the Lord. But, behold, our work is not finished; therefore they burn us not" (Alma 14:13).

I built my talk around Alma 14:13, and I pled with the youth, "Don't let this tragedy define your life! You still have your own mission, your own patriarchal blessing, and your own destiny which is just yours! Your work is not finished!"

What about those who die in such tragedies? Does that mean their work was finished? I don't think so. Apparently, there is more work to do in the spirit world. President Joseph Fielding Smith taught:

May I say for the consolation of those who mourn, and for the comfort and guidance of all of us, that no righteous man is ever taken before his time. In the case of the faithful saints, they are simply transferred to other fields of labor. The Lord's work goes on in this life, in the world of spirits, and in the kingdoms of glory where men go after their resurrection. (As cited in Robert L. Millet and Joseph Fielding McConkie, *The Life Beyond* [Salt Lake City: Bookcraft, 1986], title page)

Again, we must go back to Nephi's response to the angel— we know God loves his children! We don't know exactly why some people die and some people don't in these tragedies. Many good people and many not-so-good people die every day! But we know God loves his children, in this life and in the next.

The Prophet Joseph Smith taught that while we may still mourn, we do not mourn without hope:

> The only difference between the old and young dying is, one lives longer in heaven and eternal light and glory than the other, and is freed a little sooner from this miserable, wicked world. Notwithstanding all this glory, we for a moment lose sight of it, and mourn the loss, but we do not mourn as those without hope. (*Teachings of the Prophet Joseph Smith,* sel. Joseph Fielding Smith [Salt Lake City: Deseret Book, 1976], 197)

The important thing to remember is that if you are here, your earthly work is not finished. I believe the Lord will hold us accountable for what we did with our lives whether we have trials or not, whether we marry or not, and whether our life is easy or not. Alma and Amulek had to go on, and so do we. Alma and Amulek must have relied on the atonement of Christ to get them through the sadness, the nightmares, and the emotional trauma of the tragedy in Ammonihah, and we must rely on the Atonement to help us through our personal tragedies as well.

My father served in the Navy in World War II, and saw many battles toward the end of the war. His two years in the service deeply affected him. Sometimes I think of the life of

Reference	Age	Event
Mormon 2:2	16	Leading the armies against the Lamanites
Mormon 2:9	20	Attacked by an army of 44,000
Mormon 2:15	34	"I saw thousands hewn down in open rebellion against their God"
Mormon 2:22	36	The Lamanites attack again
Mormon 2:28	40	Nephites retake lands, make a treaty with Lamanites
Mormon 3:4	50	The Lamanites attack again
Mormon 3:7	51	Lamanites attack the city of Desolation
Mormon 3:8	52	Lamanites come down to battle again
Mormon 4:1	53	Nephites go up and attack Lamanites
Mormon 4:7	54	Lamanites attack Teancum
Mormon 4:15	57	Nephites attack Lamanites
Mormon 4:16	65	Innumerable army of Lamanites attack
Mormon 5:6	70	Lamanites attack again
Mormon 6:5	74	Nephites gather at Cumorah for tremendous battle

Mormon, who took over the Nephite armies at sixteen, and I wonder how his life of war must have affected him.

If you look at the chart on the previous page, you'll see that Mormon spent nearly his whole life, from age sixteen to seventy-four, in the business of defending the Nephites. He witnessed the violent deaths of tens of thousands, yet he was filled with love. Try to imagine a large, powerful, battle-hardened career General standing up in testimony meeting and saying this:

> Charity is the pure love of Christ, and it endureth forever; and whoso is found possessed of it at the last day, it shall be well with him.
>
> Wherefore, my beloved brethren, pray unto the Father with all the energy of heart, that ye may be filled with this love, which he hath bestowed upon all who are true followers of his Son, Jesus Christ; that ye may become the sons of God; that when he shall appear we shall be like him, for we shall see him as he is; that we may have this hope; that we may be purified even as he is pure. Amen. (Moroni 7:47–48)

How did Mormon manage to keep his spiritual sensitivity while growing up in an environment of war? He must have been renewed by the atonement, which can take away not only the pain from our sins, but also the pain from things that happen to us over which we have no control (see Alma 7:11; remember the discussion from the Assembly chapter?).

4. One Day, the Lord Will Reveal All Things (D&C 101:32–36)

We may never have all the answers in this life. The newspapers, the news networks, and the politicians will be debating about solutions to these kinds of problems for years. We will look for our answers in books where the answers don't change. One day, the Lord will return and answer all our questions: (Notice the list of things he'll tell us about!)

Yea, verily I say unto you, in that day when the Lord shall come, he shall reveal all things—

Things which have passed, and hidden things which no man knew, things of the earth, by which it was made, and the purpose and the end thereof—

Things most precious, things that are above, and things that are beneath, things that are in the earth, and upon the earth, and in heaven.

And all they who suffer persecution for my name, and endure in faith, though they are called to lay down their lives for my sake yet shall they partake of all this glory.

Wherefore, fear not even unto death; for in this world your joy is not full, but in me your joy is full. (D&C 101:32–36)

Indeed, this world is "Act II," full of tests, trials, temptations, and sometimes even tragedies, but in Christ our joy is full. Jesus is the Master Teacher, and he has a Teacher's Edition with all the answers.

Have you ever done needlepoint? Have you ever noticed that it's important which side of the fabric you display? One side is full of knots and the design is difficult to recognize. I have always loved this little poem about a needlepoint or weaving design. It helps me to trust God when I can't understand why things happen the way they do.

The Weaver

My life is but a weaving, between my Lord and me;
I cannot choose the colors, He worketh steadily.
Ofttimes He weaveth sorrow, and I in foolish pride,
Forget that He seeth the upper, and I the underside.
Not till the loom is silent, and the shuttles cease to fly,

Shall God unroll the canvas and explain the reason why.
The dark threads are as needful in the Weaver's skillful hand,
As the threads of gold and silver in the pattern He has
*   planned.*
(In *Sourcebook of Poetry,* Al Bryant, comp. [Grand Rapids,
    Mich.: Zondervan Publishing House, 1968], 664.)

Someone once said that in this life, suffering is mandatory, but misery is optional. No one's going to make it out of here alive. We're all going to pass through some trials, and perhaps even some tragedies. Just remember to keep your perspective. God loves his children, part of his plan is to allow evil to exist in the world, we have a work to accomplish, and one day he will answer all our questions, and wipe away all our tears (Revelation 7:17).

EXTRA CREDIT

Why Bad Things Happen to Good People, Brent L. Top (Salt Lake City: Bookcraft, 1991).

Second Semester

Orientation

Welcome Back!

Orientation

Welcome Back!

Hi, I'm glad you're back in school. It will be fun to talk with you again. There is so much to learn and explore and discover, and you, my fellow explorer, can do it all because you can read! I love the power of books. (You know, new books *smell* good too. Go ahead, stick your nose in here and take a whiff. Nice, huh?)

You've finished the first half of the "crash course" and whizzed through summer school, but we haven't covered a few things, some of the deeper things. Let me explain. No, there is too much. Let me sum up. Once I attended a fireside. A wonderful talk was given, and there was a peaceful, thoughtful spirit in the chapel. Everyone in attendance was "turned inward." The youth were sitting quietly, thinking about personal, spiritual things. You know the feeling—I know this has happened to you. It was very interesting because the closing hymn was over, the closing prayer was said, but no one left. The dance was starting in the other room, but no one wanted to leave the chapel! The overwhelming feeling shared by everyone in the room seemed to be, "I want to soak this feeling in for a few minutes." It was written on every face. The youth whispered to one another. No one told them to whisper; they just did. Why do you suppose that was? The music began to play in the gym, but no one seemed to care. Some even got a pained look on their faces when they heard the beat through the partition. Kind of a "well, back to the real world" look. *I love it when that happens!* I love it when the youth notice the difference between the feeling of the Spirit and the feeling of the world. (I get that same "back to the real world" feeling every time I leave the temple and go back to my car.)

Now, here's the problem. A few youth still had unanswered questions. Important questions. I know they did, because it was written all over their faces. So a few of us stayed in the chapel and talked. We had a wonderful discussion while the majority of the group jumped around and perspired in the gym.

There are some questions that people ask only when they are on that deep-down level. That's where those young people were. They wanted to know about heaven, about Heavenly Father, about Jesus. Some of them weren't sure what they wanted, except that they wanted more—more of that sweet feeling that seemed to stay in the room. They had a wonderful case of "celestial homesickness." Some of those great teens had questions that they didn't want to ask in front of the others. (I wonder how many questions about important things don't get asked because people are too afraid?) Would you like to know some of their questions? How about this one: "How do I repent?" Is that an important question, or what? A little more important than which fork to use on a date, isn't it? How about this one: "How do I know if I've felt the Spirit?" and, "How can I feel it more often?" I can't tell you how thrilled I was, having lived a few more years but remembering my teenage years like they were yesterday, to sit with those five or six young people and talk about the weightier things of the gospel for the next two and a half hours. I think I would rather do that than attend any youth conference dance, or any amusement park, or any movie, anytime.

Well, my friends, I've tried my hardest to find answers to

the deep-down questions and put them in the rest of this book. I'm giving you fair warning, because there may be times when you look up from the pages and say, "Wow. This is serious stuff!" And it is. I don't know much myself, so I've looked for answers in the scriptures and from the words of the prophets. If I missed any of *your* deep-down questions, those are the best places for you to look too.

Let's get to work! Go get a highlighter, your scriptures, and a favorite beverage, and let's finish this book. You might even want to take the phone off the hook. (Right, like you would really take the phone off the hook.) Anyway, turn off the TV and read, and I'll try to make it as interesting as I can.

Well, that's it for Second Semester Orientation. *It's back-to-school time!* First Period is about to start—I'll see you in class!

First Period: Motivation 101

The Three Attitudes

And they were all young men, and they were exceedingly valiant for courage, and also for strength and activity; but behold, this was not all—they were men who were true at all times in whatsoever thing they were entrusted.
—Alma 53:20

You know the story. You may have even lived the story. Big family leaves on big trip and leaves something big behind. It's happened to your family, it's happened to my family, and it happened to Lehi and Sariah and their family. "Oh, great. We traveled two hundred miles, but we have to go back and get the plates. You know, the brass ones. Boys, would you please go back and get the plates?"

What's the difference between Nephi and Laman and Lemuel? Notice the different responses to exactly the same request. Laman and Lemuel, say it's too hard: "It is a hard thing which [you] have required" (1 Nephi 3:5). (Today's ordinary teenagers would probably ask, "Is this gonna be fun?") Nephi, however, says, "I will go and do" (1 Nephi 3:7). Same request, opposite attitudes.

In fact, as you go through the Book of Mormon, you'll find that Laman and Lemuel usually ended up doing the same things Nephi did—they just had a bad attitude about it. That "little" difference, that difference in attitude, seemed to be passed down through many generations who felt they were "wronged in the wilderness," and it ended up affecting the destiny of both the Nephite and Lamanite civilizations.

No one wants to be labeled. But whether we like it or not, we label *ourselves* by our attitudes and actions. Laman and Lemuel labeled themselves, Nephi labeled himself, and every day we label ourselves by the things we say and do.

We give Laman and Lemuel a pretty hard time, but think

about it—*walking* two hundred miles to get something (from someone who doesn't want to give it to you), and then walking another two hundred miles to bring it back is a little inconvenient. And that makes Nephi's "I will go and do" response even more impressive. But it's not just the big things that show what's inside of us. We also tell on ourselves by the little things we do. President David O. McKay shared this interesting little poem in general conference back in 1969:

> *You tell on yourself by the friends you seek,*
> *By the very manner in which you speak,*
> *By the way you employ your leisure time,*
> *By the use you make of dollar and dime;*
> *You tell what you are by the things you wear,*
> *And even by the way you wear your hair,*
> *By the kind of things at which you laugh,*
> *By the records you play on your phonograph*
> [ancient predecessor of the CD player].
> *You tell what you are by the way you walk,*
> *By the things of which you delight to talk,*
> *By the manner in which you bury deceit,*
> *By so simple a thing as how you eat.*
> *By the books you choose from the well-filled shelf;*
> *In these ways and more you tell on yourself.*
> (In Conference Report, October 1969, 87)

As you know, earth life is full of rules, requirements, commandments, dress codes, honor codes, Morse codes, and so on. When someone starts explaining the rules, an amazing thing happens. People begin to "tell on themselves" by their reactions. You'll see obedient, "I-will-go-and-do" types; whining, "It-is-a-hard-thing" types; and everything in between. For now, we're going to narrow the field down to three different groups or attitudes. We'll call them the "three attitudes."

(You've heard of the *beatitudes?* Well, these are the *three-attitudes.*)

HOW BAD CAN I BE?

I once attended a standards lesson during which anonymous questions were gathered in a shoebox and submitted to a panel of leaders. One of the questions, to our surprise, was, "How far can you go before you have to see the bishop?" Whoa. Nice attitude. Stated another way, the question was, "How bad can I be?" I guess this person wanted to know exactly where "bad" began so he or she wouldn't miss out on anything. A youth asking, "How far can I go before it's bad?" is like asking how deep can I swim before I have to come up for air? The person who asked that question didn't realize that where "bad" *really* begins is in the attitude, which reveals itself through bad behavior.

One way people show their membership in the "how-bad-can-I-be" group is by their strong reactions to things like dress standards, which are simply an attempt to draw the line on what is acceptable. They want to know exactly where that line is. For instance, they want to know exactly where the knee begins, or where "long hair" begins, so that they can get as close to being in violation of the code as possible and still be admitted to the dance. They may be secretly excited when they can "get away with" something, because that's the attitude: "What can I get away with?"

They tell on themselves another way by choosing music and entertainment that are right on the line as well. They say, "It wasn't that bad," or "I've seen other movies with a better rating that were worse." Once again, they live right next to the danger zone, not realizing that the most dangerous thing is the attitude itself.

They may say things like, "Hey, nobody's perfect"—which is true, but they're not trying to be perfect. They're not even trying to be good! They want to know how bad they can be. Elder Richard J. Clarke commented:

> Those who excuse transgressions by saying, "Well, I'm not perfect" may be reminded that conscious sin is a long way from perfection. We would do best to consider this counsel of President Brigham Young. "Be . . . as perfect as [you] can, for that is all you can do. . . . The sin . . . is [not doing] as well as [you know] how" (*Journal of Discourses* 2:129–30). (*Ensign,* May 1991, 42)

If you were to ask someone with this attitude why they attend church or seminary, they might respond, "'Cause I have to." I *have* to do this, I *have* to do that. They see life as a big set of unfair rules, and obedience is an irritation.

HOW GOOD DO WE HAVE TO BE?

The next group wants to know, "How good do we have to be?" At first, that attitude might sound okay. It's a little better, but not much. Members of this group want to do what they're supposed to do. In fact, if you asked them, "Why do you go to seminary?" they would say, "'Cause I'm *post* to." (Some people pronounce the word "supposed" as "post.") These are good people. They do what they're "post" to, they go to church and attend meetings. They're willing to be good. Good for them. And, hey, being good is good! But that's all it is—good. It's not great, it's not valiant; it's just, you know, good. Sister Ardeth Kapp said:

> It has been my observation, and it is my confession as a former participant, that many people drift along with the crowd in the Church. Many *good* people drift to sacrament meeting and Sunday School, even family home evening, and they drift through a casual study of the scriptures. . . . [They] step into the mainstream, getting deeply involved with Church activity and floating

with the current, comfortable with a sense of false security that they are in the right place. (In *Woman to Woman: Selected Talks from the BYU Women's Conferences* [Salt Lake City: Deseret Book, 1986], 53; emphasis added)

"See, here I am, bein' good, doin' what I'm post to. Call me the post-man, 'cause I do what I'm post to." Yup. It's good to be good, but it's better to be *better* than good.

Now, here's the problem. Sometimes, for this group, being good has its limits. They wouldn't want to go too far. I was once asked by a Young Women leader to challenge a group of teens to give up a certain TV show named after a zip code. We discussed the thirteenth Article of Faith, "If there is anything virtuous, lovely, or of good report or praiseworthy, we seek after these things." After realizing that many television programs failed to fit in those categories, most of the youth present willingly accepted my challenge. Some had uncomfortable looks on their faces. One girl whispered to her friend, "I want to be good, but I don't want to be *that* good." Ouch. Can you see how dangerous that attitude is? Yes indeed. Heaven forbid we become *too* good—we might get too many blessings. Elder Carlos E. Asay told the young men in a priesthood session of general conference:

> There is a lie—a vicious lie—circulating among the Latter-day Saints and taking its toll among the young. And it is that a "balanced man" is one who deliberately guards against becoming too righteous. (*Ensign,* May 1992, 41)

Yeah, we wouldn't want to be a Molly Mormon or a Sammy Seminary (I believe heaven will be full of Mollys and Sams). Elder Joseph B. Wirthlin taught:

> [Some] claim to be obedient to God's commandments

but do not feel at all uncomfortable about purchasing food at the store on Sunday and then asking the Lord to bless it. Some say they would give their lives for the Lord, yet they refuse to serve in the nursery. The Savior spoke very explicitly about people who "draw near to me with their mouth, and with their lips do honour me, but have removed their heart far from me." (*Ensign*, November 1992, 35)

But President Ezra Taft Benson said we need to be more than just good:

> We have too many potential spiritual giants who should be more vigorously lifting their homes, the kingdom, and the country. We have many who feel they are *good* men, but they need to be good for something—stronger patriarchs, courageous missionaries, valiant genealogists and temple workers, dedicated patriots, devoted quorum members. [Okay, here's my favorite part:] In short, we must be shakened and awakened from a spiritual snooze. (*Teachings of Ezra Taft Benson* [Salt Lake City: Bookcraft, 1988], 403–4; emphasis added)

Too many people continually hit the snooze button on the clock radio of their personal spirituality. They hear the alarm, but they say, "I'll be better someday, but for now, I don't wanna be too good, I'll just snooze. Someday I'll start a scripture study program, someday I'll say my daily prayers, someday I'll do what I'm post to, but not now. I'll just snooze for a while."

If we don't want to be in the "How-bad-can-I-be" group, or the "How-good-am-I-post-to-be" group, then where should we be? It's time to talk about the third attitude, and you, my friend, know all about this group. It's the group where you can find fine teenagers like you.

I WANT TO BE VALIANT!

I love this group, and you're in it! This group doesn't ask, "How bad can I be?" They have absolutely no interest in what is bad. And *good* isn't enough for them, either. They want something better than good. Their question is on a higher plane: "Is it *valiant?* Is it better than average? Is it high class? That's where I want to be. That's where I *belong.* I want to be valiant." No one has to remind these young people about rules. No one has to tell these young men they need a necktie at the sacrament table, or these young women exactly where their knee is. They carry their desire to please their Heavenly Father everywhere they go. Like the others, they tell on themselves. The quality of their spirit shines brightly through their attitude.

Valiant people have no problem with dress codes. They usually agree with them. And even if they don't agree, they follow them anyway. That's the way valiant people are. They're more interested in being obedient than in knowing all the reasons for the rules. They get up on Sunday morning and think to themselves, "What should I wear today? Then they ask one more question: What does the Lord deserve? He deserves the best. Yeah, that's it. Sunday best." Valiant young women dress carefully because they realize they can attract young men in one of two ways: to themselves, or to their bodies; to who they are inside, or to how they look on the outside. They also realize that inner beauty is more, yes, *more* powerful in the long run than external beauty will ever be.

If you were to ask an "is-it-valiant" type teenager, "Why do you go to seminary?" they would give you that "what-a-strange-question" look and answer, "Because *I want to.* I love it. It's the best part of my day." And when they get to seminary, they stay awake, and they stay focused. They don't expect to be entertained. They expect to learn! And they don't just listen to their instructor, they *help* their instructor by being involved in the class. They are always part of the solution, and never part of the problem.

"Is-it-valiant" teenagers are missionaries from the moment they get up in the morning. Just being around them makes you want to be better. President David O. McKay said:

> Every man and every person who lives in this world wields an influence, whether for good or for evil. It is not what he says alone; it is not alone what he does. It is what he is. Every man, every person radiates what he or she really is. . . . It is what we are and what we *radiate* that affects the people around us. (*Man May Know for Himself,* comp. Clare Middlemiss [Salt Lake City: Deseret Book, 1967], 108)

You just can't hide it when you're valiant! It radiates!

If you want to be valiant, and you need a model to follow, think about Jesus. Jesus was a teen at one time. We have very little information about his teenage years. All we really have is summed up in one scripture: "And Jesus increased in wisdom and stature, and in favour with God and man" (Luke 2:52).

Imagine what the Savior was like when he was young. Think how he would have "radiated." Next time you wonder how to live your life, think about being the kind of young person Jesus must have been. He would have been valiant—obedient to his parents, a good worker, and kind and respectful to everyone. Valiant people focus on the Savior and try to live the words of the Primary song:

So, little children,
Let's you and I
Try to be like him,
Try, try, try.
(*Children's Songbook,* 55)

Did Jesus ever ask, "How bad can I be?" or "How good am I supposed to be?" Did he do things because he had to, or because he was supposed to? Let's ask President Howard W. Hunter:

[Jesus] was perfect and sinless, not because he had to be, but rather because he clearly and determinedly wanted to be. *(Ensign,* November 1976, 19)

Why is it so important to be valiant? Well, those in the terrestrial kingdom are described like this:

These are they who are *not valiant* in the testimony of Jesus; wherefore, they obtain not the crown over the kingdom of our God. (D&C 76:79; emphasis added)

Like Nephi, Laman, and Lemuel, you will find that much of your life and your eternal destiny will be determined by your attitude. We'll talk more as this semester continues about being valiant, about having our hearts changed so that we sincerely *want* to be valiant, all the time. And now that you've been introduced to the three attitudes, tuck them away in your mind because we'll be referring to them again.

We'll close with an appeal from President Howard W. Hunter:

We must know Christ better than we know him; we must remember him more often than we remember him; we must serve him more *valiantly* than we serve him. . . . What manner of men and women ought we to be? Even as he is. (*Ensign,* May 1994, 64; emphasis added)

Well, you've told on yourself again, because you just finished First Period. You must be reading this book because you *want* to. You must be one of those valiant ones, because you want to learn! So, my fellow Nephi, let's "go and do" Second Period—not because we have to, or because we're post to, but because we want to.

Second Period:
Spiritual Health 101

Hand Soap and Heart Transplants

*I say unto you, can ye look up to God at that
day with a pure heart and clean hands?
I say unto you, can you look up, having the
image of God engraven upon your countenances?*
—Alma 5:19

If you were to look up the term *Service Project* in the dictionary of Latter-day Saint jargon, it might look something like this:

Service Project—*Sur' vis Proj' ekt* (LDS): 1. An event usually advertised as "something really fun, but we're not going to tell you what it is." Followed by, "Wear grubbies and show up at the church. P.S. Bring a shovel." The *Service Project* is usually followed by a caffeine-free beverage and/or pastry (see *Refreshments*). 2. Some teens may moan when hearing *Service Project,* but they always end up enjoying the experience.

One summer, I found myself involved in one of those service projects in San Antonio, Texas. About a hundred of us were busy painting a widow's home. We were having a good time. It's amazing how quickly you can get a major job done when there are a hundred people doing it. The "is-it-valiant" group were working their hearts out, the "how-good-are-we-post-to-be" group were doing what they were post to, and the "how-bad-can-I-be" group were telling on themselves by playing around with the water hose. I was three or four rungs up a ladder painting one side of the house. (People driving by thought, "Hey, it must be the ladder-days." Ha, ha.)

Anyway, I was painting near the rain gutter, which I accidentally bumped with my hand. Apparently the rain gutters hadn't been cleaned in a while, and bumping them showered my face with dirt and dust. I closed my eyes just in time, but the dirt went everywhere else, and I looked as if I had been bobbing for potting soil. With the sleeves of my T-shirt I wiped the lovely combination of dirt and perspiration from my face. Yuck. It was incredibly hot and humid that day, but I kept painting, because I knew there was a high-pressure shower and a big bar of deodorant soap in my future.

Things got worse before they got better. I continued to paint, finding in my path what looked like a vacant wasps' nest. It wasn't vacant. After my paintbrush sideswiped the nest, everything went into slow motion. An irritated wasp flew out and landed on my hand. I remember thinking, "Oh, lookie there. There's a wasp on my hand." Then he stuck his little behind *in,* not on, the back of my hand. I thought to myself, "He's gonna sting me," and he did. And it hurt. In a reflex action, I let go of the paintbrush, which, on its way to the ground, hit a member of the teachers quorum squarely on the back. I felt awful. I stepped off the ladder, face filthy, hand stinging, and apologized up and down to the young man whose shirt I had just ruined.

But we weren't done yet. Now we had to paint the metal bars around all the windows with a coat of black enamel. That was fine, except that I have a problem: whenever I'm working with a liquid, I always seem to get it on my hands. I remember when I was a kindergartner, whenever my family had pancakes for breakfast, the syrup would somehow magically creep up my fork and knife and get on my fingers. One morning at school someone asked, "Did you have pancakes for breakfast?" (I guess they could smell the syrup.) "No," I responded, "that's my new cologne, 'Mrs. Butterworth for Men.'" (Just kidding.)

So now we're painting with black paint, and you can guess what happened. Yes, it crept up the brush and got all over my hands. Black paint. On my hands. Gross. When we arrived, the house was a mess and we were clean. Now we were a mess and the house was clean. All we did that afternoon was transfer messes! And I for one was anxious to transfer my mess again to a paint-thinner rag and a hot shower. Try to imagine it. It's hot. It's humid. Drops of perspiration and muck drip freely off my face, my T-shirt is soaked and filthy, and my hands are sticky with half-dried black paint. I was looking forward to a shower like it was the celestial kingdom.

What if the youth conference chairperson had stood up at that point and announced, "Brothers and sisters, we don't have time for you to take a shower before the fireside. Your clean clothes have been taken to the changing rooms at the church, and we'd like you to go straight there and put on your clean white shirts and your fresh clean dresses. Wear them over your filth and sweat, and go directly to the chapel for the fireside."

How would that make you feel—sitting there with clean, fresh clothes but feeling gross and sweaty and dirty underneath? Remember that feeling for a second, okay?

One time, when I was in college, I had to give a priesthood blessing at about 5:30 in the morning. A sister in my ward was really sick. We got dressed quickly and ran over to her apartment. My roommate did the anointing, and then it was my turn. I remember placing my hands on her head and then pausing. For whatever reason, I remembered the lyrics of a song my dad used to play on Sunday mornings. I remembered especially the chorus: "He that hath clean hands, and a pure heart." I looked it up later. The chorus is the answer to a question:

> Who shall ascend into the hill of the Lord? or who shall stand in his holy place?
> He that hath clean hands, and a pure heart. (Psalm 24:3–4)

As I stood over this young woman with my hands on her head, I wondered, Are my hands clean? Is my spirit filthy and gross in any way? *Do I really have the priesthood today?*

> That [the rights of the priesthood] may be conferred upon us, it is true; but when we undertake to cover our sins, or to gratify our pride, . . . the heavens withdraw themselves; the Spirit of the Lord is grieved; and when it is withdrawn, Amen [or, "that's the end"] to the priesthood or the authority of that man. (D&C 121:37)

I reviewed my life for a moment. I thought about my sins, about my attempts to repent and change, about the purity of my heart and motives, and about my prayers the night before. *Have I looked at a magazine that has stained my hands? Have I pushed a video into the machine that has soiled my spiritual fingers?* You young men will do this every time you're asked to give a blessing. Every time.

It is a wonderful feeling to go through this thought process, look at your hands, and think, "I'm okay. I can do this." It's nice to know when you're asked to break the bread at the sacrament table to know that your hands are clean. It is wonderful to kneel before the ward and hear the words "O God, the Eternal Father, we ask thee in the name of thy Son . . ." come out of a mouth that is clean, that does not use profanity or tell raunchy jokes or stories.

It's true. Nothing feels as good as the peace that comes with being clean. Nothing! There is no sin that feels as good as being clean. Nothing can compare with the feeling that if you were to die today, you could face the Lord with clean hands and a pure heart. That's what peace is.

Now, here's an important point to consider. Repentance is like soap. Repentance is like a hot shower that washes away all the sweat and the filth, leaving you fresh and clean. Some sins require very strong soap. But even that kind of soap is available from your bishop and from the Lord. The Savior is so powerful. He can make us clean. He's the only one who can do that. No one else can bring us real peace. No one. We need Jesus. We all need him. We can't be with him again unless we're absolutely clean. We've talked about clean hands, *but there's more.*

Let's say you had to teach Sunday School one day, and you asked your class, "Why do we love Jesus?" What kind of responses would you get? Your list would probably look like this:

Because he died for us.

Because he loved us.

Because he makes it possible to return to our Father in Heaven.

Because he showed us how to live.

Because he can make us clean.

All of those answers are right. We must be made clean, because no unclean thing can enter into the kingdom of heaven, *but there's more.*

CLEAN HANDS AND A PURE HEART

Sometimes we focus so much on the fact that Jesus can make us clean, and that he died for us, that we forget another powerful part of his wonderful atonement. It is amazing and miraculous, and we've talked a little bit about it already. Would you like to know what it is?

Remember that when I was about to give a blessing to that young woman in my ward, the scripture I thought of as I stared at my hands said, "He that hath clean hands, and a pure heart" (Psalm 24:4). Look at it closely. There's something more than just "clean hands" in that verse, isn't there? What is a "pure heart"? What exactly does that mean? Perhaps the atonement of Jesus does two things: it cleanses our hands *and* purifies our hearts. Clean hands and pure hearts are obviously not the same thing. If I'm cleansed from my sins but my heart isn't pure, then I'm just a sinner who hasn't sinned recently (see Stephen E. Robinson, *Believing Christ* [Salt Lake City: Deseret Book, 1992], 27–28). That's not enough! Elder Dallin H. Oaks explained it beautifully:

> A person who sins is like a tree that bends easily in the wind. On a windy and rainy day the tree bends so deeply against the ground that the leaves become soiled with mud, like sin. If we only focus on cleaning the leaves, the weakness in the tree that allowed it to bend and soil its leaves may remain. Merely cleaning the leaves does not strengthen the tree. ("Sin and Suffering," Brigham Young University seventeen-stake fireside, 5 August 1990)

I love that analogy. (I think it's fun that Elder *Oaks* would use a tree as an example.) If the tree is cleaned, that's nice, we have a clean tree. But what happens when another storm comes? Right. The tree just gets soiled again. The tree must be strengthened. It must be changed. Just cleaning the tree isn't enough! Clean leaves are like clean hands, and the strengthened tree is like a purified heart.

I gave my brother one of my kidneys a few years back. It was a remarkable experience, a miraculous experience. For a few weeks, my whole family felt very close. It was wonderful. I wouldn't want to do it again, though. Come to think of it, I don't think it's possible to do it again. I'm fresh out of spare kidneys. Kidneys are essential equipment, but what you, and I, and everyone else needs just as critically is a new heart. We all need a "heart transplant," and through the power of the Atonement, we can get one.

When the scriptures speak about the heart, they're normally not referring to the four-chambered pump. They're referring to our innermost desires and motives, or something even deeper, like our "nature." When we talk about purifying our hearts, we're not talking about being cleansed for individual sins. We're talking about changing our "sinfulness," or our desire to sin. The brother of Jared explained it this way: "Because of the fall, our natures have become evil continually" (Ether 3:2). Do you see that? *All* of us have been affected by the Fall. We all need a new heart.

Think for a moment: What would you give to be really close to God? Would you give your money? Hmmm, the Lord doesn't need your money. In fact, he doesn't need any worldly possessions. Would you give up the worldly shows and movies you watch? Would you give up gossiping? Would you give up complaining or being rude to members of your family? Are there any other "favorite sins" you can think of? What is the price tag for this new heart transplant, anyway? Well, it's a high price. It's not just our favorite sins—it's all of them. It's our whole fallen nature.

A Lamanite king set a fine example of being willing to do anything to know God. His prayer is beautiful. It's interesting that one of the most inspiring prayers in all of the scriptures was offered by a Lamanite investigator:

> O God, Aaron hath told me that there is a God; and if there is a God, and if thou art God, wilt thou make thyself known unto me, and I will give away all my sins to know thee. (Alma 22:18)

I love that. "I will give away all my sins." King Lamoni's father wanted to pay the price. I'll give up my old heart for a new one that has no desire to sin. Sounds like a good trade, doesn't it? Who does that heart transplant? Can you do surgery on yourself? No. Let's look at a few verses and discover *who* actually performs the heart transplants.

Scene One, about 124 B.C.: Look! King Benjamin is speaking to his people:

> And they had viewed themselves in their own carnal state, even less than the dust of the earth. And they all cried aloud with one voice, saying: O have mercy, and apply the atoning blood of Christ that we may receive forgiveness of our sins [clean hands], and our hearts may be purified [pure hearts]; for we believe in Jesus Christ, the Son of God, who created heaven and earth, and all things; who shall come down among the children of men. (Mosiah 4:2)

Scene Two, about 124 B.C.: Look! Now they're noticing their change of heart:

> And they all cried with one voice, saying: Yea, we believe all the words which thou hast spoken unto us; and also, we know of their surety and truth, because of the Spirit of the Lord Omnipotent, which has wrought a mighty change in us, or in our hearts, that we have no more disposition to do evil, but to do good continually. (Mosiah 5:2)

Scene Three, about 83 B.C.: See that? Alma the Younger is speaking of the people who were baptized by Alma the Elder:

> Behold, he [God] changed their hearts; yea, he awakened them out of a deep sleep [a spiritual snooze], and they awoke unto God. (Alma 5:7)

So how do we—you and I—receive this change of heart? How do we get to the point where the question we ask is not, "How bad can I be?" but, "How good can I be?" The answers are in examples one through three above. We *desire* to reach that point, we *work* for it, and we *pray* for it. Every day! And we have the faith that the Lord can take us there.

Many teenagers feel like they don't have a strong enough

testimony, because they haven't had some huge spiritual experience. Please be careful that you don't get discouraged. Some people, like Paul, Enos, and King Benjamin's people, had their hearts changed in an instant. They actually lost their desire for sin in a split second. For others of us, it may take a lifetime. President Ezra Taft Benson made me feel much better when he explained:

> But we must be cautious as we discuss these remarkable examples. Though they are real and powerful, they are the exception more than the rule. For every Paul, for every Enos, and for every King Lamoni, there are hundreds and thousands of people who find the process of repentance much more subtle, much more imperceptible. Day by day they move closer to the Lord, little realizing they are building a godlike life. They live quiet lives of goodness, service, and commitment. They are like the Lamanites, who the Lord said "were baptized with fire and with the Holy Ghost, *and they knew it not.*" (3 Nephi 9:20; italics added.) (In *Repentance* [Salt Lake City: Deseret Book, 1990], 6–7)

Every time you pray, you can ask the Lord not only to cleanse you from your sins but to change your heart so that you can lose your desire to sin. I like to use Nephi's words when I pray: "O Lord, . . . wilt thou make me that I may shake at the appearance of sin" (2 Nephi 4:31). *Make me shake.* Isn't that great? Once again, remember that every verse in the Book of Mormon was handpicked for us in our day. Perhaps Nephi was sharing with us the way he prayed so that we could use it too. Why else would he tell us? Here's an example of how you might use Nephi's words:

> O Lord, I'm going to school today, and in my gym class some guys always get out some bad magazines. O Lord, please make me shake! Please take away my desire

to sin, please change my heart so that I have no more disposition to do evil but to do good continually. Please, Lord, make me shake at the appearance of sin!

Or how about this one:

O Father, I have some friends who like to gossip. Sometimes it's hard to get out of it. Sometimes, in a strange way, the gossip seems to make us closer, but I know it's wrong. O Lord, please make me shake! Please change my heart. Please help me lose all my desire to sin!

Do you see what I mean? You don't have to fight temptation all by yourself. The best way to fight temptation is to do everything you can and then add God's power. Pray for a new heart, plead for it, and believe God can give it to you—every single day.

I often hear teenagers say, "My parents don't trust me." I love it when they say that! Because I love to show them this quote from President Gordon B. Hinckley:

I am reminded of what I heard from a man—a great, strong, and wise man—who served in the presidency of this Church years ago. His daughter was going out on a date, and her father said to her, "Be careful. Be careful of how you act and what you say."

She replied, "Daddy, don't you trust me?"

He responded, "I don't entirely trust myself. One never gets too old nor too high in the Church that the adversary gives up on him." ("Trust and Accountability," Brigham Young University devotional address, 13 October 1992)

And the adversary won't give up on you, either. That's why we must never give up praying for assistance.

As you know, there is a dangerous attitude that is spreading like a virus among many young people. It's called the "sin now, repent later" idea. Elder Dean L. Larsen taught:

There appears to be an increasing tendency and temptation for young people to sample the forbidden things of the world, not with the intent to embrace them permanently, but with the knowing decision to indulge in them momentarily as though they held a value of some kind too important or exciting to pass by. (*Ensign,* May 1983, 35)

President Ezra Taft Benson said it this way:

Yes, one can repent of moral transgression. The miracle of forgiveness is real, and true repentance is accepted of the Lord. But it is not pleasing to the Lord prior to a mission, or at any time, to sow one's wild oats, to engage in sexual transgression of any nature, and then to expect that planned confession and quick repentance will satisfy the Lord. (*Ensign,* May 1986, 44–45)

People who embrace the "sin now, repent later" idea obviously believe in Jesus, but it seems they don't love him very much. Such people believe that the Atonement can "clean our hands," but they somehow forget the "pure heart" part. A heart that asks, "How bad can I be?" is not a pure heart. A heart that has "sought to do wickedly" (see 1 Nephi 10:21) and is "procrastinating the day of repentance" (see Alma 34:33–34) is not clean.

Wherefore, if ye have sought to do wickedly [asking "how bad can I be?"] in the days of your probation, then ye are found unclean before the judgment-seat of God; and no unclean thing can dwell with God; wherefore, ye must be cast off forever. (1 Nephi 10:21)

Uncleanness is not what we're after. Filthiness isn't fun. We want to be clean. I'm convinced that most of the youth reading this book really desire to be clean. I am amazed and often intimidated by some of the young people I've met in this church. I recall attending a youth conference at a small university near Arkadelphia, Arkansas. Several stakes were in attendance. The youth were so excited to be there! They had never been surrounded by so many Latter-day Saints in their life! When the time for workshops came, they sat in the front. They opened their scriptures and sat on the edge of their seats. They listened, they took notes, they smiled. I was a new teacher, and I was overwhelmed. I just loved them—and I knew that the Lord loved them even more.

Later, I sat in amazement and witnessed a testimony meeting that lasted for four hours. Young people, eager to share their feelings, were lined up on both sides of the auditorium, and the lines were still there when the meeting had to be closed. I was so overwhelmed I couldn't speak. I had never seen anything like it. At that moment I began to understand what prophets had been saying for years about this chosen generation. I was reminded of the hymn we sing, "As Zion's youth in latter days, we stand with *valiant heart*" (*Hymns,* no. 256; emphasis added). And they did.

It seemed to me that many of those young people had already received a heart transplant. Even at their young age, it seemed they had lost their desire to sin. They came to earth with the potential to be valiant, and they gave up their old heart and their desire to sin for a new heart that just wanted to be pure.

You see, repentance is a process, and repentance has steps, but it's also an attitude. Some people want to repent, but they're not *repentant*—in other words, they feel they should go through the steps of repentance because they're "post" to, or because that was part of their plan, but they haven't really been convinced of the awfulness of sin and rebellion against God. They want to repent, but they have no plans to change their attitude, at least not yet. They want clean hands, but their hearts are not yet pure.

They are confused. Somewhere, they got the idea that the

choice is between repenting or not repenting. That's not the choice. The choice is "repent or suffer." And we're not talking about just any kind of suffering, but the kind Jesus endured, "which suffering caused myself, even God, the greatest of all, to tremble because of pain, and to bleed at every pore, and to suffer both body and spirit" (D&C 19:18).

When people really want to repent, they, well, really want to repent! They are more concerned with what Father in Heaven thinks than with what their friends or the world will think. The embarrassment doesn't stop them, the "what will the bishop think" doesn't stop them; they won't let anything stop them. Their hearts want to be clean and at peace, and they're willing to give whatever it takes. They, like King Lamoni's father, are willing to "give away all [their] sins to know [God]" (Alma 22:18).

It's amazing to think that there will come a day when we will stand before the Lord, face to face, and account for our lives. We will remember everything, and we will have to account for it. When I think about that day (which may be closer than we think), Alma's question becomes the most important question of all (watch for the words "look up" in both of these verses):

> I say unto you, can ye look up to God at that day with a pure heart and clean hands? I say unto you, can you look up, having the image of God engraven upon your countenances? (Alma 5:19)

Alma gives us the other option if we don't repent:

> For our words will condemn us, yea, all our works will condemn us; we shall not be found spotless; and our thoughts will also condemn us; and in this awful state we shall not dare to look up to our God; and we would fain be glad if we could command the rocks and the mountains to fall upon us to hide us from his presence. (Alma 12:14)

Can you imagine being so ashamed that you want the mountains to fall on you to hide you? Wow. Let's take another look at Alma 12:14 and include some modern terms that show a heart that isn't pure:

> For our *profanity and gossip* will condemn us, yea, all our *deliberate sin* will condemn us; we shall not be found spotless; and our *movies and music* will also condemn us; and in this awful state we shall not dare to look up to our God; and we would fain be glad if we could command the rocks and the mountains to fall upon us to hide us from his presence.

Sometimes I think about all the things I want. I wish I were 6' 4." I wish my job paid better. I wish I had a newer car. But then I go to church, or anywhere else where the Spirit is present, and something changes inside. In those times, if you were to ask me what I want more than anything else in the world, I could tell you in five words: "I want to look up."

Well, my friend, I'm going to heaven, and I'm taking my family with me. And I want you to be there too. There is no way I'm going to let the filth in this world stain my hands and poison my heart. Let's *all* go back, okay? Nephi was so positive when he said, "And I pray the Father in the name of Christ that many of us, if not all, may be saved in his kingdom at that great and last day" (2 Nephi 33:12). I hope that all of us—you and me, my friend—at that day can come into Jesus' presence and "look up" with clean hands and a pure heart.

Well, it's almost time for Third Period. I'll see you then.

EXTRA CREDIT

Life in Christ, Robert L. Millet (Salt Lake City: Bookcraft, 1990), especially chapter 9.

Third Period: Purity 101

How Do I Repent?

*Every soul confined to a concentration camp of sin
and guilt has a key to the gate. The adversary
cannot hold them if they know how to use it.
The key is labeled repentance.*
—Boyd K. Packer

This chapter was a challenge to write, but I did so because of a letter I once received. Here it is:

Dear Brother Bytheway:

I cannot begin to tell you my failings, the list would be too long. I hate being wicked and un-Christlike. I want to be clean and Christlike. I wish I could feel comfortable talking to my bishop, but I cannot.

How can I be forgiven? How do I repent? These questions may sound stupid, but I do not know how to repent. I love my Heavenly Father and Jesus Christ with all my heart. I want to return to my eternal family so much. This Church is as true as true can be. I know the Book of Mormon is true because I have prayed about it and I know.

I have hated my life so much sometimes that I just cry and wish I was dead. I want to serve a mission, be married in the temple, and replenish the earth. I cannot do any of these things until I learn how to repent. I want to be clean and I want to feel loved every day of my life. Please, help me to repent.

Thank you for listening.

Love,

Nicole [not her real name]

I'm so proud of Nicole for asking, "How do I repent?" I wonder if she realizes how much progress she has made already. She's not resisting repentance—she wants it. It sounds like she's already working on the first step.

In President Spencer W. Kimball's wonderful book, *Faith Precedes the Miracle,* he gives an excellent explanation of the steps required for repentance (Salt Lake City: Deseret Book, 1972, 180).

Repentance could well fall into five steps:

1. Conviction of and sorrow for sin
2. Abandonment of sin
3. Confession of sin
4. Restitution for sin
5. Doing the will of the Lord

President Kimball goes into more depth, but let's stop here for a minute. I have a feeling that many people, adults and teens alike, stop right there and think that the "steps of repentance" *are* repentance. They're not! The steps are just the tip of the iceberg. The tip of the iceberg, the visible part, is *not* the iceberg—it's evidence that there's something much larger beneath the surface. In the same way, the steps of repentance by themselves are not repentance. A superficial run-through of those steps is not repentance. True repentance is a deep, involved process. When someone is truly repenting, yes, they *will* go through the steps of repentance, but those steps are merely the visible evidence that something much larger is going on beneath the surface.

And what is that "something much larger" going on beneath the surface? Well, to use the words we've already used in this book, it's the heart transplant, the "change of heart." It's going from the "how-bad-can-I-be" attitude, or the "how-good-am-I-post-to-be" attitude, to the "I-want-to-be-valiant" attitude. It's when we begin to love righteousness more than sin.

Now, back to the steps of repentance. Elder Theodore M. Burton said this:

Many times a bishop will write: "I feel he has suffered enough!" But suffering is not repentance. Suffering comes from *lack* of complete repentance. A stake president will write: "I feel he has been punished enough!" But punishment is not repentance. Punishment *follows* disobedience and *precedes* repentance. A husband will write: "My wife has confessed everything!" But confession is not repentance. Confession is an admission of guilt that occurs *as* repentance begins. A wife will write: "My husband is filled with remorse!" But remorse is not repentance. Remorse and sorrow continue because a person has *not* yet fully repented. But if suffering, punishment, confession, remorse, and sorrow are not repentance, what *is* repentance? (In *Repentance* [Salt Lake City: Deseret Book, 1990], 10–11)

Good question. *What is repentance?* President Kimball said that the first step of repentance is conviction of and sorrow for sin.

1. CONVICTION OF AND SORROW FOR SIN

That doesn't mean just saying, "Oh, I'm supposed to be sorry? Oh, okay. I'm sorry." It's a little more involved than that. Go ahead and read President Kimball's explanation:

To be sorry for our sin, we must know something of its serious implications. . . . We are sorry. We are willing to make amends, pay penalties, to suffer excommunication, if necessary. . . .

If one is sorry only because his sin was uncovered, his repentance is not complete. Godly sorrow causes one to harness desire and to determine to do right regardless of consequences; this kind of sorrow brings righteousness and will work toward forgiveness. (*Faith Precedes the Miracle,* 180)

That's what it means to really be sorry. You'd be willing to do anything needed to get things cleared up. Yes, even seeing the bishop. Some people carry around serious burdens and regrets for years because they're too embarrassed to talk with their bishop. They are worried that their parents or friends will find out, and I guess that's understandable. But if we're more worried about what our peers think than what the Lord thinks, we're not truly sorry. When we are filled with godly sorrow, we will be willing to do *anything* the Lord requires.

So, guilt can be good! My car has a little warning light that says, "Service Engine Soon." Some maintenance on my car I can do myself, but other things require outside help. Sorrow and guilt are like a little warning light telling us there's something wrong that needs to be fixed. And, as with my car, some repairs we can't do by ourselves. We'll talk more about that when we get to confession. Just remember, *acting* sorry is not the same as *being* sorry. Okay, let's go back to President Kimball and talk about the second step:

2. ABANDONMENT OF SIN

One discontinues his error when he has a full realization of the gravity of his sin and when he is willing to comply with the laws of God. The thief may abandon his evil in prison, but true repentance would have him forsake it before his arrest and return his booty without enforcement. The sex offender as well as any other transgressor who voluntarily ceases his unholy practices is headed toward forgiveness. (Kimball, *Faith Precedes the Miracle*, 180)

Let's look at that last phrase again: "any . . . transgressor who voluntarily ceases his unholy practices is headed toward forgiveness." President Kimball touches on two important concepts there. First, if you go voluntarily to confess, it's much better than if you had no intention of confessing and you just got caught. The second idea is that a person who ceases sinning "is headed toward forgiveness." In other words, repentance isn't over yet, but the person is on the path.

Let me explain with a little math problem. What does math have to do with abandoning a sin? You'll see what I'm doing in a minute. Let's say you have a math problem. You're supposed to take a number, and add and subtract some other numbers. We'll start with the number 5. Now watch this carefully, okay?

Start with five: 5
1. Now add twelve to it: 5 + 12 = 17
2. Subtract four from it: 17 - 4 = 13
3. Add six to it: 13 + 6 = 18
4. Subtract five from it: 18 - 5 = 13
5. Add ten to it: 13 + 10 = 23
6. Now subtract four from it: 23 - 4 = 19
7. Add ten to it: 19 + 10 = 29

Have you noticed anything? Look closely. Right! We made a mistake back there on step 3. Thirteen plus six equals *nineteen,* not eighteen. We can continue with step 4 and keep going as long as we want to, adding and subtracting more numbers, but it won't come out right, because we made a mistake on step 3.

The point is, some people believe that if they simply stop doing the sin, that's repentance. "Well, I haven't done that for a long time, so I'm probably forgiven." It doesn't work that way. You have to go back and correct the mistake. Like in our math problem, if you *don't* go back and correct the mistake, you'll never come out right in the end. Forsaking the sin is not enough. You have to completely correct it by repentance. Get it?

It *is* important to forsake our sins, though. The Lord said,

"Go your ways and sin no more; but unto that soul who sin-neth shall the former sins return" (D&C 82:7).

That idea scares a lot of people. They don't want to sin anymore, but they're afraid that they might, somewhere down the road. This is one of those instances where I believe the Lord looks on our hearts. He knows we can't become per-fect overnight. But if we're fully committed in our heart not to sin again, I believe the Lord accepts that kind of repen-tance. On the other hand, if our heart is saying, "I just want to get through these steps and see what happens," then per-haps we're not really sorry.

Here's a common question:

The part about forsaking the sin and never doing it again always scares me. For example, if I get mad at my sister, and I repent, how can I know I will never get mad at her again? How can I be sure? It makes it so I don't want to repent because I can't promise it won't happen again.

Hmmm, that's an excellent question. I think we can answer it from the scriptures. In Mosiah 26:30, the Lord told Alma, "Yea, and as often as my people repent will I forgive them their trespasses against me."

Does this seem a little confusing? On the one hand we're saying, "If you sin and repent, you can't do it again," and on the other hand we're saying, "but if you do, you can repent." I have had this question myself, but I found the answer in my *Book of Mormon Student Manual.* Let's read what it says about Mosiah 26:30:

How Long-Suffering Is the Lord?

Even though a mighty change occurs at rebirth, no one becomes perfect overnight. So the principle of repentance is needed as one endeavors to go on unto perfection (Hebrews 6:1) and as he endures to the end.

Satan would have him believe that, once forgiven, any mis-step is fatal and irreparable. But this passage shows that Satan is a liar. *Every young person should have this pas-sage memorized as a source of hope.* But he should under-stand that it is not a license to commit willful sin or try to take unrighteous advantage of the Lord's mercy, for the Lord has also said, "but unto that soul who sinneth shall the former sins return." (D&C 82:7.) Though at first these two scriptures (Mosiah 26:30; D&C 82:7) may seem contradictory, together they teach the true mercy and justice of the Lord. (Manual for *Religion 121–122* [Salt Lake City: The Church of Jesus Christ of Latter-day Saints, 1979], 201; emphasis added)

Does that help? So you repent with all your heart, and you don't plan on repeating that sin. But if you do, you start the repentance process again. The main question becomes, what's in your heart? Did you approach it with a lazy, "I'll-probably-do-it-again" attitude, or was it a serious, "I'm-really-going-to-try-to-forsake-that-sin" attitude? The Lord doesn't require you to be perfect right now, but he wants you to be trying. Okay, step three from President Kimball.

3. CONFESSION OF SIN

The confession of sin is an important element in repentance. Many offenders have seemed to feel that a few prayers to the Lord were sufficient and they have thus justified themselves in hiding their sins. The Proverbs tell us:

"He that covereth his sins shall not prosper: but whoso confesseth and forsaketh them shall have mercy." (Proverbs 28:13.)

"By this ye may know if a man repenteth of his sins—behold, he will confess them and forsake them." (D&C 58:43.)

Especially grave errors such as sexual sins shall be

confessed to the bishop as well as to the Lord. There are two remissions that one might wish to have: first, the forgiveness from the Lord, and second, the forgiveness of the Lord's church through its leaders. (Kimball, *Faith Precedes the Miracle,* 181)

All sins, great or small, must be confessed to the Lord. As you've probably already figured out, the Lord knows what your sins are. You're not going to surprise him or tell him anything new. But you still need to acknowledge to the Lord that you have sinned. You also need to confess to anyone you may have hurt or injured because of your sin. And, as President Kimball mentioned, especially serious sins need to be confessed to the bishop. Why? Well, the Lord said to Alma, "If he confess his sins before thee and me, and repenteth in the sincerity of his heart, him shall ye forgive, and I will forgive him also" (Mosiah 26:29).

Why does the bishop have to be involved? The simple answer is that the bishop can help guide you through the repentance process. But there's more; let's take another look at my excellent *Book of Mormon Student Manual:*

When a member's sins have been discovered by or reported to Church leaders, they are duty bound to take action for three reasons: [1] to preserve the good name of the Church [to show the world that it does not condone sin], [2] to help the sinner, [3] and to assure the righteous that Church leaders are not trying to hide or overlook the sins of some while punishing the sins of others. A confession of guilt is required on these occasions as part of the proof of repentance. (201)

In case you're still not sure why the bishop needs to be involved, I'll put it another way. One time I had a persistent sore throat. I tried everything to get rid of it: gargling, lozenges, plenty of liquids, throat sprays, everything! But it wouldn't go away. Finally I got smart and went to the doctor. He had medicine that I couldn't get on my own. Are you listening with your spiritual ears? *He had medicine that I couldn't get on my own,* and he had authority to get that medicine for me. Can you imagine me saying, "Well, I'd like to get rid of this sore throat but I just can't go see a doctor." That's crazy. Saying, "I can't go see the bishop, I'm too ashamed!" is like saying, "I can't go see the doctor, I'm too sick!"

Of course, anyone grappling with major sins may feel reluctant to confess to the bishop. But everyone I know who has actually followed through, confessed to the bishop, and repented has said that although it was difficult, it was a wonderful and positive experience. And they always came out of the bishop's office rejoicing, feeling renewed gratitude for the Atonement, and feeling like a tremendous load had been taken from their shoulders. Most of them say, "I wish I had gone sooner." And so does the Lord. He is constantly inviting us to repent.

Here's another common question:

Exactly what sins have to be confessed to the bishop?

Good question. As a rule of thumb, if you think a sin is serious but you're not sure if you should talk to the bishop, talk to the bishop. In another book, *The Miracle of Forgiveness,* President Kimball gave a fairly specific list:

> The confession of . . . major sins to a proper Church authority is one of those requirements made by the Lord. These sins include adultery, fornication, other sexual transgressions, and sins of comparable seriousness. (Salt Lake City: Bookcraft, 1969, 179)

As you can see, for the most part, the sins involving sexual purity are the ones that need to be confessed to the bishop. Here's another question:

I feel like I need to talk to my bishop, but I'm too embar-
rassed. He's my relative, and I'm afraid my whole family
and everyone else will find out.

First of all, the bishop is under a sacred obligation to keep confessions confidential, and to discuss them only with those who were directly involved. (Now, maybe you've heard of cases where this didn't happen, but if those stories are true, they are the exception and not the rule.) If your personal situation makes you feel that it is not possible for you to go to your bishop, then make an appointment with the stake president and clear things up. Don't procrastinate and stew and figure out all the worst things that could happen. The worst has already happened, and now it's time to seek forgiveness and put it behind you. And about the embarrassment thing—you can have a little embarrassment now or a lot of embarrassment later. Elder Richard G. Scott taught:

> Do not take comfort in the fact that your transgressions are not known by others. That is like an ostrich with his head buried in the sand. He sees only darkness and feels comfortably hidden. In reality he is ridiculously conspicuous. Likewise our every act is seen by our Father in Heaven and His Beloved Son. They know everything about us. . . . If you have seriously transgressed, you will not find any lasting satisfaction or comfort in what you have done. Excusing transgression with a cover-up may appear to fix the problem, but it does not. The tempter is intent on making public your most embarrassing acts at the most harmful time. Lies weave a pattern that is ever more confining and becomes a trap that Satan will spring to your detriment. (*Ensign,* May 1995, 77)

If you need to repent, this is no time to try to hide your sins. If you really want repentance, if you really want to feel clean, no amount of anticipated embarrassment will keep you from the bishop's office. And once you are there, tell him everything! Elder Vaughn J. Featherstone has said:

A bishop may be deceived, but the Holy Ghost cannot. . . . What a tragedy when someone finally gets enough courage to go to the bishop and then leaves his office having only partially confessed. (In *Repentance,* 58)

President Kimball continues:

The bishop may be one's best earthly friend. He will hear the problems, judge the seriousness thereof, determine the degree of adjustment, and decide if it warrants an eventual forgiveness. He does this as the earthly representative of God, who is the master physician, the master psychologist, the master psychiatrist. If repentance is sufficient, he may waive penalties, which is tantamount to forgiveness so far as the church organization is concerned. The bishop claims no authority to absolve sins, but he does share the burden, waive penalties, relieve tension and strain, and he may assure a continuation of church activity. He will keep the whole matter most confidential. (*Faith Precedes the Miracle,* 182)

4. RESTITUTION FOR SIN

You probably already know what *restitution* means; another word for it might be *restoration.* When we repent, we try to "restore" what was taken away. Let's continue reading from *Faith Precedes the Miracle:*

When one is humble in sorrow, has unconditionally abandoned the evil, and confesses to those assigned by the Lord, he should next restore insofar as possible that which was damaged. If he burglarized, he should return to the rightful owner that which was stolen. Perhaps one reason murder is unforgivable is that having taken a life, the murderer cannot restore it. Restitution in full is not always possible. Virginity is impossible to give back.

However, the truly repentant soul will usually find things that can be done to restore to some extent. The true spirit of repentance demands this. Ezekiel taught:

If the wicked . . . give again that he had robbed, walk in the statutes of life, without committing iniquity; he shall surely live. . . . (Ezekiel 33:15.) . . .

A pleading sinner must also forgive all people of all offenses committed against himself. The Lord is under no obligation to forgive us unless our hearts are fully purged of all hate, bitterness, and accusations against others. (182–83)

You may have wondered why adultery is a sin next to murder in seriousness. When you think about restitution, it may help you answer the question. A murderer cannot restore life, and one who commits a sexual sin cannot restore purity. But the Lord, because of his mercy, still allows a way to make restitution from the serious sin of immorality through the wonderful and powerful doctrine of repentance. Much of that restitution comes from the next step.

After all we've talked about, it may seem like the most difficult part of repentance is over. It isn't. Confession takes real courage, but the hardest part is yet to come. President Kimball continues with step five:

5. DO THE WILL OF THE FATHER

The Lord in his preface to modern revelations gave us the fifth and one of the most difficult requirements to forgiveness. He says:

"For I the Lord cannot look upon sin with the least degree of allowance;

Nevertheless, he that repents *and does the command-ments of the Lord* shall be forgiven." (D&C 1:31–32; emphasis added.)

Under the humiliation of a guilty conscience, with the possibility of detection and consequent scandal and shame, with a striving spirit urging toward adjustment, the first steps of sorrow, abandonment, confession, and restitution must now be followed by the never-ending requirement of doing the commandments. Obviously this can hardly be done in a day, a week, a month, or a year. This is an effort extending through the balance of life. (*Faith Precedes the Miracle*, 183)

So there's the toughest part: Do the will of the Father, and live the gospel from now on! It reminds me of Jesus' words to the woman taken in adultery: "Go, and sin no more" (John 8:11).

We've managed to cover the five steps of repentance out-lined by President Kimball. Does it all make sense? It's a sobering subject, isn't it? It would be a lot simpler to just avoid sinning. I like the saying often quoted by President Ezra Taft Benson: "It is better to prepare and prevent than it is to repair and repent" (in *Speaking Out on Moral Issues* [Salt Lake City: Bookcraft, 1992], 87).

Here are some other common questions:

How do you know when you're forgiven? How long does it take?

Well, that's a good one. As you know, we live in a world of drive-through dining, instant cocoa, and microwave dinners. We want everything right now! But there are a few things that cannot be rushed that will always take time. How much time? With repentance, it's not possible to give a blanket answer. We cannot dictate our timetable to the Lord. He will answer our prayers in his own way and in his own time, but we have a few hints from the scriptures. Enos prayed all day and into the night to receive forgiveness of his sins. And Alma the Younger, in one of the most wonderful stories of repentance ever told, said that he was "racked . . . with the pains of a damned soul" for three days and three nights before he received forgiveness (Alma 36:16).

Elder Henry B. Eyring told of a young man who had gone through deep and painful repentance. This young man was scheduled to be married in the temple, but he wanted to know he was forgiven. He wanted to be the best he could be for his new bride. He asked Elder Eyring, who was his bishop at that time, how he could be *sure* the Lord had forgiven him. Bishop Eyring said he would try to find out. A few days later, the bishop was in the company of then Elder Spencer W. Kimball (whom we've quoted so much in this chapter). He explained the situation, and asked:

> "How can he get that revelation? How can he know whether his sins are remitted?"
>
> I thought Elder Kimball would talk to me about fasting or prayer or listening for the still small voice. But he surprised me. Instead he said, "Tell me something about the young man."
>
> I said, "What would you like to know?"
>
> And then he began a series of the most simple questions. Some of the ones I remember were:
>
> "Does he come to his priesthood meetings?"
>
> I said, after a moment's thought, "Yes."
>
> "Does he come early?"
>
> "Yes."
>
> "Does he sit down front?"
>
> I thought for a moment and then realized, to my amazement, that he did.
>
> "Does he home teach?"
>
> "Yes."

"Does he go early in the month?"

"Yes, he does."

"Does he go more than once?"

"Yes."

I can't remember the other questions. But they were all like that—little things, simple acts of obedience, of submission. And for each question I was surprised that my answer was always yes. Yes, he wasn't just at all his meetings: he was early; he was smiling; he was there not only with his whole heart, but the broken heart of a little child, as he was every time the Lord asked anything of him. And after I had said yes to each of his questions, Elder Kimball looked at me, paused, and then very quietly said, "There is your revelation." (*To Draw Closer to God: A Collection of Discourses* [Salt Lake City: Deseret Book, 1997], 56)

Is Elder Eyring saying that all you have to do to be forgiven is go early to meetings and smile a lot? Of course not! This is a perfect example of the "tip-of-the-iceberg" concept we talked about earlier. The simple acts of obedience by this young man were evidence that something much larger was going on beneath the surface. His heart was changing. He wanted to be valiant! He wouldn't *think* of asking, "How bad can I be?" He wanted to be the best he could be.

If you want to learn more about repentance, go to the Book of Mormon. Alma teaches us so much about repentance in Alma 36. For example, we know that the Lord will not remember our sins when we sincerely repent: "Behold, he who has repented of his sins, the same is forgiven, and I, the Lord, remember them no more" (D&C 58:42). But what about us? Do *we* remember them? Let's read from Alma:

Now, as my mind caught hold upon this thought, I cried within my heart: O Jesus, thou Son of God, have mercy on me, who am in the gall of bitterness, and am encircled about by the everlasting chains of death.

And now, behold, when I thought this, *I could remember my pains no more;* yea, I was harrowed up by the memory of my sins no more.

And oh, what joy, and what marvelous light I did behold; yea, my soul was filled with joy as exceeding as was my pain! (Alma 36:18–20; emphasis added)

It sounds to me as if we will *remember* our sins, but the memory of them will not cause us *pain* anymore! Perhaps this is another way we can know we are forgiven. We'll remember our sins, but we will know we have sincerely repented and put them behind us. We won't be "harrowed up" by their memory anymore.

In another place in the Book of Mormon, we read that King Benjamin's people knew they were forgiven because they felt peace:

And it came to pass that after they had spoken these words the Spirit of the Lord came upon them, and they were filled with joy, having received a remission of their sins, and having *peace of conscience,* because of the exceeding faith which they had in Jesus Christ who should come. (Mosiah 4:3; emphasis added)

A young friend of mine wrote, "I hope that through all I have experienced I may be able to influence others to steer clear of sin. It is not a happy path. It may seem fun, but one mistake leads to others, and it's just a slippery slide that ends in the mud, and it's so hard to climb out."

She's right. Sin is like mud. Elder Richard G. Scott gave a very beautiful and tender talk called "We Love You—Please Come Back." He talked about mud too, and how we should deal with our memories of past mistakes:

If you, through poor judgment, were to cover your shoes with mud, would you leave them that way? Of course not. You would cleanse and restore them. Would you then gather the residue of mud and place it in an envelope to show others the mistake that you made? No. Neither should you continue to relive forgiven sin. Every time such thoughts come into your mind, turn your heart in gratitude to the Savior, who gave His life that we, through faith in Him and obedience to His teachings, can overcome transgression and conquer its depressing influence in our lives. *(Ensign,* May 1986, 12)

Nine years later, Elder Scott gave another beautiful talk about repentance. He used President Kimball's five steps and then added a sixth:

6. RECOGNITION OF THE SAVIOR

Of all the necessary steps to repentance, I testify that the most critically important is for you to have a conviction that forgiveness comes because of the Redeemer. (Richard G. Scott, *Ensign,* May 1986, 12)

As you grow older, you will find that you become more and more sensitive to the fact that sin separates you from God. And because of this, you'll become more and more grateful for Jesus Christ, and for his power to rescue us, and help us, and cleanse us. I am comforted by the words of one of my most honored and respected heroes, Nephi. He was amazing to me. Someone once said, "The closer we get to God, the further away we'll realize we really are," and I think of that whenever I read Nephi's lament:

O wretched man that I am! Yea, my heart sorroweth because of my flesh; my soul grieveth because of mine iniquities.

I am encompassed about, because of the temptations and the sins which do so easily beset me.

And when I desire to rejoice, my heart groaneth because of my sins; nevertheless, I know in whom I have trusted.

My God hath been my support. (2 Nephi 4:17–20)

There's that last step. We must focus on Jesus, and when we do, our love for him will grow, because we will always remember him and what he has done for us to make us clean.

Wow, this has been a long chapter, but let's look at one more question:

Sometimes when I read or hear stories about repentance, it sounds so hard. I want to know how willing God is to forgive us.

God does not want anyone to suffer. He wants us to repent. Jesus has already suffered for us if we repent. There are so many scriptures I could show you to answer this question, but none better than Luke 15, the story of the prodigal son. Read this carefully, and you'll be able to see for yourself how willing Heavenly Father is to take us back from sin when we repent:

And he said, A certain man had two sons:

And the younger of them said to his father, Father, give me the portion of goods that falleth to me. And he divided unto them his living.

And not many days after the younger son gathered all together, and took his journey into a far country, and there wasted his substance with riotous living. (Vv. 11–13)

Sorry to interrupt, but what does "riotous living" mean? Right. He was living a sinful life. Okay, keep going.

And when he had spent all, there arose a mighty famine in that land; and he began to be in want.

And he went and joined himself to a citizen of that country; and he sent him into his fields to feed swine.

And he would fain have filled his belly with the husks that the swine did eat: and no man gave unto him.

And when he came to himself, he said, How many hired servants of my father's have bread enough and to spare, and I perish with hunger! (Vv. 14–17)

Isn't that a great phrase: "He came to himself"! In other words, he figured out how empty and hollow and wrong his behavior had been. Okay, back to the story . . .

I will arise and go to my father, and will say unto him, Father, I have sinned against heaven, and before thee,

And am no more worthy to be called thy son: make me as one of thy hired servants.

And he arose, and came to his father. But when he was yet a great way off, his father saw him, and had compassion, and ran, and fell on his neck, and kissed him. (Vv. 18–20)

Are you listening? "When he was yet *a great way off,* his father saw him." Remember that, okay?

And the son said unto him, Father, I have sinned against heaven, and in thy sight, and am no more worthy to be called thy son.

But the father said to his servants, Bring forth the best robe, and put it on him; and put a ring on his hand, and shoes on his feet:

And bring hither the fatted calf, and kill it; and let us eat, and be merry:

For this my son was dead, and is alive again; he was lost, and is found. And they began to be merry. (Vv. 21–24)

What does all this mean? To begin with, obviously the

father in this story represents our Father in Heaven. Now, I have a question for you. You remember that the prodigal son's father saw him when he was "yet a great way off." So, where was his father? Was he in the house, doing something else, not caring about whether his child ever returned? No, no. His father must have been *looking for him,* searching the horizon, waiting, watching, and wondering, "Will he ever come back?" And one day, the son turned around and began the journey home. And as soon as his father saw him, he *ran.* He didn't stay on the porch and wait for his son to walk all the way back, and he didn't just walk out to meet him. He ran! Then, together, they walked home. Do you see what is being taught here?

How willing is our Father to forgive us? He is so willing that when we "arise, and come to our Father," he will run out to help us come back. Is our repentance finished? Not at all. But once our Father in Heaven sees that we have turned around and are heading home, he will run out to be with us to help us through each of the steps of repentance. What love he must have for us, to run to us and bring us home!

Well, I hope we answered Nicole's questions—and maybe some of yours, too. Just remember that repentance isn't just some steps. Real repentance is hard. It hurts. As President Kimball once said, "If a person hasn't suffered, he hasn't repented. . . . The Savior can do almost anything in the world, but he can't forgive somebody who hasn't repented" (*Teachings of Spencer W. Kimball,* Edward L. Kimball, ed. [Salt Lake City: Bookcraft, 1981], 99).

Here's another letter from Nicole, and it was written several months after the first one. *(Yes, this really is a second letter from the same young woman.)*

Dear John:
. . . As I said before, I was having a lot of problems

with my life. I loved the Lord but I was not happy. I had sinned and I felt like just asking for forgiveness was not enough. I had to do more. I got a lot of strength and help from my seminary teacher. He suggested I talk to my bishop. When I told him my feelings, he called my bishop and arranged an appointment. From there, there was no backing down. I wanted it bad enough that I wouldn't back down either.

My bishop was very understanding. . . . Since then, my bishop has become a dear friend I can go to in times of need. I really did feel good afterwards. I believe now that he has the true healing power of God. . . .

Your sister in the gospel,

Nicole

Isn't that great? She followed through and now she is so much happier. It reminds me of a scripture: "Likewise, I say unto you, there is joy in the presence of the angels of God over one sinner that repenteth" (Luke 15:10).

I guess that's a nice way to end Third Period. The older I get, the more I realize how much I really need the principle of repentance. I am grateful to President Spencer W. Kimball who wrote so much about repentance so that we could all understand. And most of all, I am grateful for the Savior, who suffered in Gethsemane and on Golgotha, and took all of our pains, sicknesses, transgressions, and sins upon himself, so that we could repent and change and be clean and be able to "look up" to him again someday.

I'll see you in Fourth Period.

EXTRA CREDIT

Faith Precedes the Miracle, Spencer W. Kimball (Salt Lake City: Deseret Book, 1972).

The Miracle of Forgiveness, Spencer W. Kimball (Salt Lake City: Bookcraft, 1969).

"Finding Forgiveness," Richard G. Scott, *Ensign,* May 1995, 75–77.

Believing Christ, Stephen E. Robinson (Salt Lake City: Deseret Book, 1992).

Within Reach, Robert L. Millet (Salt Lake City: Deseret Book, 1995).

Lunch Break

A Visit to Zarahemla Burger

Well, we covered some pretty heavy subjects in the last three classes, so I think you deserve a break today. Whaddaya say we go get some lunch? Do you like fast food? Good—I'll drive.

"Hi, Honda, I'm home!" Hop in, it's unlocked. So, where do you want to go? Do you want me to choose? Okay. Books can take you anywhere you want to go. We can go anywhere (or should I say any*when*) we want to. How about some fast food in ancient America? We'll have to talk a little differently, okay? Let's see, I gotta get in the mood here. . . . Behold, I see the place of feeding, and it is exceedingly close. Yea, it is called Zarahemla Burger. Behold, I will pull into the drive-up window, near the speaker, and we will place our order.

Behold, welcome to Zarahemla Burger. May I take your order, please?

Yes—I mean, Yea, we are exceedingly hungry. I'll have an Ammon Cheese, a cold Laman-ade, and an order of Nephries. But behold, this is not all. My friend has to order too. Canst thou wait whilst my friend decides?

Behold, I will wait even until thy friend orders. Just speak when ready, and I will record all thy words, and will give thee thy price.

Well, what dost thou desire? It's hard to read that reformed Egyptian menu, isn't it? I'll ask her for some help.

Behold, canst thou tell me all that thy restaurant offers?

Behold, we have many selections from the Nephi's Broken Bow (1 Nephi 16:18) Vegetarian Section. Thou mayest start with a Sariah Salad . . .

Dost thou have dressing with that?

Yea, we have Rameumptom (Alma 31:21) Ranch, Hagoth (Alma 63:5) Thousand Island, and Gadianton (Helaman 3:23) dressing.

Gadianton dressing—what's in that?

I cannot tell thee; it is a secret combination.

Oh, okay. Dost thou still have lamb chops?

Nay, for behold, all of our sheep have been chased away from the waters of Sebus (Alma 18:7). But behold, Ammon is out gathering the flocks to the place of water. Soon we will have leg of lamb again. (Apparently, we will also have Arm of Bandit, but I doubt that will be on the menu.)

Wow-uh-okay, canst thou describe the Brother of Jared Burrito?

Yea, it is peaked at the ends, and tight like unto a dish (Ether 2:17).

What about the Promised Land Breakfast?

Yea, it is just flowing with milk and honey (D&C 38:18).

And what's the Brass Plate Special?

Behold, it is exceedingly good. People have walked two hundred miles in a desert to get it (1 Nephi 3:24).

I think we'll just have another Ammon Cheese, with a Laman-ade and Nephries.

Wouldst thou like that in our Ish-meal combo? Behold, it is cheaper that way.

Yea, that is acceptable. Behold, what are thy drink sizes? For verily we have traveled far and thirsted much.

We have small, medium, large, and our 32-ounce Waters of Mormon (Mosiah 18:30). Surely it will quench thy thirst.

Behold, I believe all thy words, but please don't call me Shirley. We'll have two Waters-of-Mormon Laman-ades. Wilt thou accept a check?

Yea: cash, checks, and the Amaron (Omni 1:4) Express card.

Behold, that sounds good. Thank thee.

Please pull forward, and it will come to pass that I will give thee thy total at the place of payment. . . . Behold, the total comes to one senum (Alma 11:3).

One senum, okay, here you go—I mean, um, here thou goest.

Behold, here is thy food, and here is thy change—a shib-lum and a leah. Have a nice day, and may it come to pass that we will see thee again at Zarahemla Burger.

Thou wilt. Thank thee and farewell!

Hey, that was fun. Let's park the car and go sit at the table underneath that tree. Our visit to Zarahemla Burger wouldn't be complete unless we play the games they print on these bags. It looks like you got the "exceedingly simple" games, and I got the "exceedingly challenging" games. Let's try yours first:

EXCEEDINGLY *SIMPLE* GAME #1

There is a cleverly hidden message inside this
baffling word puzzle! See if you can find it!
(Time limit: 20 minutes.)

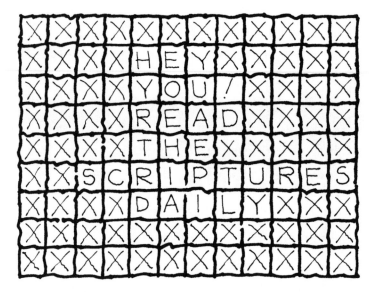

EXCEEDINGLY *SIMPLE* GAME #2

OPTICAL ILLUSION!
See if you can tell which object is bigger!
(Time limit: 5 minutes.)

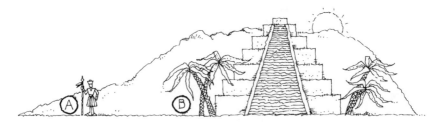

Answer: B

EXCEEDINGLY *CHALLENGING* GAME #1

There are six women mentioned by
name in the Book of Mormon: Who are they?

1. _____ (Hint: She was the first woman—1 Nephi 5:11)

2. _____ (Hint: She had several sons, including Sam, Jacob, and Joseph—1 Nephi 8:14, 1 Nephi 18:19)

3. _____ (Hint: She and Joseph journeyed to Bethlehem—Mosiah 3:8)

4. _____ (Hint: She saw Ammon and King Lamoni unconscious—Alma 19:16)

5. _____ (Corianton was scolded about her by his father—Alma 39:3)

6. _____ (She was Isaac's mother—2 Nephi 8:2)

EXCEEDINGLY *CHALLENGING* GAME #2

Ammon and King Lamoni
Crossword Puzzle

1. Alma 17:25   Ammon did not immediately announce that he was a missionary. Instead, he offered to be a _____ to King Lamoni.

2. Alma 17:26   The flocks drank of the water of _____.

3. Alma 17:29   Ammon wanted to win the _____ of his fellow servants so that they would believe on his words.

4. Alma 17:35   The Lord promised _____ that Ammon would not be harmed.

5. Alma 17:37   Ammon withstood the blows of those who came to scatter the flocks, and they began to be _____.

6. Alma 18:2   The king thought Ammon might be the _____ Spirit.

7. Alma 18:9   While the servants were explaining to the king what had happened at the watering place, Ammon was feeding the king's _____.

8. Alma 18:23   The king told Ammon he would believe all his _____.

9. Alma 18:39   Alma taught the king the gospel, including the plan of salvation, or in other words, the plan of _____.

Note: Completing this crossword puzzle does <u>not</u> count as your daily scripture reading.

So, did you enjoy the games? Did you like your Laman-ade? Ah yes, the only drink that rebels when you try to swallow it. Next time we'll try the Lemuel-lime, "the beverage with an attitude." But now I think it's time to get back to class. 'Bye, Zarahemla Burger! Push the lighter thingy in, close your eyes, and think, "Back to Fourth Period."

Click . . . POP! Here we are, back to the real world. We'll visit our imagination again before this day (this book, I mean) is over. I'll see you back in class!

Fourth Period: Listening Skills 101

Recognizing the Spirit

God does not send thunder if a still, small voice is enough.
—Neal A. Maxwell

Have you ever felt like a spiritual amoeba? Have you ever said, "How come I never have any spiritual experiences?" Perhaps you've wondered if you have ever really "felt the Spirit" at all. Well, my guess is that you've had many spiritual experiences—you just haven't recognized them as such. I hope Fourth Period will help.

I remember a very interesting poster I saw a few years ago. It was a drawing of an old man dancing around some train tracks holding a small radio near his ear. Underneath the picture it read: "Those who danced were thought to be quite insane by those who could not hear the music."

I've thought about that poster many times as I've sat in youth testimony meetings and heard a fine young man or a fine young woman (like you) talk about how their friends think they're strange because they get up long before sunrise and go to seminary. Or about their friends who don't understand why people like us would even consider going on a mission for no pay. Or they wonder why we won't drink, or party, or why we want to save our affections before marriage. I suppose they think we are quite insane, because they cannot "hear the music." Well, our job is to help them hear the beautiful music of the gospel. Many of them would like to "tune in" to this station on their spiritual radio, but they "know not where to find it" (see D&C 123:12).

What is that music? What is it that pulls us out of bed for early-morning seminary? (Besides your mother.) What is that feeling inside that makes us want to be better—not better looking, or more popular, but just better? Back in the Orientation for this semester, I mentioned a fireside I attended, remember? There was such a nice, calm feeling in the chapel that no one wanted to leave. The fireside was over, and the dance was starting in the gym, but no one seemed to want to go. I believe that many of the youth in attendance were feeling the Spirit. I also believe that many of them had felt it before, but this time they *recognized* it. They *knew* it felt different than the feeling of watching a movie or jumping around at a dance. It was a quiet feeling, and it made you think. It made you think about where you were going in your life, and it even told you things that you should do. I could see it in their faces. Inside, I know they were feeling things like, "I need to say my prayers," or "I need to change my attitude," or "I want to be clean." I believe that most of the youth stayed in the chapel—when refreshments, socializing, and dancing were only a few steps outside the door—because they wanted to *remember.* They knew they were feeling something real, and they wanted to remember what it felt like. I don't blame them! These type of impressive spiritual experiences really don't come very often.

Sometimes, at firesides or in sacrament meetings or other places, we get the wrong message. Speakers in Church meetings often share their most powerful spiritual experiences, or the most powerful spiritual experiences of someone else. Those experiences are nice, and they inspire us. But if we're not careful, we may think, "Wow. Nothing like that has ever happened to me. I guess I've never felt the Spirit."

That's the wrong message to get. We enjoy hearing about other people's spiritual experiences, but we must be careful to remember that really powerful spiritual experiences don't happen very often. We shouldn't be discouraged! Listen to this next quote: "I have learned that strong, impressive spiritual experiences do not come to us very frequently." Who do you suppose said that? Me? My home teacher? Someone who doesn't feel the Spirit very often? No. It was an *apostle,* Elder Boyd K. Packer! This is an *apostle* saying that "strong, impressive spiritual experiences do not come to us very frequently"! Listen to what else he taught:

> The Spirit does not get our attention by shouting or shaking us with a heavy hand. Rather it whispers. It caresses so gently that if we are preoccupied we may not feel it at all. . . .
>
> Occasionally it will press just firmly enough for us to pay heed. But most of the time, if we do not heed the gentle feeling, the Spirit will withdraw and wait until we come seeking and listening. (*Ensign,* January 1983, 53)

So the Spirit does not always speak with a loud and booming voice. More often, it is a *still small* voice. In fact, it's so still and small that "if we are preoccupied we may not feel it at all." Wow.

May I be bold for a minute? Do you think we could ever feel the Spirit in the middle of watching a sitcom? Or during an immoral or violent movie? What about a few hours later, when the images and feelings from those shows are still with us?

As you know, you feel more comfortable with some people than with others. Some people you can be with all day long, and they never make you feel uncomfortable. We have a word for such people: we call them "friends." I had missionary companions who were friends. Some of them were Filipino elders. We were different in so many ways! Our backgrounds, our eating and sleeping habits, the way we talked or expressed ourselves were all different. But I felt totally comfortable with them, and they with me. Why? Because Elder Perez and Elder

Casinillo knew that I would never tell an off-color joke, or offer them a beer, or anything like that. We had the gospel in common, and that was all we needed.

Now, are you ready for a new thought? Here it comes. Do you think the Spirit of the Lord might be like that? Do you think that the Spirit of the Lord may simply feel more comfortable dwelling with some people than with others? Back when I was a junior in high school, I attended a camp with some other students. One of the camp counselors used the most profane and disgusting language I had ever heard in my life. I remember having to leave his presence several times because I literally became sick to my stomach. I didn't know that mere words could make me sick.

Similarly, if someone's thoughts are full of prime-time filth and immoral song lyrics, do you think the Spirit can feel *comfortable* with that person? To put it a little irreverently, I think it would make the Spirit sick, and cause him to leave.

Someone once said that the gospel is here to "comfort the afflicted, and afflict the comfortable." This next quote from Brigham Young has a tendency to "afflict the comfortable." Brace yourself (this is great):

> Pray the Lord to inspire your hearts. Ask for wisdom and knowledge. It is our duty to seek after it. Let us seek, and we shall find. . . . But as for His coming down here to pour His Spirit upon you, while you are aiming after the vain and frivolous things of the world [*Baywatch leaps to mind*]; indulging in all the vanity, nonsense, and foolery which surrounds you [Dare I say WWF?]; drinking in all the filthy abomination which should be spurned from every community on the earth—so long as you continue in this course, *rest assured He will not come near you.* (*Journal of Discourses,* 1:120; emphasis in original)

As you may have guessed, Brigham Young didn't mention any TV shows in his quote. These days you don't have to see the shows to know what they're about. You can just listen to the commercials:

> *Tonight, in an all-star line-up, you'll never guess who winds up with who. . . . Yes, tonight, the truths and values you embrace will be mocked on every hand! Get hooked! Join us at 8:00 Central/7:00 Pacific.*

Okay, they don't really say that, but they might as well. Go back to the Brigham Young quote—do you remember the last part? *"Rest assured—[the Spirit] will not come near you!"* Why not? Because it would be too "uncomfortable." So what's the point of all this? The point is, we need to do the work necessary to be prepared to feel the Spirit of the Lord before we can feel it. We need to be doing our best to keep the commandments. We need to be in places where the Spirit can come. We need to be clean! To be filthy is to be weak:

> And they saw that they had become weak, like unto their brethren, the Lamanites, and that the Spirit of the Lord did no more preserve them; yea, it had withdrawn from them because *the Spirit of the Lord doth not dwell in unholy temples.* (Helaman 4:24; emphasis added)

> *And he doth not dwell in unholy temples;* neither can filthiness or anything which is unclean be received into the kingdom of God; therefore I say unto you the time shall come, yea, and it shall be at the last day, that he who is filthy shall remain in his filthiness. (Alma 7:21; emphasis added)

HOW DOES THE SPIRIT SPEAK TO US?

As a junior in high school, I found myself one afternoon at the bowling alley with some friends. I rented a pair of lovely, high-fashion bowling shoes, chose a bowling ball, and waited for my turn. As I stood ready to deliver my ball down the lane, I noticed the little lighted number "11" at the end of the lane just above the pins. I was puzzled. Usually, you'll see a little number 1, indicating that this is your first ball. Well, to me, it looked like an 11. I squinted, and contorted my face, and the little green number 11 "morphed" into a number 1, and then back to a number 11. This was the first time I realized I needed glasses. I had always wanted to be a fighter pilot, but without 20-20 vision, I would have to settle for something else (but that's another story).

A few days later, I stood in the eye doctor's office and put on my new glasses for the first time. It was great. I looked out the window at billboard advertisements, and I was surprised at how sharp and clear they appeared. I could read the stenciled letters on the dumpster in the parking lot! And the next time I went bowling, I watched that 11 merge into a sharp and clear number 1. I repeatedly took off and put on my glasses and watched the number go from blurry to clear.

Why the bowling story? Well, I think one of the most common ways we feel the Spirit is that it makes things go from blurry to clear—just like putting on glasses. When the Spirit is with us we can "see" better than before. The word often used in the scriptures is *enlighten.*

> Verily, Verily, I say unto you, I will impart unto you of my Spirit, which shall *enlighten* your mind, which shall fill your soul with joy. (D&C 11:13; emphasis added)

> Behold, thou knowest that thou hast inquired of me and I did *enlighten* thy mind; and now I tell thee these things that thou mayest know that thou hast been *enlightened* by the Spirit of truth. (D&C 6:15; emphasis added)

For by my Spirit will I *enlighten* them, and by my power will I make known unto them the secrets of my will—yea, even those things which eye has not seen, nor ear heard, nor yet entered into the heart of man. (D&C 76:10; emphasis added)

For my Spirit is sent forth into the world to *enlighten* the humble and contrite, and to the condemnation of the ungodly. (D&C 136:33; emphasis added)

I've often sat in meetings where I felt "enlightened." There was no burning feeling, and no glorious vision, but the Spirit was present nonetheless. Inside, I felt enlightened and instructed. Everything became clear. "John," my thoughts would say, "you need to do better on your scripture reading." Or, "John, you need to do better in your prayers." Nephi's younger brother Jacob taught, "The Spirit speaketh the truth and lieth not. Wherefore, it speaketh of things as they really are, and of things as they really will be; wherefore, these things are manifested unto us plainly, for the salvation of our souls" (Jacob 4:13). That's the way it is. The Spirit makes things plain.

I have also noticed that when I feel "enlightened," I sometimes feel a little bit scolded. The Spirit seems to be saying, "John, you can do better, and you know it." I guess I don't mind being scolded in these situations. Elder Neal A. Maxwell said, "When conscience calls to us from the next ridge, it is not solely to scold but also to beckon" (*Ensign,* November 1976, 14). That "scolding" is the Spirit beckoning me to do better. "C'mon, John. Come up to higher ground. You can do better. You can *be* better!" I absolutely love it when I have this feeling. I know I make my best decisions under its influence, and I want to feel it as often as I can. That's why this is one of my favorite quotes:

Men are mortal and beset by human frailties. . . . When they are under the influence of an exalted occasion, they make high resolves. They firmly determine to avoid past mistakes and to do better. But gone out from under the spell of that influence and absorbed in the complicated pursuits of life, they find difficulty in holding fast to their noble purposes. . . . *So it is essential that they come again, and frequently, under the influence which kindles anew the warmth of spirit in which good resolutions are begotten,* that they may go out fortified to withstand the pressures of temptation which lure them into false ways. Happily, *if they refresh themselves frequently enough* under ennobling influences, the spirit of repentance will be at work with them, and they will make conquest of some temptations—rise above them—and advance thus far toward their final goal. (Albert E. Bowen, cited by Dean L. Larsen, *Ensign,* November 1989, 62)

That was a long quote, but did you catch the main message? *"Come again, and frequently!"* To me, this quote says that if we want to feel those "enlightening" moments, we need to take advantage of every chance we have to feel the Spirit—every opportunity to attend a fireside, a standards night, our Sunday meetings, and our family home evenings; every opportunity we have to attend seminary, read our scriptures, listen to good music, watch Church videos. Every opportunity we have to make our thoughts go from blurry to clear, we need to take it!

When it comes to matters of the Spirit, we need to be careful not to compare ourselves to others too much. Some people seem to think that the Spirit affects everyone the same way. For example, some may believe that "whoever cries the most is the most spiritual," and that's not necessarily true. For some people, the presence of the Spirit may bring tears. For others it doesn't. You may feel the Spirit very strongly and not shed any tears at all. Some may confuse strong emotion for the Spirit. Elder Boyd K. Packer said:

> The spiritual part of us and the emotional part of us are so closely linked that it is possible to mistake an emotional impulse for something spiritual. We occasionally find people who receive what they assume to be spiritual promptings from God, when those promptings are either centered in the emotions or are from the adversary. (*Ensign,* January 1983, 56)

If I had one thing to say to teenagers about recognizing the Spirit, it would be this: "Be patient, be clean, and don't give up." This is a difficult topic to write about, because I feel like I'm still learning to understand how the Spirit works in my life—and I'm old!

In the April 1989 *Ensign,* there is an excellent article titled "Have I Received an Answer from the Spirit?" In this article, Brother Jay E. Jensen outlines several different ways the Spirit may communicate with us. The Spirit:

1. Speaks peace to the mind
2. Causes the bosom to burn
3. Tells us in our minds and our hearts
4. Comes as a voice in the mind
5. Leads us to do something
6. Occupies our minds and presses upon our feelings
7. Constrains us from dangerous or improper things

As we go through this list, I bet you'll remember times when the Spirit has helped you. Let's talk about each one for a minute.

1. The Spirit speaks peace to the mind. The Spirit can bring peace, calmness, and tranquillity. It can remove turmoil and anxious feelings. The Lord answered one of Oliver Cowdery's prayers by sending a feeling of peace. This is interesting:

Later, the Lord gave Oliver a revelation to inform him that he had already received a revelation!

> Verily, verily, I say unto you, if you desire a further witness, cast your mind upon the night that you cried unto me in your heart, that you might know concerning the truth of these things.
>
> Did I not speak peace to your mind concerning the matter? What greater witness can you have than from God?
>
> And now, behold, you have received a witness; for if I have told you things which no man knoweth have you not received a witness? (D&C 6:22–24)

Jesus is the "Prince of Peace" (Isaiah 9:6), and he spoke to his disciples about peace:

> Peace I leave with you, my peace I give unto you: not as the world giveth, give I unto you. Let not your heart be troubled, neither let it be afraid. (John 14:27)

2. The Spirit causes the bosom to burn. After Jesus was resurrected, he walked with two of his disciples on the road to Emmaus. He talked with them for a while, and then left. They didn't recognize him when he was with them, but after he left they said, "Did not our heart burn within us, while he talked with us by the way, and while he opened to us the scriptures?" (Luke 24:32).

Don't be too discouraged if you've never felt this warm feeling. Because of the wonderful counsel given to Oliver Cowdery in Doctrine and Covenants section 9, many have felt like spiritual misfits if they have never experienced the "burning in the bosom." Elder Dallin H. Oaks explained:

> This may be one of the most important and misunderstood teachings in all the Doctrine and Covenants. The teachings of the Spirit often come as feelings. That

fact is of the utmost importance, yet some misunderstand what it means. I have met persons who told me they have never had a witness from the Holy Ghost because they have never felt their bosom "burn within" them.

What does a "burning in the bosom" mean? Does it need to be a feeling of caloric heat, like the burning produced by combustion? If that is the meaning, I have never had a burning in the bosom. Surely, the word "burning" in this scripture signifies a feeling of comfort and serenity. That is the witness many receive. That is the way revelation works.

Truly, the still, small voice is just that, "still" and "small." (*Ensign,* March 1997, 13)

3. The Spirit tells us in our minds and hearts. I spent a lot of time on this one earlier in the chapter, because I believe it is the most common way we feel the Spirit. When the Spirit speaks to our minds and hearts, we are "enlightened" and things become clear. The Lord told Oliver Cowdery, "Yea, behold, I will tell you in your mind and in your heart, by the Holy Ghost, which shall come upon you and which shall dwell in your heart" (D&C 8:2). Not only do things make sense in our minds but also they feel right in our hearts. I think that's why the scripture says mind *and* heart.

4. The Spirit comes as a voice in the mind. President David O. McKay has said that the Holy Ghost speaks through the conscience of the members of the Church who are in the line of their duty. Most people's thoughts are in their own voice, and when thoughts come into your mind, it may be hard to distinguish between your own voice and the Spirit of the Lord. Others times it may be very clear that the "voice" came from somewhere else. Elder Jensen continues:

At times, a person may actually hear an audible voice;

at other times, a person may have an impression or a thought come into his mind expressed in one or more complete sentences. Enos reported that while he was "struggling in the spirit, behold, the voice of the Lord came into [his] mind." (Enos 1:10.) (*Ensign*, April 1989, 23)

5. The Spirit leads us to do something. This is another common way that the Spirit influences us. I'm sure you've heard stories about someone who "felt impressed" to make a phone call, or visit someone, or do a favor for someone, and it turned out that the person really needed that service at that time. You may have even been led by the Spirit to say "hi" to someone at school, or to keep someone company who was having a hard day. The Spirit can lead you to do these things.

I remember attending a very rowdy Scout meeting one Tuesday night many years ago. Our Scoutmaster was doing his best to teach us about the Citizenship in the World merit badge, but we were bouncing off the walls. He did what he could to explain the requirements, but we were being totally obnoxious. He finally finished and asked someone to give the prayer. With my head bowed, I remember feeling like something was wrong. I watched my Scoutmaster putting away his things after the prayer, and I felt bad. Something—I believe it was the Spirit—told me that he felt like he had failed. I decided that I would go home and work on that merit badge until I earned it. I wanted my Scoutmaster to know that I did not ignore all his work that night.

The Lord told Hyrum Smith:

> And now, verily, verily, I say unto thee, put your trust in that Spirit which leadeth to do good—yea, to do justly, to walk humbly, to judge righteously; and this is my Spirit. (D&C 11:12)

That may seem like a simple scripture, but it's important

to emphasize that the Spirit leads us to do *good*. If someone says something like, "The Spirit led me to slug my little brother," or "The Spirit told me not to listen to the prophet," I think you can know it's not the Spirit of the Lord. The prophet Mormon gave us a key for how to judge if a prompting comes from the Spirit of the Lord or the spirit of the devil:

> But behold, that which is of God inviteth and enticeth to do good continually; wherefore, every thing which inviteth and enticeth to do good, and to love God, and to serve him, is inspired of God. . . .
>
> But whatsoever thing persuadeth men to do evil, and believe not in Christ, and deny him, and serve not God, then ye may know with a perfect knowledge it is of the devil; for after this manner doth the devil work, for he persuadeth no man to do good, no, not one; neither do his angels; neither do they who subject themselves unto him. (Moroni 7:13, 17)

Some people are deceived and even leave the Church because they are confused in this area. They may think they have been given a "higher law." They may suddenly feel that they are more entitled to inspiration than the leaders of the Church. The Spirit would not tell anyone to go against the prophet and leave the Church. Sorry, folks, it's just not going to happen. If they knew the scriptures, they would know they had been deceived. President Wilford Woodruff said:

> The Lord will never permit me or any other man who stands as President of this Church to lead you astray. It is not in the programme. It is not in the mind of God. If I were to attempt that, the Lord would remove me out of my place, and so He will any other man who attempts to lead the children of men astray from the oracles of God and from their duty. (Doctrine and Covenants, Official Declaration 1, note)

One of the reasons I love to watch general conference is because I know that if I listen to the prophet and follow him, I will not be led astray.

6. The Spirit occupies our minds and presses upon our feelings. I love to read Joseph Smith's testimony. You'll remember that he read from the book of James, "If any of you lack wisdom, let him ask of God" (James 1:5). Once he'd read that verse, he couldn't get it out of his mind! Listen to his own words:

> Never did any passage of scripture come with more power to the heart of man than this did at this time to mine. It seemed to enter with great force into every feeling of my heart. I reflected on it again and again, knowing that if any person needed wisdom from God, I did. (Joseph Smith—History 1:12)

The Spirit of the Lord was telling Joseph that this verse was important. Many sections of the Doctrine and Covenants were revealed after the Prophet was impressed to meditate and ponder about a certain subject for a long time.

In the same way, if *you* seem to be reflecting on something again and again, maybe the Lord is trying to tell you something too.

7. The Spirit constrains us from dangerous or improper things. Many years ago, my brother David was driving to a party up Emigration Canyon near Salt Lake City. Suddenly, a feeling came over him that he should turn around and go home. So he turned around and headed back. But then he started to think, "They're expecting me, they're waiting for me, and they'll be worried if I don't show up," so he turned around and started back up the canyon. The feeling came again, "Turn around and go home." So he turned around and headed home again. But the same objections arose in his mind. This time David stopped the car, knelt down, and prayed. He told the Lord that he felt he was getting promptings from the Spirit, but that people were waiting for him, and he needed to go. He told the Lord, however, that if he felt the prompting again, he would head home with no more questions. The Lord seemed to let him continue this time, but David knew something was wrong at that party, because the Lord had warned him. When David arrived, he found that there *was* something wrong, and that he needed to get out of there. He stayed long enough to persuade two of his friends to get in the car, and the three of them drove home.

When I was on my mission, many times I would get a feeling that I shouldn't go to certain places. Sometimes I would think, "Was that my own thoughts or the Spirit?" When the feeling seemed to come out of nowhere, I obeyed. I don't know what would have happened if I had ignored the Spirit on those occasions, but that's not the point. The point is, follow the Spirit when it constrains! It's smarter than you are!

A FEW CLOSING THOUGHTS

As I have tried to learn how to recognize and use the Spirit in my life, I have been motivated by the words of Nephi. I have heard people say, "I don't think I've ever felt the Spirit, and I'm not going to do anything until I do!" or "I'll wait until the Lord tells me *exactly* what to do." Nephi, on the other hand, had a different approach. He was willing to *move,* full of faith that the Lord would guide him when he needed it. In 1 Nephi 4:6 we read, "And I was led by the Spirit, *not knowing beforehand* the things which I should do" (emphasis added). Nephi was a man of action. Nephi said, "I will go and do," not "I will sit and stew." Elder Marion G. Romney agreed with this approach: "While the Lord will magnify us in both subtle and dramatic ways, he can only guide our footsteps when we move our feet" (*Ensign,* May 1981, 91). If you want to feel the Spirit, you've got to move your feet!

Remember to be patient. Sometimes it seems as if the Lord waits until the last possible second before sending his inspiration. "And it shall be given thee in the very moment what thou shalt speak and write" (D&C 24:6). There have been times in my life when I have begged and pleaded for guidance and felt as if I received nothing. Months later I have looked back and realized that I was being guided all along—that my prayers *had* been heard by the Lord. I realized that "as often as [I] inquired . . . [I] received instruction of [the] Spirit" (D&C 6:14). So be patient, purify your life, and keep the faith. The Lord will speak to you in his own way and in his own time.

There's one more important thing about the Spirit that I'd like to mention before we're done. Some people think the Spirit is just a "good feeling." And it is, but it's more than that. If the Spirit were only a good feeling, it would be nothing more than "background music" to life. But the Spirit is much more than background music. I believe the Spirit is more like the phone ringing. It needs to be answered! My seminary-teacher friend Bill Carpenter is fond of saying, "The Spirit of the Lord is a call to action, and the action you take is your answer to God." I agree. Whenever I've felt the Spirit, I've always felt as if I should *do* something! I've felt that I should take action in some way. I've felt that I want to repent, be clean, and change my heart and motives. And the action I take is my answer to God. So when you hear the phone ringing, answer it!

Learning to recognize and understand the Spirit is perhaps one of the most important goals you will ever have in your life. To paraphrase President Ezra Taft Benson, The Lord can make a lot more out of your life than you can (see *The Teachings of Ezra Taft Benson* [Salt Lake City: Bookcraft, 1988], 361). You will need to know how to follow the Spirit to receive that help. When you live your life by high standards, and desire with all your heart to be valiant, you will eventually gain respect from the people you admire most. Others may think you are insane, but that's only because they can't hear the music. Stay tuned—or, in other words, stay "in tune"—and you will be able to hear the soothing and motivating music of the Spirit. It will guide you through all of life's hazards and take you all the way home to your Father in Heaven.

EXTRA CREDIT

"Teaching and Learning by the Spirit," Dallin H. Oaks, *Ensign,* March 1997, 6–14.

"Have I Received an Answer from the Spirit?" Jay E. Jensen, *Ensign,* April 1989, 21–25.

"Revelation," Dallin H. Oaks, *New Era,* September 1982, 38–46.

"I Have a Question," Dallin H. Oaks, *Ensign,* June 1983, 27.

"Learning to Recognize Answers to Prayer," Richard G. Scott, *Ensign,* November 1989, 30–32.

"Prayers and Answers," Boyd K. Packer, in *That All May be Edified* (Salt Lake City: Bookcraft, 1982), 9–15.

"The Candle of the Lord," Boyd K. Packer, *Ensign,* January 1983, 51–56.

Understanding Personal Revelation, talk on cassette, Joseph Fielding McConkie (Salt Lake City: Deseret Book, 1991).

Receiving Answers to Our Prayers, talk on cassette, Gene R. Cook (Salt Lake City: Deseret Book, 1991).

Fifth Period: Communications 101

Improving Your Prayers

Prayer can solve more problems, alleviate more suffering,
prevent more transgression, and bring about greater
peace and contentment in the human soul than can be
obtained in any other way.
—*Thomas S. Monson*

et's play a guessing game, okay? I'm thinking of something—an event. Your job is to guess what it is. Are you ready? I'll give you a few clues:

- Because of this event, you are reading this book.

- Because of this event, hundreds of thousands of the world's best teenagers get up before the sun rises and go to seminary before school starts.

- Because of this event, thousands of men, women, and children endured unbelievable hardship and walked across a continent.

- Today, even as we speak, sixty thousand young men and women have left their homes to teach people all over the world about this event for no pay.

- Because of this event, millions are familiar with the names Nephi, Alma, and Moroni.

- Because of this event, the whole world has been changed. The priesthood of God has been restored, baptism by immersion for the remission of sins is available, and families can be sealed together forever.

- Because of this event, millions of people will endure whatever persecutions or hardships come their way as they watch and wait for the second coming of Jesus Christ to the earth.

What is this remarkable, amazing, powerful event that has changed the whole world forever?

The prayer of a teenager.

That's it. The prayer of a fourteen-year-old farm boy back in 1820 changed the world, and it will never be the same. The point? *Don't ever underestimate the power of prayer.* The Father and the Son appeared to Joseph Smith in the spring of 1820 because of his faithful response to a beautiful scripture: "If any of you lack wisdom, let him ask of God, that giveth to all men liberally, and upbraideth not; and it shall be given him" (James 1:5).

Sometimes it seems like the answer to every question in Sunday School is "pray and read your scriptures." Well, that's good advice, because that's exactly what young Joseph Smith did, and because he did, the world is a different place today.

DON'T EVER STOP PRAYING

Prayer is so important that if you're not praying twice a day, the President of the Church may be fearful for you! Are you on his worry list? This is what President Heber J. Grant said:

> I have little or no fear for the . . . young man or the young woman, who honestly and conscientiously sup-plicate God twice a day for the guidance of His Spirit. (*Gospel Standards* [Salt Lake City: Improvement Era, 1942], 26)

Is President Grant saying that all you have to do is pray twice a day and everything will be fine? No—he said he has little fear for you if you are *already* praying twice a day. Usually, when people are having a tough time, struggling with sin, or bordering on inactivity, what's one of the first things they stop doing? Right! They stop praying. I've met many young people who are still attending seminary and church, but who have stopped praying. Everything may appear fine on the outside, but inside they are struggling. I think that

President Grant is saying that if you are praying twice a day, he has little fear for you because the other things in your life are probably all right.

Why do people stop praying? I don't know—probably many reasons. I met a young woman once who said she hadn't really prayed in months. She said the blessing on the food when she was asked to, and she said opening prayers in seminary and Sunday School classes, but she offered no personal prayers. When I asked her why, she looked at the ground and explained, "Well, I've made a lot of mistakes in my life, and I've done some things, and I don't see why Heavenly Father would listen to me, 'cause I've done so many dumb things."

Do you have to be perfect to pray? Satan wants you to think so. Nephi taught:

> For if ye would hearken unto the Spirit which teacheth a man to pray ye would know that ye must pray; for the evil spirit teacheth not a man to pray, but teacheth him that he must not pray.
>
> But behold, I say unto you that ye must pray always, and not faint. (2 Nephi 32:8–9)

In other words, if you ever have that feeling that you can't pray, now you know where it comes from. It isn't from God. He always wants you to pray. It comes from "the evil spirit."

Of course, it's easier to say that than to believe it. When we've made a big mistake, or when we've sinned, it's much harder to pray. I know that. But that's also the most important time to keep in touch with our Heavenly Father. He knows what we've done. We're not going to surprise him.

If you find that it's really hard to pray, don't tell your friends, tell your Father! You might say, "Heavenly Father, this is really hard for me to do. I know I'm not perfect, and I've made some mistakes, but thou hast a commandment to pray, so here I am." That kind of prayer is remarkably similar to a prayer spoken by the brother of Jared. Listen to how humble he is:

> Now behold, O Lord, and do not be angry with thy servant because of his weakness before thee; for we know that thou art holy and dwellest in the heavens, and that we are unworthy before thee; because of the fall our natures have become evil continually; nevertheless, O Lord, thou hast given us a commandment that we must call upon thee, that from thee we may receive according to our desires. (Ether 3:2)

What if the brother of Jared had thought, "Oh, well, I'm not worthy, so I won't pray." Or, "I'll just forget about praying until I'm perfect." As a matter of fact, it so happens that the brother of Jared *did* forget to pray for a while, and what do you think happened? He got scolded for *three hours!*

> And it came to pass at the end of four years that the Lord came again unto the brother of Jared, and stood in a cloud and talked with him. And for the space of three hours did the Lord talk with the brother of Jared, and chastened him because he remembered not to call upon the name of the Lord. (Ether 2:14)

Perhaps you're thinking, "Yeah, but I'm not the Brother of Jared—I'm not that important." H. Burke Peterson, a former member of the presiding bishopric, said this:

> I want you to know that I know that whenever one of Heavenly Father's children kneels and talks to him, he listens. I know this as well as I know anything in this world—that Heavenly Father listens to every prayer from his children. I know our prayers ascend to heaven. *No matter what we may have done wrong, he listens to us.* (*Ensign,* June 1981, 73; emphasis added)

So let's just dispense with the ridiculous little "I-don't-think-God-listens-to-me" comments. You don't have to be perfect to be heard, and you don't have to pray perfectly. The most important thing is that you try.

WE KNOW WE CAN DO BETTER IN OUR PERSONAL PRAYERS

A young woman once told me, "I pray, but I don't feel anything." At first I wanted to say, "Well, welcome to the club." As we learned in fourth period, strong and impressive spiritual experiences do not come to us very often. Perhaps you're different from me, but I would say I feel things in my prayers only maybe 2 or 3 percent of the time. Not very often. But I *know* God is there, and I will *never* stop praying.

This chapter is not intended to teach anyone how to pray. I imagine whoever is out there reading this book already knows the basic steps to prayer. This chapter is intended to motivate us to try harder, and to make our personal prayers a more important part of our day. The problem is, sometimes you and I (guilty sigh) are simply not doing our best in our personal prayers. We've fallen into a routine. What we need is a gentle (or maybe a not-so-gentle) reminder of what we already know. Sometimes we're simply not concentrating on improving the quality of our prayers.

Let's imagine it. You get home late, you kneel down by the side of your bed—wait a minute, you are kneeling, aren't you? You're not just lying on your back and looking toward heaven and expecting to stay awake? If you're praying like that, you'll fall asleep in the middle of your prayers. Then you'll wake up and look at your clock at 2 A.M. and say, "Um . . . um . . . Amen! Wow, that was a long one." I don't think that counts for much.

Okay, so you *kneel* down by your bed. A note of caution here: when you kneel down, don't just do a "face plant" into the mattress. I've done that before when I've started to pray, but sometimes, when I'm really tired, my thoughts begin to drift. At first I'm praying, but after a while I become lost in La-La Land. And I hate to tell you this, but I've thought and said some of the weirdest things in the middle of my prayers. How embarrassing! Has that ever happened to you? When you finally realize where you are, that you're on your knees next to your bed, it hits you that you were in the middle of praying! Isn't it embarrassing at that point when you have to say, "Oh . . . sorry, Heavenly Father—um—bless the sick and the afflicted . . ." This may be a little irreverent, but I wonder if Father isn't thinking, "I'd like to afflict you! Then maybe you'd remember me, and pray with a little more intent!"

> And thus we see that except the Lord doth chasten his people with many afflictions, yea, except he doth visit them with death and with terror, and with famine and with all manner of pestilence, they will not remember him. (Helaman 12:3)

You've probably heard the saying, "There are no atheists in foxholes." Yup. When the crisis is on, watch people get religious. We must be sure that we are praying not only in the tough times, but when things are easy and life is good. Elder Howard W. Hunter said:

> If prayer is only a spasmodic cry at the time of crisis, then it is utterly selfish, and we come to think of God as a repairman or a service agency to help us only in our emergencies. (*Ensign,* November 1977, 52)

Imagine if you were looking down on this world, and knew that only a small fraction of your children would kneel and talk to you at the end of the day. That's a sad thought, isn't it? Let's you and I commit to pray morning and night, in good times and bad, okay?

OPEN THE DOOR!

At one time or another, you've probably seen a painting of Jesus knocking on a door. I can recall three different versions of that painting. We had one in our house when I was growing up. I remember my dad asking me when I was very young, "John, what is different about this door?" I looked at it as closely as I could, but couldn't find anything unusual. "Keep looking," my dad said. Finally, I noticed that there was no doorknob! I said, "Oh, there's no handle!" And my dad said, "That's right. Do you know why?" I didn't, but I studied it some more, and finally my dad said, "If you want Jesus to come in, *you* have to open the door." The scripture that inspired that painting comes from Revelation 3:20: "Behold, I stand at the door, and knock: if any man hear my voice, and open the door, I will come in to him."

In other scriptures, the situation is reversed: We are at the door, and we do the knocking. For example: "Draw near unto me and I will draw near unto you; seek me diligently and ye shall find me; ask, and ye shall receive; knock, and it shall be opened unto you" (D&C 88:63). There are some wonderful principles in there. Let's examine this scripture in a more visual way:

WHERE YOU ARE: WHERE GOD IS:

Draw near unto me ■   ■ and I will draw near unto you;

seek me diligently ■   ■ and ye shall find me;

ask, ■   ■ and ye shall receive;

knock ■   ■ and it shall be opened unto you.

Now, what have you noticed? With every action you take, you move closer to the Lord, and he can move closer to you! But there's something more important. In every case, guess who has to move first? *You do!* Someone once said, "If you feel farther away from God today than you were yesterday, you can be sure who moved." It's true. If you want to be closer to the Lord, you have to *move* closer! You may be asking, "How do you seek, ask, and knock?" Good question. Now we'll give some examples and become even more visual:

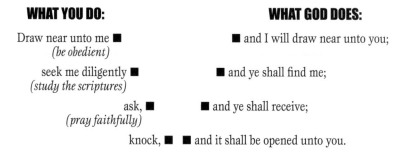

WHAT YOU DO: **WHAT GOD DOES:**

Draw near unto me ■   ■ and I will draw near unto you;
    (be obedient)

   seek me diligently ■   ■ and ye shall find me;
   (study the scriptures)

       ask, ■   ■ and ye shall receive;
    (pray faithfully)

        knock, ■   ■ and it shall be opened unto you.

See how that works? Now, I know that you are a very polite person, and you would not barge in on a party where you were not invited. In the same way, Heavenly Father respects our agency enough that he will not go where he's not invited. He will wait for us to move closer to him through obedience and prayer. And when we do, he has promised he will move closer to us.

The opposite is also true. You've seen how obedience can bring us closer to the Lord. What do you suppose disobedience would do? Let's take a look.

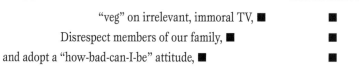

IF YOU AND I: **WHERE GOD IS:**

      "veg" on irrelevant, immoral TV, ■   ■

    Disrespect members of our family, ■   ■

and adopt a "how-bad-can-I-be" attitude, ■   ■

Through disobedience, we "draw away" from God! And we distance ourselves from the influence of his Spirit. Remember? "The Spirit of the Lord doth not dwell in unholy temples" (Helaman 4:24). With every activity, every day, we either draw closer to God or move farther away from him.

BE PERSISTENT AND CONSISTENT

One day I was waiting in line at the grocery store. I was behind a mom and a little boy. Moms are known for being able to do about 47 million things at once, and this mom was no different. She was conversing with the cashier, filling out a check with her right hand, and with her left hand holding the wrist of a hyper little boy who was struggling to get away. He was just out of reach of a display of candy bars. When he realized that he couldn't reach them by himself, he stopped trying to pull away, stepped close to his mother's side, and started tugging on her coat. "Mom?" (tug, tug, tug, tug). *"Mom?"* (tug, tug, tug). "MOM!" (tug, tug). At this point, the little boy put all his weight on his left foot, fixed his gaze on the ceiling, and put it on automatic: "Mom (tug) Mom (tug) Mom (tug) Mom (tug) Mom (tug) Mom (tug) Mom (tug) Mom (tug) . . ." Finally the mother, obviously ruffled, turned and answered, *"What?"* At this point the boy pointed to his left and said something like, "Nestle's Crunch!" I almost broke out laughing. Then I thought, "How perfect! I could use this in a talk!" (That's why I'm telling you about it now.) I'm hoping that you listened to that story with your spiritual ears, and you know what I'm going to say.

The boy wanted something, and he knew he couldn't get it by himself. He looked to a higher power, but got no response after a few tries. Very determined, he fixed his eyes upward and tugged and tugged until he got an answer. As I witnessed this event, I was reminded of something Joseph Smith said: "Weary [the Lord] until he blesses you" (in *Words of Joseph Smith,* Andrew F. Ehat and Lyndon W. Cook, eds. [Orem, Utah: Grandin Book Co., 1993], 15). Sometimes, in our prayers, we say, "Father?" (tug, tug, tug, tug). *"Father?"* (tug, tug, tug). "FATHER!" (tug, tug). Then we say to ourselves as we hit the pillow to go to sleep, "He just doesn't answer my prayers." Hmmm. I think we need to be more like that little boy and "weary the Lord." The boy knew that if he tugged long enough and hard enough, he would get his mother's attention. In the same way, if we tug long and hard, I believe the Lord will, in his own way and time, send us an answer (see Luke 18:1–8).

Perhaps the Lord will let us pray for a certain blessing for weeks, months, or even years. But this kind of struggling will build our faith and our spiritual muscles, and make us more humble and aware of our dependence on him. At these times we need to trust him, and believe in him, and "be still and know that [he is] God" (D&C 101:16).

AVOID VAIN REPETITION

You've probably heard the story of the man who was asked to offer a prayer at a prison. Because he was in the habit of using some of the same words and phrases in his prayers, he said, "We're thankful for this beautiful building we have to meet in, and we hope that those who are not here will be here next time . . ." Oops. Brother Jack Marshall talks about how we might prepare an ice-cream sundae, full of fat and refined sugar, and drenched with chocolate syrup. Then we bow our heads and ask the Lord to bless it to "nourish and strengthen our bodies." Oops again.

"Vain repetition" means using the same phrases over and over in our prayers without really meaning or thinking about what we are saying. Of course, it is fine to thank the Lord for a beautiful building to meet in, and to ask him to bless our food that it will nourish and strengthen us, if that's what we really mean. The key is sincerity. When prayers become just a habit, and we don't invest any real concentration and effort, then we are guilty of vain repetition. President Ezra Taft Benson said:

> Our prayers should be meaningful and pertinent. . . .
> Do not use the same phrases at each prayer. Each of us

would become disturbed if a friend said the same words to us each day, treated the conversation as a chore, and could hardly wait to finish in order to turn on the TV and forget us. (*God, Family, Country* [Salt Lake City: Deseret Book, 1974], 121–22)

I remember that, as a boy, I felt I should go down the list of everyone in the family and ask the Lord to bless them. After a while, I thought of a more "efficient" prayer. I remember telling my older brother how quickly I could bless a large number of people. I would say, "Please bless everyone I know, and everyone I've ever seen." Fortunately, I grew up, and I no longer treat the Lord like a servant who needs a "to-do" list from me.

Sometimes, when things are tough in my life, I don't even know what to say in my prayers. And do you know what? That's okay. Sometimes we don't even need words to pray.

> Likewise the Spirit also helpeth our infirmities: for we know not what we should pray for as we ought: but the Spirit itself maketh intercession for us with groanings which cannot be uttered. (Romans 8:26)

Even if we can't find the words, the Lord knows what we need. And this kind of prayer, though it may be more feelings than words, will reach heaven much easier than one full of vain repetition. Once again, the test is our sincerity, our intent. Mormon warned:

> And likewise also is it counted evil unto a man, if he shall pray and not with real intent of heart; yea, and it profiteth him nothing, for God receiveth none such. (Moroni 7:9)

WHO LISTENS TO, AND WHO ANSWERS, OUR PRAYERS?

A young woman once asked me, "Do Heavenly Father and Jesus listen when we pray, or just Heavenly Father?" Good question. We know that Jesus prayed very often while he was on the earth, and he told the Nephites, "Therefore ye must always pray unto the Father in my name" (3 Nephi 18:19). We know that we address our prayers to our Father in Heaven. As to whether Jesus hears them too, let's read what Elder Bruce R. McConkie wrote:

> It is true that when we pray to the Father, the answer comes from the Son, because "there is . . . one mediator between God and men, the man Christ Jesus." (1 Timothy 2:5.) Joseph Smith, for instance, asked the Father, in the name of the Son, for answers to questions, and the answering voice was not that of the Father but of the Son, because Christ is our advocate, our intercessor, the God (under the Father) who rules and regulates this earth. . . .
>
> But what we must have perfectly clear is that we *always* pray to the Father, not the Son, and we *always* pray in the name of the Son. (In *Prayer* [Salt Lake City: Deseret Book, 1977], 10)

We don't know exactly how, but in some way our prayers are conveyed to the Son so that he may answer us. He also sends the Holy Ghost, or the Comforter, to answer our prayers. Jesus said, "But the Comforter, which is the Holy Ghost, whom the Father will send in my name, he shall teach you all things, and bring all things to your remembrance, whatsoever I have said unto you" (John 14:26).

WHAT SHOULD WE PRAY FOR?

As a little boy, I remember praying very hard one night for a bicycle. I bowed my head and prayed very earnestly for a bike to be sitting in my room when I looked up. I'd pray, and look up, then I'd pray some more, and look up. I prayed for quite a while, as I remember, while my brother slept in the bunk below. (I don't know how I would have explained it to him if a bike had appeared.)

I have since learned that we must be careful what we pray for, and that we should always add "Thy will be done" in our prayers. Sometimes we pray for things that wouldn't be good for us, and fortunately, in those cases, we often don't get what we want. (You may have heard a country music song with the words, "Sometimes I thank God for unanswered prayers.")

At a youth conference testimony meeting, a young woman told how she prayed every night to have a boyfriend. She was only fifteen, and not even old enough to begin dating, but she prayed and prayed and prayed to have a boyfriend. (We normally don't pray for things we know we shouldn't have. "Bless us that as we rob the bank we can get home in safety.") She thought having a boyfriend would make her happy. She said that the Lord finally answered her prayers by telling her that she "wouldn't be able to handle the things that would come with having a boyfriend."

This brings up another important point: We are not promised that we will receive *everything* we pray for, but we are promised every *right* thing we pray for.

> Whatsoever ye shall ask the Father in my name, *which is right,* believing that ye shall receive, behold it shall be given unto you. (3 Nephi 18:20; emphasis added)

> Whatsoever ye ask the Father in my name it shall be given unto you, that is expedient for you. (D&C 88:64)

Do you know what *expedient* means? The dictionary says, "useful for effecting a desired result." Because Heavenly Father knows us better than we know ourselves, he also knows what's best for us, and what our "desired results" ought to be. Though at times it may seem he is not answering our prayers, it may be that he wants us to wait for something even better. Jesus taught:

> What man is there of you, who, if his son ask bread, will give him a stone?
>
> Or if he ask a fish, will he give him a serpent?
>
> If ye then, being evil, know how to give good gifts unto your children, how much more shall your Father who is in heaven give good things to them that ask him? (3 Nephi 14:9–11)

What a beautiful thought. Our Father in Heaven is willing to give good gifts to them that ask him. So what should we ask for? Do you want a list? Okay, fine, I'll give you one. Actually, it's Amulek's list from Alma 34, and it's great.

> Yea, cry unto him for mercy; for he is mighty to save.
>
> Yea, humble yourselves, and continue in prayer unto him.
>
> Cry unto him when ye are in your fields, yea, over all your flocks.
>
> Cry unto him in your houses, yea, over all your household, both morning, mid-day, and evening.
>
> Yea, cry unto him against the power of your enemies.
>
> Yea, cry unto him against the devil, who is an enemy to all righteousness.
>
> Cry unto him over the crops of your fields, that ye may prosper in them.
>
> Cry over the flocks of your fields, that they may increase.
>
> But this is not all; ye must pour out your souls in your closets, and your secret places, and in your wilderness.
>
> Yea, and when you do not cry unto the Lord, let your hearts be full, drawn out in prayer unto him continually

for your welfare, and also for the welfare of those who are around you. (Alma 34:18–27)

By now you may be saying, "John, I don't have any fields, and I don't have any flocks, and I don't have any crops." Well, neither do I. So, let's do as Nephi recommended, and "liken all scriptures unto [ourselves]" (1 Nephi 19:23). What *do* you have? You may not be able to pray in your field over your flocks, but can you pray in school over your books? You may not work with crops in your field, but you may have peer pressure where you *do* work. You may not have your own household, but imagine the power you can have in your own family if, when you offer the family prayer, you mention your parents and each of your brothers and sisters by name, and lovingly pray for them. And if there isn't regular family prayer in your home, imagine the power you can have to bless your family if *you* organize it. Be a Nephi and take charge! Da-da-da-dat, da-dah! (That was the sound of a bugle playing *"Charge!"*)

GET IN THE HABIT

Evening prayers have never been a problem for me. I never forget. But there was a time, I'm embarrassed to admit, when I would forget, skip, or run out of time for my morning prayers. Finally I formed a habit. You need to find your own way, of course, but this is what I do. The instant I get up, I drop to my knees and pray. If I try to wait until I'm dressed, or showered, or something like that, I always seem to run out of time. So I say my prayers first thing.

That method works for me. You'll have to find one that works for you, but find one! You can't afford to miss that morning time with your Father in Heaven. Elder H. Burke Peterson shares with us how he formed a good habit:

When I was a boy, I couldn't always remember to say

my prayers at night. I wanted to, but sometimes I would forget because I'd be too sleepy. When I got older, I had a great idea.

If I were you, I would go out in the field and find a rock about the size of your fist. I'd wash it clean and put it under my pillow. Then, when I would get in bed at night and drop my head on my pillow—crack! I would remember to get out of bed and kneel down by it. I would then put the rock on the floor by my bed and go to sleep. Then, in the morning, I would jump out of bed, and as my foot would come down on the rock—"Ouch!" And I would remember to kneel down and say my morning prayers. Sometimes we need reminders to form good habits. (*Ensign,* November 1981, 35)

Because of Bishop Peterson's talk, many young people throughout the Church have made "Prayer Rocks" to help them remember to pray. (Other ideas, like the ill-fated "Prayer Cactus," didn't catch on as well.)

SHOULD I ASK A BLESSING ON THE FOOD IN A RESTAURANT?

Do you bless the food when you're on a date? If you pray over your food in a public place, will it show your obedience to the principle of prayer, or might it just look like you are showing off? Elder Bruce R. McConkie wrote:

The practice of the Church in our day is to have family prayer twice daily, plus our daily personal prayers, plus a blessing on our food at mealtimes (except in those public or other circumstances where it would be ostentatious or inappropriate to do so), plus proper prayers in our meetings. (In *Prayer,* 12)

There's a key. Be careful about praying in public if it feels inappropriate or ostentatious. Do you know what *ostentatious* means? My dictionary says it means a "showy display." Yes, indeed. The "I'm-more-spiritual-than-you-are" display is not appropriate. So you'll just have to use your best judgment on this one. (My friend Brad Wilcox does what he calls the "Bayer Prayer." He bows his head and rubs his temples as if he has a headache that needs an aspirin, and offers a silent prayer on his food.)

THE BEST FOR LAST

As you know, the best place to learn about prayer—or any other subject, for that matter—is in the scriptures. So, to conclude this chapter, I'm going to include some classic scriptures about prayer. The Savior was an incredible teacher. He could teach great principles in just a few words. Listen to how beautifully Jesus taught the Nephites:

> And when thou prayest thou shalt not do as the hypocrites, for they love to pray, standing in the synagogues and in the corners of the streets, that they may be seen of men. Verily I say unto you, they have their reward.
>
> But thou, when thou prayest, enter into thy closet, and when thou hast shut thy door, pray to thy Father who is in secret; and thy Father, who seeth in secret, shall reward thee openly.
>
> But when ye pray, use not vain repetitions, as the heathen, for they think that they shall be heard for their much speaking.
>
> Be not ye therefore like unto them, for your Father knoweth what things ye have need of before ye ask him. (3 Nephi 13:5–8)

I have found that one of the best and fastest ways to get to know people is to ask them what their favorite scriptures are. These next verses are some of my very favorite. One of the first times I felt the Spirit, and *knew* I was feeling it, was when I was reading this passage of scripture. I was a sophomore in high school, and we were studying Church history and the Doctrine and Covenants in seminary. Just before bedtime one night, I was reading these verses in my Doctrine and Covenants:

> Pray always, and I will pour out my Spirit upon you, and great shall be your blessing—yea, even more than if you should obtain treasures of earth and corruptibleness to the extent thereof.
>
> Behold, canst thou read this without rejoicing and lifting up thy heart for gladness?
>
> Or canst thou run about longer as a blind guide?
>
> Or canst thou be humble and meek, and conduct thyself wisely before me? Yea, come unto me thy Savior. Amen. (D&C 19:38–41)

Did you catch that? You can become as rich as you want to in this world, but the Lord says you will have more joy if you will just "pray always." And can you read that without rejoicing? Wow. One of the weapons you'll need in your personal battles against Satan is prayer. Here's another great verse from the Doctrine and Covenants:

> Pray always, that you may come off conqueror; yea, that you may conquer Satan, and that you may escape the hands of the servants of Satan that do uphold his work. (D&C 10:5)

At the beginning of this chapter, we looked at James 1:5, the scripture that led Joseph Smith to pray. In James 1:6, it says: "But let him ask in faith, nothing wavering." We must learn to pray more earnestly, with more faith, with real intent, and with all of the energy and strength of our souls. Mormon taught, "Pray unto the Father with all the energy of heart" (Moroni 7:48).

Earlier, I joked about some of our half-hearted prayers— the "face-plant-in-the-mattress" thing. I'm embarrassed about those times when my prayers weren't with "real intent." Writing and preparing to write this chapter has helped me want to do better. I especially felt a new resolve to try harder when I read this beautiful counsel from Elder H. Burke Peterson:

> As you feel the need to confide in the Lord or to improve the quality of your visits with him . . . may I suggest a process to follow: go where you can be alone, where you can think, where you can kneel, where you can speak out loud to him. The bedroom, the bathroom, or a closet will do. Now, picture him in your mind's eye. Think to whom you are speaking. Control your thoughts—don't let them wander. Address him as your Father and your friend. Now tell him things you really feel to tell him—not trite phrases that have little meaning, but have a sincere, heartfelt conversation with him. Confide in him. Ask him for forgiveness. Plead with him. Enjoy him. Thank him. Express your love to him. Then listen for his answers. Listening is an essential part of praying. Answers from the Lord come quietly, ever so quietly. In fact, few hear his answers audibly with their ears. We must be listening carefully or we will never recognize them. Most answers from the Lord are felt in our heart as a warm, comfortable expression, or they may come as thoughts to our mind. They come to those who are prepared and who are patient. (In *Prayer,* 108)

I don't know if there is any way I can express how grateful I am that a fourteen-year-old boy offered a prayer in a sacred grove so many years ago. That prayer, and everything that has happened since, has changed my life. Because of that prayer, Samuel Alexander Pagan Kelsey and his wife, my fourth great-grandparents, crossed the plains and came to Utah. Because of that prayer, my father joined the Church when he was twenty-four years old. Because of that prayer, my brother David was given a powerful blessing with the priesthood of God before he underwent a kidney transplant. Because of that prayer, I had the opportunity to serve a mission in the Philippines. So I am very, very grateful. Don't ever underestimate the power of prayer.

See you in Sixth Period!

EXTRA CREDIT

Prayer, various General Authorities (Salt Lake City: Deseret Book, 1977).

"Learning to Recognize Answers to Prayer," Richard G. Scott, *Ensign,* November 1989, 30–32.

Sixth Period: Geography 101

The Imagi-Nation

You see things and you say, "Why?" But I dream things that never were, and I say, "Why not?"
—George Bernard Shaw

We're going on a trip! Yes, we're going to see another nation. It's not a European nation, or an African nation, but a nation more interesting and exciting than anything you've ever seen. Airfare is free, you never get jet lag, and you can be there in a second. In fact, you can leave whenever you want, on a moment's notice! You can go there when you're feeling bad, or when you're feeling glad. Where is this nation? It's in the "State of Mind" right there in your head. It's the Imagi-Nation.

The Imagi-Nation is your own private country. You own it! It's every bit as beautiful and exciting as you can—um—imagine. You've been there before, but you may have forgotten a few things.

Some people stop traveling to their Imagi-Nation as they get older. They say it's only for kids. They prefer a place they call "Reality." It's another nation in the State of Mind. Those who live there want everyone else to live there too. They say, "C'mon, get back to Reality."

Other people live in a place they call "The Past." You've probably heard someone say, "Hey, you're living in The Past!" Well, that's what they mean. It's the third nation in the State of Mind. Some people never seem to leave The Past. They don't try to go anywhere else, because they believe things will always be the way they've been in The Past. So they give up their passport, and never visit their

Imagi-Nation. If you stay in The Past too long, you might get depressed. My advice is, don't live in The Past.

Where do most people live? I'm not sure. Probably in The Past with a daily commute to Reality. The most successful and happy people in the world, however, young and old, spend a lot of time in their Imagi-Nation.

Imagi-Nation is divided into counties called "Dreams," cities called "Goals," and freeways called "Success." (Notice that "Success" is a freeway, not a city.) In Reality, freeways go from city to city, with a new city always ahead. In Imagi-Nation, Success means going from goal to goal, with a new goal always ahead! You can never see all of your Imagi-Nation, but boy-oh-boy, it's sure fun trying. No matter how far you travel, there's always more Imagi-Nation left!

There's something very special about your Imagi-Nation. You can bring things from there into Reality. In fact, almost everything you find in Reality came from Imagi-Nation. You can make the things you imagine become real; some people call this "making your dreams come true."

One day, a little boy was wandering around in his Imagi-Nation, and his teacher had to bring him back to Reality. It happened at the Jefferson School in Cedar Rapids in 1878. Miss Ida Palmer, the teacher, noticed a seven-year-old boy hunched over his desk fiddling with two pieces of wood. He was definitely somewhere in his Imagi-Nation. Miss Palmer asked him what he was doing. He answered "that he was assembling the parts of a flying machine, a larger version of which might enable him to fly with his brother." Miss Palmer knew the wonders of Imagi-Nation, so she didn't take the craft from the little boy, but she did tell him to come back to Reality. Later, Orville and his brother Wilbur visited Imagi-Nation again. And on December 17, 1903, the Wright Brothers flew a part of their Imagi-Nation into Reality (Tom D. Crouch, *The*

Bishop's Boys: A Life of Wilbur and Orville Wright [New York: W. W. Norton & Co., 1989], 57).

You too can make your dreams come true. If you can make it in your Imagi-Nation, you can make it in Reality. But, as with any trip, you have to do some planning. In Reality, you can go to a gas station and get a map to help you plan your journey, to make sure you don't miss the best stops along the way. There are plenty of gas stations in the Imagi-Nation too, and they all have maps. Gas stations give us the fuel to travel, and maps tell us the best cities to visit. Gas stations are the Church, and maps are the gospel. The gospel map gives us a recommended tour, with stops along the way. You can visit any place you want in your Imagi-Nation, but the gospel map says, "Whatever you do, don't miss these cities!"

Some people travel without maps. They have no plans for their journey. It's unbelievable, but some people spend more time planning a vacation than they do planning their whole lives! You, however, are different. You have a map with specific goals. And somewhere on your map there is a drawing of a compass that tells you where "north" is, that gives you direction. You see, some people live in their Imagi-Nation, but they go in the wrong direction. Big mistake.

What direction should we take when we enter our Imagi-Nation? I'll tell you: "Seek ye first the kingdom of God and his righteousness, and all these things shall be added unto you" (3 Nephi 13:33). That short scripture, which is also found in Matthew 6:33, is the greatest success formula there is. Seek the kingdom of God first. What good does it do to work hard and set and achieve goals if you're moving in the wrong direction? Set goals for graduating from seminary, for receiving your Young Women Recognition Award or Eagle Scout Badge. Then set goals for your mission, marriage in the temple, and education. When you move in the right direction, the Lord will help you achieve your goals. If you start now, by charting your course and living by a plan, you'll have a full and rich life with many exciting stops along the way!

In Reality, it's easy to tell when you've arrived at a new city. There's always a sign that says, "Welcome to _____." And in Imagi-Nation, it's easy to tell when you've reached a new goal. If you've set a goal to receive your Young Women Recognition Award, or your Eagle Scout, there will come a time when you *know* you've achieved it. There are other kinds of goals that are harder to get a handle on. For example, what about the goal of being righteous? Can you suddenly check a box and say, "Okay, I'm righteous"? No. Why? Because righteousness is not that kind of goal. It's more like a way of life—a *direction,* or a mode of travel. You see, there are "do" goals, and there are "be" goals. Things that you *do,* you can check off when you're done. Things that you want to *be* are a little harder to measure, but they are still important.

Last semester, we talked mostly about "do" goals. This time we've been talking and will talk more about "be" goals, or direction goals. And that brings us to the next question:

ARE YOU EVERYTHING YOU WANT TO BE?

When I was only ten years old, I admired a sixth-grader in my elementary school very much. His name was Christian Johnson. He was always nice to everyone. He always seemed to be happy. He was outgoing, too. I'm not sure if I could have described why I admired him when I was ten, but now I know the right words. It's as simple as this: Christian was righteous. He was good. He glowed with the light of Christ. Can a twelve-year-old do that? You bet. Christian did. I wanted to be like that. I guess Christian was one of my first "role models."

Just before I entered seventh grade, my family moved to another part of town, but I never forgot about Christian. I still wanted to be like him. As the years went by, I remember writing down my feelings and goals from time to time, and when I did that I would think about Christian and other people I admired.

In junior high and high school, I found someone else to admire. He was outgoing and happy and good too, like Christian. His name was Richard Warr. Richard was popular—but unlike some of the others in the popular crowd, he was friendly with *all* the different social groups in the school, and everyone was friendly with him! Why? Because people of all kinds are drawn to goodness and righteousness. People are drawn to people who are happy. And nothing makes a person as happy as living the gospel can.

How about you? Is the person you *really* want to be hiding somewhere in your Imagi-Nation? You can be that person in Reality if you really want to. People do it all the time. Let me tell you about Lynette from New Mexico. No, I have a better idea—I'll let *Lynette* tell you about Lynette! Let's read her letter together:

> As a freshman and sophomore I found myself in a clique which included myself and two other Mormon girls. Starting at a new school with new friends and a whole new life it seemed like the perfect answer, not to mention the fact that "cliques" give the feeling of stability and friendship from others in the group. Well, things seemed great at first, and high school couldn't be better until I learned more about the people in my clique and how others were looked down upon and pushed away by one of the girls in the group, which made the whole group look bad. Every day it would get worse and I would just stand there in silence, partly because I knew that it was "safe" in a clique and I didn't want to be an outcast. Things went on like this for the first two years of my high school life, and people at school were always

nice to me when I was not with my friend who was always negative. Yet when I was around her I was looked at as a part of this group, and therefore I was also thought of as mean and negative.

Excuse me, but I need to interrupt and make a comment. This is the point where Lynette started to ask, "Am I everything I want to be?" Okay, keep reading. *We now return you to your regularly scheduled letter:*

It wasn't until the summer before my junior year that I decided that the way things were going and the way people were being treated was not something I was willing to let keep happening. . . . I decided to break away and be my own person. Junior year began, and I slowly started to break away from the group, which was very difficult. But in the long run it was worth it. As I slowly broke away from the clique I decided that instead of joining a new one and having the same thing happen I would try something else. From that day forward I promised myself and Heavenly Father that I would go to school every day and try my best to treat everyone (no matter who they are or what they look like) with the highest love and respect possible. Instead of joining a clique I would just be friends with everyone equally. I would go around to each individual clique and visit with people every day and talk to them and get to know them as my brothers and sisters and children of God.

I'm moving on to my senior year now, and my life couldn't be better. This past year has been filled with trials and struggles, yet with the wonderful friendships that I have built with people—being able to see them for who and what they are—those trials have been so much easier to handle and conquer. Life just seems to take on a new meaning.

I must admit that it wasn't easy to break away from

security and comfort, even for an outgoing person (which is how I consider myself). Not having a best friend in the world can be hard at times, when you need a shoulder to cry on. But in the end I can guarantee you that when you are nice and a friend to everyone, as opposed to just those in your little clique, life will be so much better and can bring you so much more joy than you'll ever know. There are so many wonderful people out there who are just waiting for a friend.

Lynette took a hard look at herself, and her life, and asked, "Am I everything I want to be?" And the answer was "no." So she changed. She put The Past behind her, she saw what she wanted in her Imagi-Nation, and she brought it into Reality.

Well, are *you* everything *you* want to be? How would you like to be different? If you can see it in your Imagi-Nation, you can make it in Reality. One of the cop-outs we hear all the time is: "That's just the way I am." If you're like me, whenever you hear someone say that, you want to respond, "No, you're just the way you've *chosen* to be." I know people who seem to be happy all the time, and yet they have major trials and difficulties in their lives. How do they do that? Well, at some point, those people made a conscious decision to be happy no matter what. They no longer say things like "He makes me so mad" or "This weather depresses me." They have taken control of their feelings.

On top of your TV or VCR or DVD, there's probably a remote control. With a remote control, you can "control" your TV from a "remote" location. If the TV is too loud, you can turn the volume down or even push the "mute" button. (I've tried pointing the remote at people and pushing the "mute" button when they get too loud, but it doesn't work.)

When you let others control how you feel, it is as if you

have given out a remote control that has a button on it for each of your moods. If you walk past someone in the hall, and they don't say "hi," do you let that affect your mood? If so, you have given away your remote control—and as long as you let others keep it, they will keep affecting your moods. Does that make sense?

Some people give their remote controls to the dumbest things. For example, would you give a personal remote control to the Big Dipper? Some people have. It's called astrology. "Gee, I'd better check my horoscope to see what's going to happen to me today, so I'll know what kind of a mood to be in." Yup, they have given a remote control to big balls of burning gas billions of miles away. Brilliant move. These people are not living in Reality or the Imagi-Nation. It's more like the "Halluci-Nation."

Anyway, here's the point: You need self-control, not remote control. *Take back the remote!* If you want to make a major stride forward as a teenager, decide now that you will be the kind of person you want to be, and that you will stop blaming everyone and everything outside of you for your moods and circumstances. Of course there are trials in life, but there are a million examples of people who have succeeded in spite of their trials. You can too! Or you can (as many people do) blame the government, high taxes, bad weather, your family, your genes, your teacher, your luck, your birth order, or the Big Dipper for your problems.

I have a friend named Greg. I heard him teach a class once in which he shared his amazing personal story of "taking back the remote." I should start by saying that Greg looks like one of those guys on the cover of a J. Crew catalog. No exaggeration. I wouldn't know, but the girls all say he's "gorgeous." Now you'll understand why this story was so amazing to me.

Greg told of a time back in his early high school years when he had no friends and was very overweight. He didn't feel all that good about himself, and he just kind of moved along through life like everyone else. One day something interesting happened. There was a popular girl at his school who walked up to Greg and simply said, "Greg, are you everything you want to be?" (That's where I got the idea for this part of the book!) Deep inside, Greg answered to himself, "no." He knew he could be better. This simple question from a wise young woman served as a wake-up call for Greg. He knew he was more than he was demonstrating. Greg took back the remote. All that summer, he worked. He exercised like crazy and lost a lot of weight. He changed his diet and built up some muscle by working out. When Greg went back to school in the fall, he looked totally different. Nobody recognized him! They thought he was a new kid who had just moved in. He made a lot of friends, and soon became one of the most popular boys at the school.

Greg humbly explained that he kind of got caught up in his newfound popularity. After a while, unfortunately, he wasn't treating people as well as he should have. Once again, this amazing young woman came to Greg and asked him the same question: "Greg, are you everything you want to be?" And once again, Greg answered "no." He looked deep inside. He had already changed his appearance, but perhaps there was more remodeling to be done. Now he had to work on his heart. He decided he would talk to everyone, not just those in the popular group, and he would start treating everyone with kindness and respect. And he did!

I really love this story. It happened because a young woman repeatedly asked a very good question: "Are you everything you want to be?" and because an honest young man was willing to answer the question, then take charge and change what needed to be changed.

DAILY REMINDERS, OR "DON'T FORGET TO REMEMBER!"

How do we make sure we're going in the right direction as we travel through the Imagi-Nation? Well, asking ourselves certain questions every day, like the one Greg's friend asked, can really help. In my own life, I try to remind myself *every day* of certain things. On my bathroom mirror, I have a picture of the *Christus,* the beautiful statue of the Savior in the Temple Square visitors' center. Underneath it are printed the words, "He is so powerful." This is a daily reminder to me to have faith in Jesus Christ. I love him, and I know that he has the power and the will to order all things for my good as fast as I am able to receive them (see D&C 111:11).

Daily reminders help keep us moving in the right direction. One of the reasons we're told to read the scriptures *every day* is because doing so will allow the Spirit of the Lord to be with us *every day.* The same applies to daily prayers.

May I suggest a daily reminder that you might like to use? I was once watching a television show about the Notre Dame football team. When the team leaves the locker room to go out onto the playing field, they go down a long staircase. Above the stairs is a sign that reads, "Play like a champion today." Each player, as he goes down the stairs, reaches up and touches the sign. Why? you ask. Because just *looking* at the sign might not have the same impact as touching it. Touching the sign forces them to concentrate and internalize the message, *"Play like a champion today!"*

I love this idea, and I've thought about it a lot. I thought about how I might make a similar sign, and I remembered a classic talk given by Elder Robert D. Hales when he was the Presiding Bishop. He said:

As a young man, I had an opportunity to serve in the U.S. Air Force as a jet-fighter pilot. Each unit in our squadron had a motto that would inspire its efforts. Our unit motto—displayed on the side of our aircraft—was "Return with Honor." This motto was a constant reminder to us of our determination to return to our home base with honor only after having expended all of our efforts to successfully complete every aspect of our mission.

This same motto, "Return with Honor," can be applied to each of us in our eternal plan of progression. Having lived with our Heavenly Father and having come to earth life, we must have determination to return with honor to our heavenly home. (*Ensign,* May 1990, 39)

I think it would be a wonderful idea if each of us displayed a "Return with Honor" sign in our rooms, right next to the light switch so we would see it every day when we left. We could even touch the sign when we leave, and have the conviction to return not only to heaven, but to our bedroom each night as clean as we were when we left in the morning. Actually, if you were here with me right now, you would see two signs on my wall: "PLAY LIKE A CHAMPION TODAY" and "RETURN WITH HONOR." These daily reminders inspire me and help me to stay on course and heading in the right direction.

The nice people at Deseret Book went to work and inserted a "Return with Honor" sign at the end of this chapter that you can use in your room. Just cut along the dotted line and hang it right up there. And you can add your own daily reminders if you want!

SUMMARY

I've told you about some of the people I admire—people like Christian, Richard, Lynette, and Greg. I'm sure you have a list of your own. And who knows—I'll bet there's someone out there watching and admiring and learning from you!

If you're living in The Past, now is the time to stop! The wonderful message of the gospel is that you can change, and repent, and be better every day. We all have to come back to Reality from time to time, but make sure you spend a lot of time in your Imagi-Nation. Are you everything you want to be? Not yet? That's okay; most people aren't. But you can get to work on it.

You've had moments when you've thought about trying to be better. So have I. Will this be the day that you decide to be better than you've ever been before? Will this be the day that you actually believe what prophets have said about you and your generation? Will this be the day that you begin to be the way you've always known you can be? As Robert Louis Stevenson said, "You cannot run away from weakness. You must sometime fight it out or perish, and if that be so, why not now, and where you stand?" *"Why not now?"* Why not, when you're finished reading this chapter, get out a paper and pencil and write down all the things you want to become! Why not now? Design the kind of life you want, visualize the kind of person you want to be in your Imagi-Nation, and you can make it happen in Reality!

EXTRA CREDIT

As a Man Thinketh, James Allen (New York: Barnes & Noble Inc., 1992).

Seventh Period: College Prep 101

Preparing for the Temple, the University of the Lord

It is the deepest desire of my heart to have every member of the Church worthy to enter the temple.
—Howard W. Hunter

If someone were to ask you, "Where is your very favorite place in the whole world?" how would you answer? When I was younger, I might have answered, "Disneyland" or "camping in the mountains" or maybe "an air show" (I love airplanes).

But now I know a better place. There is no place like it. It is "out of this world." It's the closest thing to being in the celestial kingdom that we have. In fact, a certain room within it actually represents the celestial kingdom. Telestial things are missing from this building. You could search the whole structure and not find a television, a radio, or a Nintendo. The worldly noise disappears as you enter. The sounds of the city, the traffic, and the hustle and bustle are left behind.

The moment you walk through the front doors, a feeling of peace and quiet surrounds you. Suddenly, the world is gone. Friendly, smiling faces greet you around every corner. People speak in whispers. The rooms are bright and light and spotless. You exchange your worldly costume for white clothes, and you sit in a small chapel for a while as an organist softly plays a few hymns.

Whenever I go to the temple, I hear myself say, "I *love* this place." And I really do. It is heaven on earth—the closest thing to heaven we have. Sitting there in my white clothes, feeling clean inside and out, *is* heaven. And it feels like being home with God. It is his holy place, his holy house. Elder Bruce R. McConkie taught:

When the Lord comes from heaven to the earth, as he does more frequently than is supposed, where does he make his visitations? Those whom he visits know the answer; he comes to one of his houses. Whenever the Great Jehovah visits his people, he comes, suddenly as it were, to his temple. (*The Mortal Messiah,* 4 vols. [Salt Lake City: Deseret Book, 1979–81], 1:98–99)

The temple is holy because it is literally the house of the Lord. It is also holy because of what we do there. We seal families together. Our hearts are turned to our fathers and mothers, and their hearts are turned to us. It is holy because we perform ordinances there for those who have died. Many, many people have lived and died on this earth without having received baptism. Many have married and raised children but were not sealed to them. We who are living can do this work for them in the temple. The work is very important to those who have died, and we serve them by doing it for them. One day, we will greet those people, and the reunion will be wonderful.

Horace Cummings recorded: "Concerning the work for the dead, [Joseph] said that in the resurrection those who had been worked for would fall at the feet of those who had done their work, kiss their feet, embrace their knees and manifest the most exquisite gratitude." (Truman G. Madsen, *Joseph Smith the Prophet* [Salt Lake City: Bookcraft, 1989], 99)

WHAT DOES "ENDOWMENT" MEAN?

In addition to performing baptisms for the dead and other proxy ordinances, in the temple we receive our "endowment." An *endowment* is a gift, and the temple endowment is a gift from heaven. We never talk about the specifics of the endowment, because it is sacred. Many misunderstand this concept and think it is "secret." Let me see if I can explain. Have you ever had someone make fun of something that was really important to you? I think we've all had that experience, and it can hurt very much. I can't think of anything that I consider more sacred than my understanding and feelings about the temple. It is simply not right to talk about the specifics of the temple anywhere but within its walls.

Wouldn't it feel strange if you attended a stake conference, and after singing a hymn and opening with prayer, the speakers discussed the National Football League or R.V. maintenance? It just doesn't fit! We don't talk about the endowment outside of the temple because it's simply too sacred for common conversation. It doesn't feel right to talk about it just anywhere.

There are some general things we can appropriately discuss, though. President Howard W. Hunter taught, "Let us share with our children the spiritual feelings we have in the temple. And let us teach them more earnestly and more comfortably the things we can appropriately say about the purposes of the house of the Lord" (*Ensign,* November 1994, 88). I'd like to try to do that.

One of the basic things to understand about the temple is that it is a place of instruction. In fact, the temple has sometimes been called "The University of the Lord." Elder James E. Talmage wrote:

> This course of instruction includes a recital of the most prominent events of the creative period, the condition of our first parents in the Garden of Eden, their disobedience and consequent expulsion from that blissful abode, their condition in the lone and dreary world when doomed to live by labor and sweat, the plan of redemption by which the great transgression may be atoned, the period of the great apostasy, the restoration

of the Gospel with all its ancient powers and privileges, the absolute and indispensable condition of personal purity and devotion to the right in present life, and a strict compliance with Gospel requirements. (*The House of the Lord* [Salt Lake City: Deseret Book, 1968], 83–84)

President Howard W. Hunter taught, "As we attend the temple, we learn more richly and more deeply the purpose of life and the atoning sacrifice of the Lord Jesus Christ" (*Ensign,* November 1994, 88). It's true. As a nineteen-year-old preparing for a mission, I remember some of my first impressions after I received my endowment. One of them was, "Wow. The plan of salvation is a lot more organized than I thought." And it is.

In the temple, along with the instruction, we are also given what President Joseph Fielding Smith called "keys":

Sons and daughters have access to the home where [Father in Heaven] dwells, and you cannot receive that access until you go to the temple. Why? Because you must receive certain key words as well as make covenants by which you are able to enter. If you try to get into the house, and the door is locked, how are you going to enter, if you haven't your key? You get your key in the temple, which will admit you. (*Doctrines of Salvation,* 3 vols. [Salt Lake City: Bookcraft, 1955], 2:40)

In probably the most specific and most often quoted statement about the endowment ever given, President Brigham Young said:

Your endowment is, to receive all those ordinances in the house of the Lord, which are necessary for you, after you have departed this life, to enable you to walk back to the presence of the Father, passing the angels who stand as sentinels, being enabled to give them the key words, the signs and tokens, pertaining to the holy

Priesthood, and gain your eternal exaltation in spite of earth and hell. (*Discourses of Brigham Young,* sel. John A. Widtsoe [Salt Lake City: Deseret Book, 1954], 416)

As President Joseph Fielding Smith mentioned, we make covenants with the Lord in the temple. A covenant is a two-way agreement. You are already familiar with the covenant of the sacrament. We covenant to always remember him and to keep his commandments, and in return, the Lord promises that the Saints will have his spirit to be with them. What covenants do we make in the temple? Good question. I'll let President Ezra Taft Benson answer that one:

> In the course of our visits to the temple, we are given insights into the meaning of the eternal journey of man. We see beautiful and impressive symbolisms of the most important events—past, present, and future—symbolizing man's mission in relationship to God. We are reminded of our obligations as we make solemn covenants pertaining to obedience, consecration, sacrifice, and dedicated service to our Heavenly Father. (*The Teachings of Ezra Taft Benson* [Salt Lake City: Bookcraft, 1988], 251)

HOW DO I PREPARE?

I think I've said as much as I can about what we learn and do within the temple. The more important question for us now is, "How do I prepare?" At the beginning of this chapter, you read the words of President Howard W. Hunter. Let's read more of what he said:

> It would be the deepest desire of my heart to have every member of the Church be temple worthy. I would hope that every adult member would be worthy of—and carry—a current temple recommend, even if proximity

to a temple does not allow immediate or frequent use of it. (*Ensign,* July 1994, 5)

We often use the word *someday* when we refer to the temple: "Someday I will go to the temple," or "Someday I'll be married in the house of the Lord." And that's okay. But President Hunter seems to be saying, "Yes, someday you will. But be *worthy* to enter the temple *right now.*" We should strive to live our lives so that we would *always* be worthy to enter the temple, instead of just becoming worthy "someday." That was President Hunter's challenge—for every member of the Church to be temple worthy, whether they're at the temple or not.

Being worthy "right now" is one of the main things we've talked about in this book. We're not interested in the "pre-planned sin and repentance" idea, or the "I'll do what I want now and prepare for the temple and a mission later" idea. We want to be valiant *right now.* And we want to continue being valiant all our lives, so that if we are called to go home sooner than expected, we can "look up" when we're brought to stand before God (see Alma 5:19).

One way you can try to be worthy of the temple right now is to make your home like the temple. Does that sound like a strange idea? Grab your scriptures, and let's look up "Temple" in the Bible Dictionary (it comes right after the Topical Guide in the LDS edition of the Bible). Here's what it says:

> A temple is literally a house of the Lord, a holy sanctuary in which sacred ceremonies and ordinances of the gospel are performed by and for the living and also in behalf of the dead. A place where the Lord may come, it is the most holy of any place of worship on the earth. Only the home can compare with the temple in sacredness.

PREPARING FOR THE TEMPLE, THE UNIVERSITY OF THE LORD

Only the home can compare with the temple in sacredness. The implications of that are staggering. For example, do you watch TV shows at home that you wouldn't dare show in the chapel or at the stake center? Well, according to our Bible Dictionary, the home is *more* sacred than the chapel or stake center. I think many of us (myself included) have watched things at home that we wouldn't feel comfortable showing at church. Oops.

When you walk into the temple, your brain walks in with you. All of your memories, everything you've seen on TV, including the things you wish you hadn't seen, go with you. You don't want those memories walking onto the stage of your mind when you're in the temple. If we have the goal of being prepared for the temple on our minds every day, it will help us choose what we should watch and what we shouldn't. And, of course, if that's true of television, it must be true of the music we listen to as well. Those tunes and lyrics walk into the temple with us too.

How else can we make our home more like the temple? Well, would you shout and quarrel with your brothers and sisters in the chapel? No way. You would be a little quieter, a little more patient, and a little more forgiving. Therefore, to prepare for the temple *right now,* we could be a little quieter, a little more patient, and a little more forgiving *right now.*

In short, the way to prepare for the temple is to live the gospel. Make your home as peaceful as the celestial room at the temple—a place where everyone is comfortable, where no one is threatened by the criticism or harsh words of other family members, where there is peace and happiness and prayer. Can you do this all by yourself? Of course not. But what you can do will affect every other member of your family. You can always have the temple in the back of your mind as a model for what you want your home to be.

Earlier in this book we talked about "daily reminders." President Spencer W. Kimball gave us advice on a daily reminder for the temple:

It seems to me it would be a fine thing if every set of parents would have in every bedroom in their house a picture of the temple so the boy or girl from the time he is an infant could look at the picture every day and it becomes a part of his life. When he reaches the age that he needs to make this very important decision, it will have already been made. (*The Teachings of Spencer W. Kimball,* Edward L. Kimball, ed. [Salt Lake City: Bookcraft, 1982], 301)

Maybe we could put our "Return with Honor" sign next to a picture of the temple. Of all the goals you set in life, one of the most important is that you marry in the temple. President Howard W. Hunter taught, "Let us make the temple, with temple worship and temple covenants and temple marriage, our ultimate earthly goal and the supreme mortal experience" (*Ensign,* November 1994, 88).

Somewhere out there is your future husband or wife. What do you suppose they are up to these days? Hopefully, they have a picture of the temple on their wall, and they're anticipating being in the temple on their wedding day. Hopefully, they have as their "ultimate earthly goal" being in the temple with you. And hopefully, they're concentrating on being worthy right now, not just "someday."

As you may have already figured out, I was single when I wrote the first edition of this book. I'd been to the temple many times, but one day, I knew I'd be taking my fiancée with me. I didn't yet know her name. I often wondered where she was, and what she was doing! Did she return home with honor from Friday-night dates? Did she date young men who respected her standards, who honored their priesthood? Did she love the Young Women values? I knew that she did.

I couldn't wait to meet her. I wanted to be the best I could for her. And I couldn't wait to take her to the temple. I had something I wanted to say to her that I had been planning for years. I'm sorry to get so personal, but I can't think of any other way to let you know how I felt about the temple even before participating in the most sacred of ordinances performed in that holy house. A temple marriage was always my goal. I never even considered getting married anywhere else.

What am I going to say? Well, I'll tell you part of it. I wanted to look across the altar and say, "I loved you before I even met you." What do I mean by that? Well, the best way I could show my love for my future wife was to keep myself clean during all of my "single" years. Every time I honored the law of chastity, in words or thoughts or actions, it was as if I was saying, "I love you." Every time I refused to watch an immoral TV show or movie, every time I was on a date and was careful in my thoughts and expressions of affection, I was saying, "I love you." I was saying it to the Lord, who has asked me to keep it, and I was also saying it to my future wife.

When you're married, you're supposed to say "I love you" every day. Well, I've been saying, "I love you" to my wife every day for many years, even before she was in my life to hear it. After I finally did find her, we walked into a sealing room in the house of the Lord. We knelt across a holy altar, and I held her hand, and told her face to face. It was a wonderful day.

Hang on a second while I dry my eyes. (Sniff, sniff.) Okay. So, how do you prepare for the temple? Well, whether you like it or not, you *are* preparing for the temple. Preparing for the temple isn't something you do "someday," it's something you're doing right now! And your future spouse is preparing too. You can prepare well, or you can prepare poorly. Everything you are doing now, you will take with you to your first temple recommend interview. So I challenge you to keep out of your house any media or other potentially harmful elements that you wouldn't want in the house of the Lord, because whatever you allow into your home will be carried into the temple by your memory. Make the temple your "ultimate earthly goal," and love your future spouse by keeping the commandments.

As I'm sitting here writing this, I have a current temple recommend in my back pocket. I hope I will always have a temple recommend in my back pocket. Whatever other worldly things I keep in there, along with all the plastic and identification, I always want to have this celestial "activity card" for the University of the Lord. One day you will go to the temple too. I don't know if I'll ever meet you in the celestial room, but let's do all we can to meet one day in the place that room represents: the celestial kingdom.

I hope you can see that everything we've discussed in this book has led us up to this chapter on the temple. How can we be temple worthy right now? Well, let's adopt the "I-want-to-be-valiant" attitude. Let's keep our hands clean and our hearts pure. Let's repent of our sins. Let's you and I strive to recognize and keep the Spirit as we pray with more faith. Let us imagine the kind of person we can be and bring it into reality. Let us go to the temple with honor, and return with honor to our Father in heaven.

Our second semester is ending, and I have to tell you, this has really been fun. It sounds a little corny, but I'll miss talking to you! I imagine wonderful teenagers like you in my mind as I write, and I'll miss you! I hope as soon as you put this book down, you'll go out and pick up another one. I know you're already reading your scriptures daily, so I mean another book. A television substitute. A book that will uplift you and inspire you and teach you something. You are wonderful, my friend! Thanks for attending the second semester—I hope you got answers to some of your "deep-down" questions. Hang in there, keep the faith, and I'll talk to you again soon! 'Bye!

EXTRA CREDIT

Why Say No When the World Says Yes? Randal A. Wright, comp. (Salt Lake City: Deseret Book, 1993).

The Mountain of the Lord, videocassette (Salt Lake City: The Church of Jesus Christ of Latter-day Saints, 1993).

Graduation: Goals 101

There Is Life after High School

Nephi said, "I will go and do," not "I will sit and stew."
—see 1 Nephi 3:7

Graduation: Goals 101

There Is Life after High School

Nephi said, "I will go and do," not "I will sit and stew."
—see 1 Nephi 3:7

Provo, Utah, is surrounded by gorgeous mountains that are constantly changing color with the seasons. Occasionally during my lunch break I enjoy the scenery by cruising up Provo Canyon in my car with the sunroof open, the window down, and some tunes on the stereo. It's a nice break, and it gives me an opportunity to think.

During one of my lunch-break excursions, I noticed a bunch of people floating down the Provo River in inner tubes. What a nice way to see the scenery! Jump in, enjoy the ride, and let the river take you wherever it's going. Sounds like a perfect way to spend a summer afternoon. Of course, you wouldn't want to spend *too* much time in there. It's cold, and you could go numb. Eventually, you'd need to get your feet back on the ground. Hmmm, I feel an analogy coming on.

Imagine a wide, slow-running river with millions of people floating along it in inner tubes. None of them seem to be concerned about where the river takes them; they're just along for the ride. Rivers always go to lower ground. They never climb, blaze trails, or explore. Rivers follow the course of least resistance until they get to the ocean or flow into a lake.

Let's call the river something poetic, like the "River O' Life." How beautiful. Everyone's in there (everyone who's alive, that is), and they're all calmly floating to an unknown destination. All except about 10 percent—a really annoying group of people who are continually "making waves." They

refuse to relax and "go with the flow." They're always looking around and asking questions.

"Wow, look at that mountain! What do you think's up
there? Wow, look at that grove of quaking aspens! I wonder
what it would be like to be there. Say, look at that waterfall!"

Boy. Those people are so noisy! Some of them actually
leave the river! Seriously! They paddle to the side and walk
right onto the riverbank! Can you imagine such a thing? Too
bad they can't just relax and take life as it comes.

It happens every once in a while: After floating down the
river for months or even years, a few hyper people begin to
ask, "Does anyone know where we're going? Hey, what's the
purpose of this river? Why are we all floating in here? Is there
anything more? What are we doing?"

"Hey, keep it down up there," others shout. "Just take
things as they come! Stop trying to figure things out, and go
with the flow. Everyone else is."

But they can't go with the flow. They lie awake at night
and stare at the stars, wondering and dreaming. Then one
night, one of those restless floaters says to himself, "I'm leaving."

The next day he announces his plans. "Can't you see?" he
cries. "Look up there, look at those mountains, look at those
peaks covered in white! Don't you want to know what's up
there? I do. I don't want to drift all my life. I'm outta here. I'm
going to higher ground!"

"It's too hard!" the others shout. "Don't you know you'll
have to walk? You'll get blisters! You'll stub your toes! Boy,"
they mutter to themselves, "kids these days." But he paddles
against the current in his little inner tube and finally makes it
to the shore. He stumbles out onto the sand and looks back
at the millions of people floating aimlessly down the river.
Some are laughing. Others are watching in silence—as if

maybe, for the first time, they're wondering about the purpose of the river.

"I will no longer let the river chart my course," our hero says to himself. "I will follow the stars, I will climb the mountains, I will chart my own course!" He turns, takes a few steps, and gasps, startled by what he sees on the ground. Footprints! What could this be? A trail left by others who have also left the river for higher ground! Who are these trailblazers? And where did they go?

Some people still floating in the river are now entertaining brand-new thoughts: "You mean, I can decide where I want to go? You mean, I don't *have* to go where everyone else is going, and do what everyone else is doing?" They've also noticed that as the river flows to lower ground, it gets muddier. They notice sticks, logs, debris, and sometimes even garbage here and there. But that's the way rivers are: they carry away whatever's floating in them. Rivers are simply the lowest point in the landscape, and leaving them can be difficult. Some try to step out onto the shore, but they leave one foot in the water. It won't work: If they don't get both feet on the ground, the current might pull them back in.

Our friend is now following the footprints into the mountains. Every step he takes up the mountainside allows him to see more of the river. What a view! What perspective! The thrill of new sights, new sounds, and new discoveries makes all the cuts and bruises from the climb worth it. One day, while hiking along, he discovers a small group of people who are also scaling the mountain. They welcome him with smiles, handshakes, and hugs. They share with him maps, compasses, and climbing gear. At the end of each day the little group looks out over the canyon. Such a beautiful sight! Jagged mountains, towering evergreens, quiet meadows, and cool waterfalls. And down below, way below, a slow-moving river, carrying millions of people to nowhere. How sad!

"They'll never see what we see, never know the beauty of the mountains," the leader of the hikers says. "Not unless we tell them. Maybe we should go down to the river, and see if we can persuade some people to come out onto the shore." The leader selects a few willing people to go down to the river and try to help the swimmers understand the joy of climbing.

Does this parable make any sense? Do you know what everything means?

The river: the world—the lowest point on the landscape of life.

The current: peer pressure, "current" trends, what everyone else is doing.

The debris and mud: the world's decaying values.

The stars: the constancy of God and the gospel.

The mountains: goals, dreams, plans; the "higher" plain of life.

Swimming upstream: gospel standards that appear to others like work.

Mocking floaters: those who don't understand our desire to be better than we are.

Footprints: a trail left by those who have gone before—the prophets and the scriptures!

Who are the hikers in our parable? Those who have chosen to act instead of being acted upon; to navigate instead of float (see 2 Nephi 2:14, 25). They're not satisfied with the "current" trends, and they don't want to do what everyone else is doing. They want more! You, my friend, are one of the rare individuals. You go against the current in so many ways! Here's a list:

1. Get up early for seminary
2. Wait until you're sixteen years old to date
3. Refrain from drinking, smoking, and drugs
4. Use clean language
5. Choose not to see movies that pollute your mind
6. Plan to leave home for a year and a half or two years, to show others how to leave the river
7. Remain morally clean so you can have a celestial marriage

There's a whole future ahead of you, waiting for your arrival. Do you ever wonder what will happen? Do you ever try to imagine what your life will be like? Well, the best way to know what will happen to you is to *plan* what will happen to you. We call that setting goals.

Who are the goal setters in our parable? The 10 percent that leave the river. I read somewhere that only about 10 percent of the people in this country have written goals. The other 90 percent just float along as the scenery of life passes them by.

Whenever we talk about setting goals, we're just going in circles unless we make the Lord and his gospel part of the process. You wouldn't want to spend your whole life hiking, only to realize you were on the wrong mountain! President Ezra Taft Benson promised:

> Men and women who turn their lives to God will find out that He can make a lot more out of their lives than they can. He will deepen their joys, expand their vision, quicken their minds, strengthen their muscles, lift their spirits, multiply their blessings, increase their opportunities, comfort their souls, raise up friends, and pour out peace. Whoever will lose his life to God will find he has eternal life. (*New Era,* May 1975, 20)

We use the term "setting goals" because it's a concrete

thing that you can do as an individual. But maybe you don't really "set" the most important goals. Maybe you just *remember* them. No doubt, before you came to this earth, you knew what you wanted in the end. You—and I—wanted to be with God! How do we get there? We receive all the proper ordinances, obey the commandments, and endure to the end. Fortunately for us, our prophets, the scriptures, and our patriarchal blessings refresh our eternal memories about our highest aspirations. President Spencer W. Kimball said:

> Very early, youth should have been living by a plan. They are the wise young man and the wise young woman who will profit by the experience of others, and who early set a course in their education, a mission, the finding of a pure, clean sweetheart to be a life's companion, their temple marriage and their Church service. When such a course is charted and the goal is set, it is easier to resist the many temptations and to say "no" to the first cigarette, "no" to the first drink, "no" to the car ride which will take one into the dark, lonely and hazardous places, "no" to the first improper advances which lead eventually to immoral practices. (*The Miracle of Forgiveness* [Salt Lake City: Bookcraft, 1969], 236)

President Kimball mentioned serving a mission. Every young man should serve a mission, and many young women will choose to serve as well. Do you get a mission call or do you remember it? The Prophet Joseph Smith said, "Every man who has a calling to minister to the inhabitants of the world was ordained to that very purpose in the Grand Council of heaven before this world was" (*History of the Church,* 6:364). You've already been called. And you'll love your mission because it's a short-cut to maturity; it's tithing on your life, and a perfect time to form habits of work and sacrifice that will set a pattern for the rest of your life.

Young women who remember their highest goals will perform miracles! President Ezra Taft Benson said:

> Give me a young woman who loves home and family, who reads and ponders the scriptures daily, who has a burning testimony of the Book of Mormon. Give me a young woman who faithfully attends her Church meetings, who is a seminary graduate, who has earned her Young Womanhood Recognition Award and wears it with pride! Give me a young woman who is virtuous and who has maintained her personal purity, who will not settle for less than a temple marriage, and I will give you a young woman who will perform miracles for the Lord now and throughout eternity. (*Ensign,* November 1986, 84)

When the goals of mission and marriage are firmly in place, you can set all kinds of other goals. When you do, be sure to take the advice of those who have hiked the trails before you. In the business world, large companies have a "board of directors." When the executives in the company want to make a big decision, they bring it before the board. My mission president suggested that I form a *personal* board of directors. What a great idea! Now, when I have major decisions to make in my life, I consult the board. Members of my board include my wife, my parents, my bishop, and some personal friends whom I've grown to respect and admire. Don't get stuck in the rut of trying to do everything by yourself. As you set your goals, take them to your personal board and get some advice.

A chapter about goals ought to have a goal. The purpose of Graduation: Goals 101 is to get you thinking about some of the goals you can set for your life. President Spencer W.

Kimball said, "Goals are good. Laboring with a distant aim sets the mind in a higher key and puts us at our best."

Some people travel without a map. They have no plan for their journey. It's pathetic, but most people spend more time planning a surprise party than they do planning their whole life! What they get is one surprise after another because they have no plan, no charted course, no goals. If you're just floating along in the river of life, who is steering? Who is at the helm? If all you're doing is going with the flow, where will you end up? Doing what everyone else is doing will take you only where everyone else is going. Decide that you will no longer drift with the current. Yes, my friend, you can be the captain of your inner tube! Take command, row for the shore, then get out and head for the hills! Listen to President Ezra Taft Benson:

> When we set goals we are in command. . . . Clearly understood goals bring our lives into focus just as a magnifying glass focuses a beam of light into one burning point. Without goals our efforts may be scattered and unproductive. (*The Teachings of Ezra Taft Benson* [Salt Lake City: Bookcraft, 1988], 384)

How do we set goals, anyway? Elder Joseph B. Wirthlin advised:

> You should look ahead now and decide what you want to do with your lives. Fix clearly in your mind what you want to be one year from now, five years, ten years, and beyond. Receive your patriarchal blessing and strive to live worthy of its promises. A patriarchal blessing is one of the most important guides in life that members of the Church enjoy. Write your goals and review them regularly. Keep them before you constantly, record your progress, and revise them as circumstances dictate. Your ultimate goal should be eternal life—the kind of

life God lives, the greatest of all the gifts of God. (*Ensign,*
November 1989, 73)

Get a paper and pencil and let's set some goals! Elder
Wirthlin said, "Look ahead now," and that's the best way to
start. Look ahead! It may sound strange, but look all the way
to your funeral! If you were asked to summarize your life at
your own funeral, what would you say? What will you feel
good about at the end of your life?

One of my heroes is a former First Lady of the United
States named Barbara Bush (former President George Bush's
wife, and current President George W. Bush's mother). She
spoke to graduates at the all-women Wellesley College in
Massachusetts, and asked them to "look ahead now" when
planning their lives. An Associated Press story reported:

> But while urging the graduates to pursue professional
> careers, if they so choose, Mrs. Bush warned, "At the
> end of your life, you will never regret not having passed
> one more test, winning one more verdict, or not closing
> one more deal. You will regret time not spent with a
> husband, a child, a friend, or a parent." (As cited in
> *Provo Daily Herald,* 2 June 1990, A1–A2)

Mrs. Bush is right! No one is going to look back on his or
her life and say, "Oh, I wish I had spent more time at the
office!" Instead, they'll be thinking of life's most important
things: family, church, and service. What will you look back
on?

Once I participated in a goal-setting workshop in Idaho. I
was extremely impressed with the group of teenage peer
counselors. I asked them to write what they would like to
have said about them at their funerals. After some rather
serious thought, they wrote their feelings. When they were
finished, a few of them were brave enough to read their personal "epitaphs" to the group (an epitaph is a brief statement

commemorating a deceased person). What they said was interesting, but what they *didn't* say was even more interesting. All of them mentioned being parents: "She was a wonderful wife and mother," or, "He was a father who spent time with his children." All of them mentioned service, too: "He was always there to help anyone who needed him," or, "She was always helping others." After the reading, we had a group discussion. We observed that no one mentioned how much money they had made, or even what kind of career they had. No one mentioned cars or boats or possessions of any kind. Instead, these top-notch teenagers wrote about the things that really matter. (Once again, I learned to never underestimate teenagers.)

As you set your long-range goals, think about what you want to have said about you at your funeral. When you've decided that, and written it down, write the words "Mission Statement" at the top of your paper, and you've now made a motto for your life. You may want to go back and change a few things from past tense to future tense, of course. For example, change "He was a good dad" to "He will be a good dad," and so on. Your mission statement gives you something to live for; it gives you a purpose. It says, "This is what I want my life to mean." Someone once said, "Your life is God's gift to you; what you do with your life is your gift to God." Make your life a gift to God.

A mission statement is a long-range tool, and you need to set short-range goals too. I'm afraid I'm going to have to use another personal experience to illustrate. (I have to use personal experiences about me because I don't know any personal experiences about you.) You see, the book that you're reading right now was a goal of mine. For months I worked on it "every once in a while." I made very little progress. It wasn't until I set a deadline that things began to happen. All of a sudden I felt a sense of urgency. I also realized that writing took a lot more time and was a lot harder than I thought it would be. One day I realized, "If I'm ever going to get this book done, I'd better set aside an hour or so every day until it's finished." So that's what I did. Most of this book was written between the hours of 5:30 and 8:00 A.M. Am I trying to impress you? No. You probably get up earlier than that to go to seminary. I'm just trying to illustrate something that Elder Richard G. Scott once said: "To reach a goal you have never before attained, you must do things you have never before done" (*Ensign,* May 1990, 76). Achieving goals takes work, and work takes time! You might have to give up something, like, uh, perhaps, television! Aaaah! You've probably heard of Brother Gerald R. Lund, who wrote the historical fiction series, *The Work and the Glory.* He gave a speech at Utah Valley State College, where he talked about the price of achieving goals.

Lund confessed that in order to produce his work of fiction he had to give up watching television and playing golf. Some people, he said, don't want any of the "work" but all the "glory" (see "Lund Defines the Educated Person," *Utah County Journal,* 26 March 2001).

Goals take work! A short-range goal should be divided into smaller short-range goals. I had a goal to write a book, but I divided it into a goal of writing ten chapters, one chapter every two weeks. Did everything come out exactly as planned? Not at all. But at least there was a goal to shoot for! It's okay to write your goals in pencil, because sometimes you'll need to make adjustments.

We've talked about the major goals for your life, the goals that you don't set as much as you "remember"—like mission, marriage, and eternal life. It wouldn't be right for me to tell you any other goals to set. You have to set them by yourself, with advice from your personal board of directors. You can set your goals about a million different things: school, family, sports, scripture reading, writing, music, foreign languages, hobbies, sewing, exercise, journal, computers, cooking, and on and on and on! Life is a great adventure! So get off the couch, put down the remote, and go live it! In other words, get off your inner tube and head for the hills!

AND NOW: THE CHEESY PART NEAR THE END

Well, I guess it's time to say good-bye. You're a pretty amazing teenager, you know that? You've read all the way to the last chapter! (Is there anyone out there reading this? What's that? You're the only one? Oh well. That's about right. Ninety percent of Americans don't read past the first chapter of the books they buy.) You are a rare individual. There are many more books out there, many books better than this one. Go check them out!

Thanks for reading! I respect you so much! I tried to write all the things I wish I'd known when I was in high school, but it seems I've left so much out. The more I learn, the more I realize how little I know. But I know where all the answers are, and so do you. I'm so glad we have a Father in Heaven, the prophets, and the scriptures. They teach us not to get bogged down by the little things in life. They may seem like big things now, but many of them are so little, and they won't mean much further down the road. Yes, there is life after high school. Your high school experience will be easier when you realize that.

This book had three goals; do you remember? (1) Learn things, (2) have fun, and (3) make changes. Well, did you learn things? (write answer here) _____. Did you have fun? _____. Did you, or will you make changes? What changes? you ask. Well, let's review. Our First Semester courses encouraged you to: read *For the Strength of Youth,* set your own dating standards, learn of and listen to the Savior's words, make a commitment to read the Book of Mormon, turn off the TV for a month, get into the "best books," and be full of gratitude every day. During Summer School you were encouraged to make good friends and good decisions and you learned that even though it's tough, you can endure trials and tragedies. Our Second Semester courses then encouraged you to: develop perspective and a positive attitude, clean up your life, repent, listen quietly for promptings from the Spirit, pray often, dream of the future, and prepare yourself for sacred temple ordinances. Finally, you learned that Graduation isn't the end: There is life after high school, so set some worthy goals. Phew! Did you, or will you, make changes? When? (Remember, I will go and do, not I will sit and stew!) _____.

Good! Well, I'm outta here. I've got more goals to work on. Good-bye, my friend; leave your inner tube behind and make tracks! I'll see you on the mountain!

Please come visit me sometime at www.johnbytheway.com.

EXTRA CREDIT

The 7 Habits of Highly Effective Teens: The Ultimate Teenage Success Guide, Sean Covey (New York: Simon and Schuster, 1998).

Tips for Tackling Teenage Troubles, Brad Wilcox, (Deseret Book: Salt Lake City, 1998)

OTHER BOOKS BY JOHN BYTHEWAY

How to Be an Extraordinary Teenager
Out of the Mouths of Babes & Dudes
SOS: A Teenage Survival Guide to Getting Home in Safety
What I Wish I'd Known Before My Mission
What I Wish I'd Known When I Was Single
What We Wish We'd Known When We Were Newlyweds
You're Gonna Make It!

Index

INDEX

INDEX